COMPUTER

SNAFUS

*To Steve Erickson,
A steadfast friend.
        Mac McDaniel*

COMPUTER SNAFUS

Herman McDaniel

CHICORA PUBLISHING, INC.
Myrtle Beach, S.C.

Copyright © 1998 Herman McDaniel

All rights reserved. No part of this work may be reproduced or transmitted in any form, electronic or mechanical, or by any information storage or retrieval system, except as authorized in writing by the copyright holder. Requests must be submitted in writing to the publisher. Excerpts of up to 100 words may be included in reviews, articles, and stories without obtaining written permission; such excerpts must be properly credited.

ISBN 0-9663993-0-7

Library of Congress Cataloging-in-Publication Data

McDaniel, Herman.
   Computer snafus : crashes, errors, failures, foul-ups, goofs, glitches, and other malfunctions that cause computers to go awry / Herman McDaniel.
      p.   cm.
   Includes index.
   ISBN 0-9663993-0-7
   1. Computer system failures.   I. Title.
QA76.9.F34M37 1998
004--dc21   98-23482
                                                            CIP

Chicora Publishing, Inc.
350 Wesley Street, Suite 702
Myrtle Beach, SC 29579

Printed in the United States of America

1 2 3 4 5 6 7 8 9 10

About This Book

Everyone who has ever wondered why a particular computer system did something both unintended and unexpected should read **Computer Snafus**. McDaniel explains in easy to read, jargon-free prose why such incidents occur. He then recounts hundreds of computer anomalies, crashes, errors, failures, glitches, goofs, malfunctions, and snafus.

Details of the incidents have been gleaned from public documents, newspaper articles, radio and television broadcasts, and other sources. This compilation confirms that, despite decades of experience, those who create systems still do not build-in adequate controls to prevent computer systems from going awry. The caution remains: always expect the unexpected.

About the Author

Herman McDaniel, more commonly known as "Mac" McDaniel, has observed the evolution of computing from vacuum tubes to pentium processors. And he has always been intrigued by incidents in which computers did the unexpected. This curiosity led him to study the nearly universal lack of adequate controls over automated systems. He has spoken on this specialty to thousands of people ranging from law enforcement and criminal justice personnel to art museum executives. Mac has discussed the need for better controls over computer systems with accountants, attorneys, auditors, bankers, chief executive officers, chief financial officers, diplomats, investigators, government managers, military personnel, programmers, security personnel, systems analysts--from about three-fourths of the Fortune 1000 companies plus every major federal and state government agency in the United States. He has also been a guest on the Larry King Show.

"Mac" once was in charge of computer programmer training at the Census Bureau. After John Wiley published his first book in 1968, the U.S. Civil Service Commission recruited him to manage the creation and delivery of a series of computer education programs designed to teach government executives and managers nationwide how to be intelligent users, rather than victims, of computer technology. He later founded a consulting and education company, which he managed for several years, before being recruited for a three-year stint as automation advisor in the office of the director of the Bureau of the Census.

An early retirement provided "Mac" time to write books that he had wanted for several years to write. Watch for his **Computer Crime for Fun, Profit, Revenge...** sometime in 1999.

Acknowledgements

For more than twenty years I have collected published stories about computer failures in anticipation of someday writing this book. I want to publicly thank the following people who have encouraged me, cajoled me, assisted in research, and provided material:

Bryant Benton	Grace Hopper
Buck Bloombecker	Joe Kalet
Bill Butz	Jean Linehan
Craig Carlton	Carla Liverman
Tom DiNenna	Wayne McDaniel
Patricia Emerson	Kathy Myerson
Jay Erdman	Cezarina Palting
Steve Erickson	Pat Quinney
Nevins Frankel	Jack Stivers
Jim Gorhman	Jeri Traw
John Halterman	Alan Wenberg
Douglas Head	Jerry Wirth

I especially want to thank my friend and editor, Stephen B. Slaughter, whose wit and wisdom I value greatly!

Herman McDaniel
July 1998

Table of Contents

Introduction	1
Why Do Most Major New Computer Systems Fail to Meet Expectations?	4
Can We Rely on Computers to Keep Our Military Ready?	33
What Happens When Computers Can't Communicate?	50
Can Bankers Bank on Computer Technology?	60
How Do Electrical Failures Affect Computers?	75
Are Computers Especially Susceptible to Fire?	81
Do Computers Compromise Air Traffic Safety?	96
Are Travelers Well-Served By Computers?	120
How Reliable Are Computers in the Securities Industry?	138
Is Mother Nature Unfairly Harsh With Computers?	148
Do Computers Really Kill People?	166
How Adversely Have Computer Problems Impacted Space Exploration?	177
Have Federal Government Computer-Modernization Efforts Become Impossible Missions?	206
How Common Are Computer Foul-ups?	227
Index	244

INTRODUCTION

The world's landscape is littered with debris from computer systems and programs that couldn't, wouldn't, or didn't perform as their creators hoped or expected.

With more than a hundred million computers currently in use around the globe, the severity of systems' failures ranges from humorous to life-threatening, from inconsequential to devastating. Murphy's Law certainly applies to computer systems!

The American military contributed to our vocabulary the word "snafu" (defined in dictionaries as "situation normal, all fouled-up"). For the record, the "f" in "snafu" initially did not stand for "fouled"!

During the nearly half-century in which computers have become necessities in most large organizations, they have also come to permeate the daily routine of average citizens everywhere. Computers gone awry often prevent individuals from completing such routine tasks as withdrawing cash from a bank, checking out at a retail store, obtaining a prescription refill, purchasing a ticket to almost any event, making hotel or travel reservations, renewing a driver's license, charging a credit-card purchase, buying or selling stock, dialing long-distance telephone calls, verifying whether an item is available in stock, or determining the status of an account. At any given moment, countless computers are unexpectedly and unexplainably out-of-service.

On the broader stage, computer problems have attracted world attention by preventing launches of space craft, shutting down telephone communications across vast expanses, and disrupting air traffic for long periods. Highly automated military systems have failed to perform as expected under actual battle conditions, sometimes causing the loss of human lives. Computers have been blamed for several airplane crashes resulting in hundreds of deaths. People dependent upon medical and life-support systems have died because of faulty computers.

Countless organizations have lost significant sums of money because of faulty systems, with some never realizing that they were suffering losses! Faulty computer systems at financial institutions have literally given away assets. After a few organizations endured great embarrassment following highly publicized computer goofs, some managers resorted to cover-ups, seeking to avoid public ridicule.

Fleeced taxpayers have paid billions of dollars for computer systems that either never performed as expected or were abandoned before completion. Business organizations have also routinely paid for computer equipment, systems, and programs from which they never derived the anticipated benefits.

The forces of nature have been blamed for thousands of computer failures. Hurricanes, tornadoes, lightning, flooding, even heavy snow accumulations, have wreaked havoc on such facilities around the world.

Fires have disrupted, damaged, and destroyed computer facilities at hundreds of sites, resulting in losses of tens of millions of dollars.

Savvy workers, aware that citizens have been conditioned to accept "computer error" as an explanation for almost anything that goes wrong, often blame all errors on their computer--whether warranted or not! After all, the public rarely cares whether the problems resulted from a data error, programming error, system's flaw or equipment malfunction--they lump all of these into a category they think of as computer screw-ups. Most people usually are concerned only about correcting whatever is affecting them.

In reality, every "computer goof" has its genesis in decisions made earlier by humans. Faulty analysis of problems often results in systems which fail to provide appropriate solutions. Logic unintentionally omitted from computer programs or systems often prevents computers from performing as planned. When programmers introduce errors of logic, their programs will yield unexpected results. If someone enters faulty data into a computer, its processing results will be wrong. Equipment problems, though considered rare, do occasionally cause computer systems to run amok. In short, every systems-related decision made by humans affects the computer system's performance for as long as the system is used.

Much of what is currently wrong with computer systems can be attributed to managers who, several decades ago, decided that such complex systems required few controls. They worried more about completing expensive projects on time and within budget, often settling for systems that weren't exactly on target, so long as they worked. Computer systems with inadequate controls remain commonplace, even now.

Most computer systems' short-comings probably result from unrealistic expectations. Simply put, it is impossible to attain 100% reliability of any complex system for the duration of its use. Data that is 100% accurate, 100% of the time, can never be the norm. Computer programs and systems can never be expected to include totally correct logic and formulas for any data they will be expected to process; situations invariably occur that their creators never envisioned and therefore never provided logic for. Even the most stringently-tested computer chips can fail. As Murphy warned, "Whatever can go wrong, will--at the most inopportune time."

Pogo might well have been describing management's relationship to computer systems when he uttered the now immortal words: "We have met the enemy and he is us."

1

WHY DO MOST MAJOR NEW COMPUTER SYSTEMS FAIL TO MEET EXPECTATIONS?

The simplest things cause computer systems to go awry, often creating major catastrophes. Reasons cover the gamut: faulty data, programming errors, equipment malfunctions, or system inadequacy. One that is rarely admitted is human stupidity.

Data integrity problems are perhaps the most common affliction of computer systems. In lay-reader terms these can be something as simple and universally understood as "garbage in, garbage out." If the data introduced to a computer is less than perfect, the processing result will be too. For example, if the data fails to reflect that an employee worked overtime, or doesn't specify the number of overtime hours worked, the pay data for that individual will be wrong--even though the program was correct and the equipment worked perfectly during processing. Identifying incorrect results is not easy. In fact, many people accept as valid any computer output.

Mistakes in computer programs, called "software errors", include logic inadvertently omitted from a program, logical errors within the program, even erroneous calculation formulas. If a programmer neglects to write logical steps instructing the computer how to calculate overtime pay, processing results for all employees who worked overtime will be wrong. However, the calculations for anyone working only regular hours will be unaffected by the missing logic. If the programmer instructs the computer to determine overtime pay rates by multiplying the hourly pay rate by 160%

(when, for example, it should be 150%), all overtime compensation will be wrong--even if the pay data was correct and the equipment worked normally.

Frequently referred to as "hardware problems," equipment malfunctions usually can be identified more easily than software errors. Humans notice quickly when printers fail to print, disk-drives don't spin, and magnetic tape drives don't read or write. With today's technology, equipment malfunctions frequently are traced to faulty computer chips or components.

Computer systems include all of the equipment, communications links, programs, data, operating procedures, etc. required to collect the data, process it, and provide results to designated recipients as needed. Problems are often simply reported as systems failures when investigators have not yet actually determined whether the problems arose from errors in the data, program, equipment, communications, or if they resulted from human error.

It is even possible for all parts of a system to work correctly but provide the results in less than a timely manner. In a battlefield situation, a commander is not well-served by a computer system that warns of an incoming missile sixty seconds after it has impacted!

Computer systems rushed into use often prove inadequate for their intended roles. More complex computer systems run a higher risk that some crucial component will be inadvertently omitted. Haste definitely makes waste--and too often results in computer systems that fail to meet the processing needs of an organization. If analysts fail to determine what is actually needed, whatever they design and implement may become more of a problem than a solution. Despite the massive expenditure of time, effort, and money, worthless systems will not be used. Even though constantly changing specifications make it impossible to build responsive systems, newly-placed managers tend to demand different information than their predecessors received. Newly-enacted laws frequently change requirements for some systems. In fact, so many factors can change that a particular system, designed to be ideal one year, might be totally inadequate and unacceptable three years later.

The following real-life situations cover a wide spectrum of ill-fated automation endeavors in which computer systems went awry.

Internal Revenue Service officials confirmed that "spurious energy" from Nashville's airport radar system had, in the spring of 1970, erased computer tapes containing thousands of tax returns at a nearby IRS computer center. When *Computerworld* reported the incident, January 6, 1971, the writer stated that IRS officials refused to discuss the matter with him. He related that a consulting engineer, familiar with the incident, speculated that improperly grounded metal shielding surrounding the computer equipment had failed to prevent electronic interference from the radar.

At approximately the same time, while instructing a computer to pay $27,054.49 due a Kansas City company for painting a federal courthouse, a General Services Administration (GSA) clerk mistakenly entered the employee number of a federal worker in Denver instead of the vendor's identification number. The computer printed a check payable to the Denver employee, who later said that he thought the unexpected windfall resulted from some recently-purchased stock. He prudently paid off his car, his home mortgage and two consumer loans before GSA discovered the error in 1970 and demanded that he return the money. When government investigators determined that the Denver employee had done nothing to cause the computer to send him the erroneous payment, GSA arranged for him to repay, in interest-free monthly payments of $300, the nearly $8,000 he no longer had.

Personalized, computer-generated letters were much in vogue in 1975 when Chicago's Oxford House hotel dispatched several thousand letters beginning: "Being privileged in having you as our recent guest..." to 4,000 area residents--most of whom had never set foot inside the hotel. Employees reported that more than 500 letter recipients called the hotel seeking explanations, with many wondering whether their spouses might have checked into a local hotel for extramarital sexual encounters.

Embarrassed hotel officials sent retraction letters to everyone who received the initial ones. The retractions explained that an employee at a computer firm hired to send the first letters had loaded the wrong computer tape--a sample listing of area residents--rather than the intended list of recent hotel guests.

On July 1, 1977, New York City began to implement phases of an ambitious Integrated Financial Management System they hoped would improve control of the city's finances. They were extremely pleased with the new system's handling of budget and accounting functions. But the implementation of the payroll phase proved disastrous; city workers lodged nearly 1,000 complaints of late or incorrect paychecks with New York's Labor Relation Office. Some employees reported working for months before receiving their first paycheck. Others complained that the computer failed to pay them night differential or overtime pay. Investigators concluded that differing reporting and record-keeping practices used by various city agencies were incompatible with the new computer system. They said that most of the pay discrepancies were caused by faulty data submitted by the agencies rather than by computer systems errors.

Officials of Worcester, Vermont, with an unemployment rate of 13% in the fall of 1977, expressed both surprise and outrage when they received no funds from the Economic Development Administration (EDA). EDA officials reportedly told their investigator that a computer error, which could not be fixed, caused the denial of funds for the town of 700. The investigator proceeded to file a Freedom of Information Act request for appropriate background materials from the agency's data processing department. When he reported to town officials that the instructions given to the programmers did not comply with federal law, Worcester officials, seeking their town's fair share of federal funds, filed suit again EDA.

The investigator specifically concluded that, because the federal government collected no unemployment statistics for unincorporated towns or those with populations less than 2,500, EDA employees had arbitrarily assigned a value of zero to all such towns rather than use unemployment statistics provided by local officials as federal law required. The use of zeroes instead of actual statistics deprived all such towns of their share of public funding under the $4 billion federal program.

When Worcester officials were able to prove that no computer foul-up had actually occurred but that EDA had used the computer as a smoke screen, the agency agreed to an out-of-court settlement under which Worcester would be paid $364,000.

An attempt to improve a computer program at the A. C. Nielsen Company, the television ratings giant, backfired when an undetected error caused erroneous ratings to be published for the period January 9 through February 1978. An employee of NBC reportedly discovered the discrepancy and alerted Nielsen to the problem. After correcting the programming error and reprocessing their data, the ratings company announced that the earlier results had erred by one tenth of a rating point, representing about 73,000 households.

In Canada, when the Ontario Department of Education revised its student awards program in 1978, officials ordered new computer programs written to reflect the changes. Rushed into service without sufficient testing, the programs granted 887 students more money than they were entitled to receive. Erroneous overpayments totaled $1.3 million.

Officials created a public uproar when, after discovering the error, they demanded that students immediately repay all overpayments. After the news media reported that the announced hard-nosed stand would create hardships for many students, the government relented and announced that it would require immediate repayment only from those who dropped out of college. Other recipients could either repay the overage at rates of $5 to $10 a month or postpone repayment till after graduation.

Back in the United States, when problems with a newly-installed computer system prevented New Hampshire state employees from processing welfare payments in June 1978, welfare offices at town, city and county levels across the state were forced to make unanticipated emergency payments. Although originally justified as a method to improve efficiency and speed service, the new system also increased the waiting period for food stamp recipients from fifteen to twenty-five days, forcing local government authorities to furnish assistance they had not expected to provide.

From June 22 to June 28, for reasons unknown, the system was "down". Technicians finally traced the problem to "a bug" in the compiler (a program that converts program code to machine-readable and executable form), which also had been recently changed.

When Dallas, Texas city employees changed pay scales at the beginning of a new fiscal year, October 1, 1978, city employees anticipated a 3% salary increase. An administrative judge's check contained an increase of $3,100; seven city judges were each paid $1,600 more than previously. The city controller's office reported that a keypunch error had caused the erroneous computer overpayment, which recipients had repaid.

The causes of some problems seem nearly impossible to identify. Foley's Department Stores in Houston in 1980 installed a communications line enabling the store's computer to transmit credit data immediately to its parent company's national data center in Cincinnati, where it could be processed immediately with the results being transmitted back to Texas. Foley's employees reported that for several weeks the data transmission operated almost error-free.

Then, in the fall, mysterious transmission problems developed-- especially on Thursdays and Fridays. No one could pinpoint the cause of the transmission problems, which at the end of November ceased just as mysteriously as they had begun!

Weeks later, communications experts announced that they had determined what had blocked data transmissions on Thursdays and Fridays: the Goodyear Blimp! In maneuvering around Houston to shoot aerial television pictures, the airship frequently blocked part of the microwave transmission. When football season ended and the blimp departed, all data transmission problems ceased.

"Measure twice, cut once," has long been a caution in construction. When the seventeen-story Lutheran Brotherhood Building was being built in Minneapolis in 1980, some one at a Pittsburgh glass manufacturer's computer apparently entered erroneous dimensions for some of the building's special glass panels. Builders reported that 1,278 of the panels delivered to the construction site were three inches too long. The unique opaque spandel panels could not be cut to correct size; new ones had to be manufactured.

In December 1980, a computer at Iowa's Department of Social Services, printed 42,000 unusable Medicaid identification cards. Because a critical number on each card contained one fewer digit than required, recipients could not obtain health-care services. State officials announced that a programming error was to blame and issued corrected Medicaid cards.

A few months later, a computer used in Maryland's Energy Assistance Program generated eligibility letters in February 1981 that incorrectly listed the amount of fuel benefits clients were entitled to receive. The computer reportedly also assigned some clients to the wrong fuel provider, causing some households to run out of heating oil before corrected letters could be generated and delivered.

Screw-ups sometimes remain undetected until the mistake has been repeated millions of times. Such was the case when, after mailing three-and-a-third million state income tax forms to citizens in November 1981, red-faced New York State officials discovered that every one of them contained erroneous Social Security numbers! Calls from early recipients prompted state employees to examine the computer program being used. They found that the computer was inserting a zero at the beginning of each Social Security number, then dropping the right-most digit because it would not fit into the space allowed by the program.

In addition to correcting the program's logic problem, employees also programmed the computer to print a line of number signs (#) across the bottom of the remaining 4.4 million labels. This feature would enable clerks to determine at a glance if correct Social Security numbers appeared on the labels of tax documents submitted later. The remaining labels were printed and the income tax forms dispatched without further incident.

Alleging that the City of Pittsburgh had been the victim of bad advice and unusable software, city officials in 1982 threatened a lawsuit against both Coopers and Lybrand, Inc. and Software International Corporation.

After the city controller's office had decided in 1980 to replace its accounting and financial systems, officials selected the accounting and consulting firm Coopers and Lybrand to decide what was needed. Coopers and Lybrand recommended that Software International provide both hardware and software to the city. In January 1982 Software International installed a Hewlett-Packard 3000 computer that ran proprietary software in the city controller's office.

Within a few weeks, disillusioned city employees said they had identified too many flaws in the system. They switched much of their work to alternate computers within the city government and began using an outside computer service bureau.

Before Pittsburgh officials filed their threatened lawsuit, the two contractors agreed to an out-of-court settlement of nearly $1 million. More than half of that amount reportedly involved repayment of money the city had already paid to Coopers and Lybrand.

Computerworld, in its March 7, 1983 issue, reported that two other users of the same software had determined that the system was inadequate to meet their needs. The State of Kentucky, serving as a beta test site for the software in 1982, reportedly concluded that the software product contained errors and returned it to the vendor without paying for it. The Town of Brookline, Massachusetts reportedly also beta-tested the package and decided that it did not satisfy their requirements. The software firm returned $65,000 that Brookline had paid for the software.

For Fiscal Year 1981, the U.S. Treasury Department budgeted $641 million for computer equipment, services and personnel. The department's handling of the appropriation received scathing reviews by the U.S. General Accounting Office (GAO) in 1982. Citing lack of planning and wasteful expenditures, the GAO reported that officials at the Bureau of Engraving and Printing had simply abandoned completed systems after users complained they did not meet all of their requirements.

GAO reported that the U.S. Customs Service developed a major new computerized law enforcement system using a nonstandard programming language, effectively ensuring that the system could only operate on equipment from one manufacturer.

The same report criticized the Treasury Department for continuing to use slower, obsolete equipment in the Bureau of Government Financial Operations, thereby creating constant backlogs and driving up operating costs.

In 1981 the South Dakota State Government terminated a computer lease contract signed in 1976. The leased IBM 370/158 computer, originally valued at $2.2 million, by 1981 was valued at only $150,000. However, the remaining lease payments totaled approximately $800,000. After state officials broke the contract and returned the leased equipment, they bought an identical computer for $150,000. When the company that financed the leased computer attempted in the spring of 1982 to sue South Dakota over the canceled contract, the U.S. Court of Appeals in Pierre ruled that the firm could not do so.

Because the New Jersey Division of Motor Vehicles had been unable to rent appropriate space in which to install Honeywell computer equipment, the electronic devices remained boxed and unused for eighteen months--even though the DMV was paying $22,000 a month to lease the equipment, according to a *Computerworld* report, March 28, 1983.

A DMV spokesman explained that installation of the minicomputers required space and electrical capabilities that were unavailable in many of DMV's fifty existing branch locations. He blamed the expensive and wasteful delay on the bureaucratic procedure the state used for leasing and renovating space.

Computerworld reported that twenty-two of the fifty branches were using their new system, while the remaining twenty-eight, unable to install new computer equipment in existing space, continued to use their old manual systems.

In Montana, the State Auditors Office reported in 1983 that an antiquated computer system had caused a loss of up to $2.5 million in uncollected state income tax. Auditors charged that the computer could not discern certain payment discrepancies in order to generate appropriate tax-due notices to taxpayers.

At the federal government level, the U.S. Postal Service announced in June 1984 that it was abandoning its electronic mail service, known as E-Com, after the venture reportedly lost more than $50 million during its two years of operation. Using computers and private data transmission equipment to transmit letters to twenty-five post offices where they were printed, inserted into envelopes, and delivered within two days, E-Com had not grown as hoped.

When the Postal Service's Board of Governors concluded that the E-Com rates (twenty-six cents for one page and five cents for each addition page) were insufficient to recover all expenses, they recommended rate increases. The Postal Rate Commission rejected the proposed increase and voted to double the first-page charge and triple that for subsequent pages. When the two groups could not agree on a compromise, the Board of Governors voted to end the two-and-a-half-year-old service, which had attracted fewer than 1,000 regular volume users. They ordered the service to sell or lease all of the E-Com equipment as quickly as possible.

Software errors plague even firms that produce popular software products sold publicly. Lotus Development Corporation revealed on September 16, 1985, that thousands of copies of the firm's new version of Symphony business software contained a serious flaw that could cause data loss during the performance of certain spreadsheet functions. All copies of the software shipped over an eight-week period reportedly were flawed. Lotus announced that all Symphony 1.1 purchasers would be sent a disk enabling them to easily correct the problems themselves.

When computer results are wrong, planners using those results can create nightmares. In California, state officials revealed that a programming error, discovered near the end of fiscal year 1985, had caused the state government to underestimate future revenues by $400 million.

Seeking to learn why reported vehicle registration rates were abnormally low, state officials assigned a team of employees to manually process data the computer had processed, then compare the two results. They discovered that a bug in a computer program producing monthly statistics of the Department of Motor

Vehicle's registration and driver's license transactions had failed to count nearly 900,000 transactions over a period of five months.

Officials of the Immigration and Naturalization Service (INS) gave IBM an unfair advantage during the bidding process for new computer equipment, overpaid for the equipment, and, after the contract was signed, made unauthorized changes that substantially increased the costs of a May 1984 contract, according to an April 1986 U.S. General Accounting Office report to the Congress. The report charged that INS allowed IBM to reduce the firm's bid by $3.3 million--after all bidders had submitted their best and final offers. The reduction made IBM's bid $2,713 lower than one submitted by Electronic Data Systems (EDS). When officials at EDS learned that IBM had won the procurement contract with a bid of $61.3 million, they filed an official protest with the federal government. An out-of-court settlement resulted in the transfer of the Immigration and Naturalization Service contract to EDS.

Although INS had been granted procurement authority to spend $64.4 million for the contract, less than two years after its award the General Accounting Office estimated the contract's actual cost would exceed $100 million. GAO auditors reported that the out-of-court settlement allowed EDS to add administrate charges, overhead, and profit to the cost of IBM equipment provided under the contract. The prices EDS charged INS ranged from 9% to 25% higher than the prices IBM originally bid. The audit report also concluded that EDS installed more powerful computers than the contract called for, increasing the agency's computing capabilities four-fold.

A California State Government computer, in the summer of 1986, issued checks to pay bondholders $4 million in interest that wasn't yet due. Officials quickly discovered the slipup and stopped payment on the checks. They blamed the foul-up on "a software problem."

When a programmer at the U.S. Customs Service mistakenly left blank two fields of more than 4,450 such program fields applicable to U.S. imports from China, no one noticed. After all, many of the fields were supposed to be left blank--but not this particular pair.

Because of the coding omission, a computer failed to record the importation of more than three million coats from China between June 1986 and May 1987. When the year-end numbers made it appear that the coat quota was not being filled, importers rushed to increase their order quantities.

Meanwhile, someone at Customs discovered the error, prompting the service immediately to declare that the current year's quota of 3.7 million Chinese coats had already been met. Importers protested vehemently, arguing that they had received nearly 2.5 million Chinese coats into bonded warehouses within the United States, awaiting import approval.

An over-taxing computer at California's Employment Development Department mailed 1.5 million notices to residents who had received non-wage income in 1987. In its January 23, 1988 issue, the *Los Angeles Times* reported that approximately 60,000 of those notices, involving a combination of unemployment benefits and disability payments, were grossly in error--because the computer multiplied the benefits actually paid by 100, then reported that figure on tax forms! Thus, for an individual who had actually received $4,600, the tax form indicated payment of $460,000!

A department spokesman told *The Times* that corrected forms were mailed within a week of the error's discovery. He also said that the mistake had been detected before the original forms were dispatched to the Internal Revenue Service; the federal tax service received only the corrected information.

In an earlier incident, after California's Employment Development Department completed a changeover to a new computer system in October 1986, auditors said that more than 24,000 employees contacted the department to complain about incorrect bills. At the time, the department was supposed to collect approximately $13 billion in withholding taxes each year from 700,000 state employees. In March 1988 the state Attorney General charged that bugs in the new computer system had caused the state to fail to collect $635 million of that amount.

Begun in 1980, this system sought to fully automate nineteen ledger systems. More than sixty million records were converted, along with an estimated 100,000 errors they reportedly contained. Within a year of the new system's implementation, the volume of citizens' complaints persuaded department officials to stop sending out bills based on the old, error-ridden records.

Shortly after the California Attorney General findings became public, officials at the Employment Development Department announced they had "resolved" their systems problems and had already mailed corrected bills to employees throughout the state.

The District of Columbia Government, in 1987, hired a former Social Security Administration employee to oversee the development of an automated personnel system. In addition to processing requests for promotions and similar routine actions, the new computer system would rate and rank job applicants. The schedule called for the installation of a prototype by July 26, 1988, and an operational system in September.

"The best laid plans..." axiom apparently was reinforced by events occurring while this system was supposed to be under development. Mayor Marion Barry agreed near the end of 1987 to assign District Government employees to assist the government of the U.S. Virgin Islands by helping to revamp their antiquated personnel system. The two programmers, officially assigned to work full-time on the District Government's automated personnel system, were ordered to work instead on the Virgin Islands' system.

District Government procurement officials, adhering to their original project schedule, ordered equipment for the District Government's new system so it would be available when needed. Because they were unaware that the programmers, assigned to work on the District Government's new computer system, were actually working full-time on the Virgin Islands' system, they did not realize that the schedule for the District's system would be seriously delayed.

The *Washington Post* reported February 16, 1989 that the "...expensive hardware acquired for the automated personnel system..." had not been installed, but was "gathering dust" at the Reeves Municipal Center.

A member of the Washington, D.C. City Council reportedly complained to the newspaper that the proposed furlough of some city workers would have to be delayed because the data to support such a personnel reduction had not been computerized as promised.

Computer snafus plague even companies that manufacture and sell computers. *Computerworld* reported in its June 5, 1989, issue that, because of a disastrous changeover from a Hewlett-Packard minicomputer to an IBM-compatible mainframe system, Sun Microsystems, Inc., would probably soon report its first-ever quarterly business loss. During the quarter Sun had introduced several new products which had increased the complexity of Sun's billing, ordering and shipping. Problems associated with the computer changeover, coupled with those caused by the product introductions, reportedly delayed thousands of orders that should have been included in that quarter's sales figures but instead were carried over into the next quarter. The snafus caused both sales and profits to appear lower than they actually were.

"If at first you don't succeed...". Some organizations appear to continue to throw money at problems, hoping that eventually they might wind up with a system that meets their requirements. In

California, Bank of America invested $60 million and six years of effort in a computer system which they abandoned in 1988--before ever using it! The chapter titled *Should Bankers Bank on Computers?* details that ill-fated endeavor.

Technology problems frequently affect stock prices. When IBM officials publicly admitted on March 17, 1989, that the firm had been unable to correct a manufacturing problem involving a minuscule microchip used in their IBM 3090S mainframe computers, the company's stock dropped more than five dollars. The next trading day IBM was the New York Stock Exchange's most active stock, dropping another three dollars.

By substituting logic chips capable of performing basic arithmetic functions for memory chips which merely stored data, IBM's new mainframe achieved a substantial performance advantage. The *Wall Street Journal*, relying on an unnamed computer specialist familiar with the IBM situation, reported that only fifteen to twenty percent of the logic chips being manufactured for use in the new computers were usable.

Less than three months later, IBM announced an unrelated equipment replacement recall for its PS/2 model 170 computers, because lubricating oil was leaking onto the surface of hard-disk drives. A company spokesman blamed the anomaly on a previously undetected "manufacturing glitch" at its factory in Fujisawa, Japan. Industry experts speculated that replacing an estimated 2,000 devices afflicted by this rare, but not unprecedented, lubricant leakage problem would cost IBM more than $5 million.

In July 1990 businessman Charles Hayes' bid of $45 to buy one lot of federal government surplus computer equipment was the highest submitted at an auction in Kentucky. The lot included thirteen computer terminals, nine printers, two memory units and two cartridge drives.

After Hayes removed the equipment, a technician, instructed in January to erase the memory units, informed federal authorities that he had not. Rattled officials concluded that the scrapped word processing system probably still contained sensitive information about FBI informants, federally-protected witnesses and sealed indictments! The U.S. Attorney's office in Lexington reportedly had used the discarded system to prepare and store virtually all of their documents from 1983 to 1989.

The federal government filed suit on Thursday, August 30, seeking the return of the auctioned equipment. A federal district judge ordered that the purchaser not examine, copy, or distribute any of the data stored in the devices.

Late the next day, federal marshals, armed with a search warrant, examined Hayes' equipment inventory for nine hours before seizing nine terminals and one computer memory device. When they determined that some of the lot apparently had been sold, Hayes reportedly declined to identify customers who might have purchased the missing equipment.

Hayes apparently later succumbed to government pressure. *The Associated Press* reported on September 8 that the Justice Department had announced that Hayes had, the preceding day, identified his customers, enabling federal agents to recover all of the computer equipment they feared contained sensitive government secrets.

Contracting dollar limits often appear to mean nothing. Under a headline that read "Federal Computer Contract Ran Millions Over Estimate," the *New York Times* reported September 20, 1990, that Arthur Anderson and Company had been paid almost $62 million for a contract that was intended to run $7–$10 million. In a federal government contracting maneuver that observers described as being tantamount to signing a blank check, the U.S. Department of Agriculture had, in 1983, awarded a contract to Andersen for the design of two computer systems to keep track of the government's grain holdings and processed commodities. Although originally budgeted at only $7 million, the contractor reportedly insisted that the contract must include a provision to cover "unforeseen expenses." *The Times* reported that the contractor had explained that the endeavor cost so much because the work specifications and instructions were "vague."

When wars end, citizens rush to return to their homes in the former battle zones. Soon after the Persian Gulf War of 1991 ended, Kuwait's newly-restored government barred thousands of people clamoring to enter the country because bureaucrats could not verify who should be permitted entry. Officials announced that their computer system had crashed, rendering unreadable computer files containing all citizenship and immigration data. The people begging to cross the border into Kuwait would simply have to wait until officials could determine their entry eligibility.

Luckily, someone realized that the data probably still existed, either in the computer or on storage media, and called upon an American firm known for its data recovery expertise. Ontrack Data International of Eden Prairie, Minnesota immediately dispatched two engineers to determine whether the data could be recovered. Using software they wrote on the spot, together with existing data-recovery tools they brought with them, the Americans reportedly recovered 100% of the lost data and restored the Kuwaiti computer system to normal operation within thirty-six hours.

Maintaining security over personal financial data has been a major privacy concern for years. In July 1991, six states announced that they were participants in lawsuits charging that TRW, Inc. employed inadequate controls to prevent errors in its credit data and inadequate procedures for correcting them. The states also charged that the giant credit-reporting firm illegally sold mailing lists based on consumers' credit reports. Alabama, California, Idaho and Michigan joined in a lawsuit filed by the State of Texas. New York filed a separate suit.

A spokesman for TRW Information Services vehemently denied the charges, announcing that TRW was filing countersuits in both Texas and New York seeking rulings that the company was in compliance with requirements of the federal Fair Credit Reporting Act.

Within six months, nineteen state attorneys general were participating in similar lawsuits against TRW. In a December 10, 1991, settlement, TRW agreed to improve accuracy of the consumer credit data it collected and maintained, to speedily investigate alleged errors, and (in conjunction with the Federal Trade Commission) to monitor the new procedures for five years. TRW admitted no wrongdoing.

For consumers the most important part of the settlement probably was TRW's promises to review consumer-disputed data within thirty days and to delete it upon receipt of documents from creditors confirming consumers' versions of credit incidents.

In an incident affecting computers around the world, a logic fault in Tandem Computer's time-stamping capability appeared destined to halt all machines with that feature engaged at 4:22 p.m. local time on August 27, 1991. In its September 9, 1991, issue *Computerworld* reported that faulty programming code caused the computers to interpret numbers representing the date and time as an impossible-to-execute command. If this occurred, the computer's security system would seize control of the system and lock out any attempting to use it. Even technicians attempting to fix the fault would not be granted access.

When Tandem field engineers became aware of the unusual problem, they quickly telephoned users, warning them to turn off the security feature before the deadly time of 4:22 p.m. arrived in their time zone. Because of this expedient warning, *Computerworld* reported that, worldwide, the tricky problem affected only sixty computers.

In September 1988 the National Institutes of Health (NIH) awarded IBM a ten-year, $800+ million contract for a major computer system. Although the procurement cited the critical nature of the calculations required by the agency's scientists as justification to procure the expensive computer system, the U.S. General Accounting Office reported in January 1992 that staff scientists rarely used the costly new system. Auditors had found that it was being used primarily to process administrative data rather than to perform scientific calculations as originally intended. The report concluded that the agency had spent $16 million to acquire two computers it did not need. It also charged that the computer system was extremely ill-suited for agency employees who were supposed to use it.

Newspaper publishers know that clever headlines sell papers. Using a headline reading "Computer 'fatal' to Hartford, Conn. Voters," *USA Today* made it appear that a computer had killed numerous voters in Hartford, Connecticut. What the paper actually reported under that September 30, 1992, headline was that a computer used to select federal grand juries for the U.S. District Court in Hartford had failed to select some 5,500 Hartford citizens to be sent jury questionnaires over a three-year period because of a data spill-over. Investigators, seeking to determine why Hartford residents were so under-represented on jury lists, discovered that when data had been entered into the computer, the "d" at the end of "Hartford" spilled over into an adjacent data field, where "d" meant dead! Of course, the computer had been programmed not to send jury questionnaires to deceased persons.

Computations yielding results "close enough for government work," often are not accurate enough to satisfy more stringent requirements of scientists, statisticians, mathematicians and engineers. Intel stunned computer users everywhere by the 1994 admission that their Pentium chip, used in computers manufactured by IBM, Compaq and Dell, contained a "subtle flaw" affecting division calculations requiring high precision.

After news of the previously unknown flaw surfaced on the Internet in November 1994, concerned computer buffs around the globe used the same medium to express their concerns about and frustrations with the situation. The *New York Times* reported (April 3, 1995) that Intel employees had discovered the flaw in July but decided to keep mum.

Intel confirmed in November that the Pentium chip computed results accurately through the fourth digit to the right of each decimal point. Any computational errors appeared in the fifth and subsequent digits to the right of a decimal.

To settle eleven class-action suits filed in the matter of the inaccurate chip, Intel announced in April 1995, both a chip replacement program and an agreement to pay claims of some who had used the faulty product. In situations clearly requiring higher degrees of accuracy than that provided by the flawed chips, Intel promised to pay costs of reprocessing work. The chipmaker also reimbursed an estimated $6 million in legal fees associated with the suits.

Intuit, Inc. of Menlo Park, California, purveyor of Quicken software, revealed on March 23, 1995 that its programmers had made two major blunders in the firm's tax preparation software, Macintax. Tens of thousands of tax returns that customers had prepared and transmitted to a computer Intuit maintained in Green Bay, Wisconsin, for electronic submission of returns to Internal Revenue Service were essentially "open" for browsing by any Intuit customer! First, the programmers had neglected to encrypt the returns stored in the computer--they were in a form that anyone accessing the computer could read, copy, or even delete. Secondly, the company had provided customers with software containing both the log-in identification code and a password that provided open access to the computer files.

An unidentified Macintax customer reportedly sent e-mail messages to both the *New York Times* and Intuit reporting his discovery of inadequate security for the completed tax returns.

An article in *The Times*' business section the following day indicated that an Intuit official reported finding no indication that any of the returns in the computer had been tampered with in any way. He also said that the security access to the computer had been improved. The company expected that more than a million customers would use their software to prepare tax returns for the year.

"Build it and they will use it," a widely-held management philosophy regarding massive computer systems, doesn't always hold true. The Environmental Protection Agency, in 1991, implemented a much-touted Resource Conservation and Recovery Information System to help state governments manage hazardous waste. In a 1995 report to Congress, the General Accounting Office (GAO) said that the multi-million dollar system had been virtually abandoned when intended users had opted for independent work-around systems because the EPA system had been so difficult to use. Even so, GAO reported that EPA was continuing to spend $7.5 million per year to run the little-used computer system. The GAO report concluded that EPA had replaced an older system, that was "cumbersome, difficult to use, and confusing" with the Resource Conservation and Recovery Information System, a newer system that also was "cumbersome, difficult to use, and confusing." Where was the improvement?

When a politician charges that the federal government wastes billions of dollars on something, the allegation often is not deemed newsworthy. However, Senator William S. Cohen's report charging that the federal government wasted billions of dollars on computers attracted widespread media attention. By the mid-1990s the federal government was spending more than $25 billion a year on computers and related services. From 1985 to 1995 the total exceeded $200 billion. Among the specific examples of government waste congressional investigators cited in their October 1994 report:

+ The National Institutes of Health spent $800 million to procure several mainframe computers when personal computers probably would have been preferable.

+ The Agency for International Development used forty-five different computer systems to manage operations and track property for its extensive foreign aid program. The computers could not share data with one another.

+ Internal Revenue Service's antiquated computers were blamed for the government's failure to collect $70 billion in delinquent taxes from corporations and individuals.

+ The U.S. Department of Agriculture failed to coordinate development of seventeen major computer systems to ensure that the $6.3 billion systems could communicate with one another.

Cohen also pointed out that the Social Security Administration, Federal Aviation Authority, Immigration and Naturalization Service and other government entities continued to use older, slower, less capable computer technology that hampered each agency's ability to serve the public effectively.

Many of the problems cited in the report can be attributed to the fact that the complicated process the federal government used to acquire computer systems moved at a much slower pace than the development of new automation technology. The average federal government procurement of a mainframe computer took nearly four years, long enough for computer technology to advance substantially. Many of the products, considered state-of-the-art when a procurement began, would be obsolete by the time the computer equipment was delivered.

Well, maybe not quite that fast... The world's largest computer-chip manufacturer, Intel, revealed on January 5, 1996, that a programming error had caused the company unintentionally to overstate the performance expectations of their Pentium processor by about ten percent. By then, Pentium had already become the most popular microprocessor for personal computer products.

"IBM misses chance for the gold," proclaimed the *Computerworld* headline of July 19, 1996. For the 1996 Olympic Games in Atlanta, IBM had agreed to serve as systems integrator for a hundred applications being developed by thirty vendors. IBM also agreed to donate $45 million in goods and services to the games.

The massive Olympics information system involved four IBM 390 mainframe computers, 300 networks, and 7,000 personal computers and Think-Pads. The system was supposed to support a commentator's information system providing live feeds; deliver electronic mail, schedules, weather, and athlete's biographies; maintain a web site; and support a games-management system that included coordinating 60,000 volunteers. Intended to support 150,000 users, the massive system was intended to serve 15,000 media organizations, 31,000 olympic employees, and 15,000 athletes. Over the seventeen days of the games, the system was expected to generate thirty million reports.

Computerworld cited several shortcomings of the Olympic system. Athletes reportedly were unable to access their electronic mail because the computerized information kiosks crashed and went out-of-service. News services complained of receiving considerable inaccurate information on athletes (such as age 92 instead of 22). Other descriptors such as height and weight also were frequently wrong. Background data was described as "unreliable." In a few instances, news services reported receiving final results for events that had not yet taken place. Despite the system's faults, *Computerworld* reported that a spokesman for the Atlanta Committee for the Olympic Games had suggested that IBM could pull together the infrastructure created for Atlanta and build a system for the Sydney Olympics in 2000.

Within days of publishing its ranking of America's top law schools in March 1997, *U.S. News* announced that the rankings were wrong because of a newly-discovered error in the database used to create the list. The same error reportedly also forced the publisher to print a corrected edition of *1997 America's Best Graduate Schools*.

To boldly go where such a huge company had never gone before, America Online (AOL) in December 1996 shifted from by-the-hour pricing to a flat-rate per month for its online computer services. Company officials, seeing smaller Internet providers selling services at flat rates, feared a loss of customers unless they did the same. With customers using tens of millions of computer-connect hours each month under the pay-by-the-hour pricing arrangement, no one could possibly predict the service demand created by flat rate pricing.

The new pricing policy encouraged AOL customers, once connected, to remain online--even while they paused to eat a meal, shower, run errands, or whatever. This practice ensured easy access when the customer was ready to resume using the service. The resulting electronic traffic jam denied millions of AOL customers immediate or even timely access, causing many to complain that they were not getting the online service they were paying AOL to provide. Politicians across America, some of them hungry for any news media exposure, rushed to offer criticism of AOL's handling of the unusual situation. Several state attorneys general threatened law suits.

AOL promised to spend $350 million to add new communications links and create another data center. They also promised to upgrade their entire network. Although the system's upgrading efforts caused a few service outages, customer access to AOL quickly improved.

Within three months of AOL's introduction of their flat-rate policy, the dramatic increase in the volume of e-mail challenged the capacity of other online service providers. Some reported increases of 50% in less than six months. Following several days of impaired service, on April 16, 1997, Microsoft Network shut down all e-mail service to its 2.5 million customers. A spokesman explained that the firm was adding nine new servers, doubling their system's capacity. He said that the transition should take less than forty-eight hours.

Voice mail, also growing at an unprecedented rate, suffered from serious computer glitches during this same period. Pacific Telesis Group completed, in December 1996, a move of 80,000 voice-mail boxes from a mainframe computer manufactured by Digital Sound Corporation to one manufactured by Unisys. For several weeks following the change, customers complained of problems ranging from their inability to access some mailboxes, to messages that played back too slowly, making them extremely difficult to understand.

Internet users learned on March 4, 1997 of the existence of free, down-loadable software designed to correct a just-discovered flaw in Microsoft's Internet Explorer. Countless users quickly downloaded copies from Microsoft's website. The flaw reportedly could have permitted website operators to secretly run programs or manipulate files on someone else's computer--without being detected.

State government computer systems also frequently miss their targets. In Washington, state welfare officials began an effort to computerize their welfare records in 1982. The undertaking, which cost $20 million, was abandoned in 1989 because caseworkers preferred to process work by hand rather than rely on the user-unfriendly system.

In 1991 officials began a second computerization effort, promising that this one would be "caseworker-friendly." After initial cost estimates for the Automated Client Eligibility System (ACES) reportedly doubled, legislators demanded that officials account for the anticipated cost increases. A compromise was reached and the ACES system went into service in April 1996.

Washington State also had problems with another major computer system. The *Seattle Times* reported March 22, 1997 that state legislators were deeply divided over the future of a costly computer system under development for the state's Department of Licensing. Begun in 1990, the License Application Mitigation Project (LAMP) was intended to consolidate, in one supercomputer, information of drivers licenses, vehicle registrations and boat registrations. Originally budgeted for $41 million, the project was scheduled to be completed in July 1995.

The Times reported that the cost estimate had risen to $51 million and the completion date had been delayed until November 1997. The article also reported that LAMP would then be able to provide only what the system it was supposed to replace could already do--despite an expenditures to date of $40 million and an anticipated total outlay of $51 million! Further, according to the article, the state was spending $800,000 a year to operate the present system. By contrast, operating costs for the new system were expected to exceed $5 million annually. An unnamed legislator likened the expenditure to the Pentagon's earlier purchase of toilet seats for $800 each. Unidentified computer experts reportedly told *The Times* that state officials had overestimated the benefits of the new system and underestimated its complexity.

As the twentieth century draws to a close, the most daunting challenge to computer programmers is to solve the myriad problems associated with the arrival of the year 2000.

Since computers' earliest days, programmers have tended to record years as only two digits--76, 80, 95, etc. Every one knew to assume that the two recorded digits were preceded by "19".

Without reprogramming, most existing computer programs will continue to assume the presence of 19 in front of the 00, the

01, or the 02 that appears to depict years after December 31, 1999. This oddity potentially spells trouble for any date-dependent computer processing performed in the year 2000 and beyond.

Because of the innumerable ways in which countless computer programs handle dates, there is no simple or universal fix. Many organizations continue to run programs written in languages their current employees maintain with difficulty under the best of circumstances. Finding and changing every computation involving a date will simply overwhelm them. Rewriting such huge programs costs big bucks and consumes years of effort.

Fearing the year 2000 might pose life-threatening dangers for the 19,000 veterans who wear pacemakers, the Department of Veterans Affairs announced in 1997, that a check of the devices concluded that none would be adversely affected by the date change.

On the other hand, a department spokesman indicated that VA expected to spend more than $144 million to correct computer programs used to pay benefits to more than ten million veterans and their dependents.

Some organizations have already encountered difficulties associated with the millennium bug. Corning Glass Works reported problems when their computers attempted to process contracts containing year 2000 dates. Owners of AMC movie theaters have complained that their computers would not accept credit cards expiring in 2000. As financial institutions issue tens of millions of credit cards expiring that year, this problem will become common.

In one of thousands of published articles concerning the year 2000 problem, the *New York Times*, in its November 15, 1993, issue, estimated the worldwide cost to correct this logic problem in all programs will total between $50 and $75 billion (yes, billion)!

Then, near the end of 1997, a New England research group estimated that American businesses would spend $440 billion (yes, billion) attempting to fix the problem. Federal government estimates of a mere $4 billion to correct its massive number of computer programs appear to be unrealistically low.

An extensive article in the *Seattle Times*, November 2, 1997, reported that a "knowledgeable executive" had estimated that the worldwide costs (including lawsuits) associated with the millenium problems might reach $3.6 trillion (yes, trillion!)--more than $600 for every person on earth!

The three widely disparate estimates appear to confirm that nobody really has a clue as to what the actual costs might be.

Reporters Peter Lewis and Thomas Haines, in their two-and-a-half page *Seattle Times* article, cautioned that the year 2000 problem could affect the obvious systems involving credit cards, bank cards, ATMs, stock trades, financial transactions, billing documents, numerous types of vital records, as well as mortgage and loan processing systems. They also warned that the problem could have serious implications for computer-controlled security systems, air-traffic control, satellites, weapons systems, communications, medical systems, even nuclear power plants! Embedded computer chips controlling equipment on manufacturing floors, in navigation systems, in military equipment, at medical facilities--all must be examined to determine whether they face potential problems.

Industry observers note that, even if most organizations in the United States fix their year 2000 problem in time to avoid major difficulties, the problem exists for the entire world. Economic interaction is such that a single computer failure in any major financial institution could seriously disrupt world commerce. A handful of economists have expressed fear that the millennium problem might cause a global recession.

2

CAN WE RELY ON COMPUTERS
TO KEEP OUR MILITARY READY?

American military personnel, who introduced the word "snafu" to our vocabulary, have encountered many such disorders in their own computer systems.

The computerized payroll system used by the U.S. Army to pay civilian employees dispensed three billion dollars in salaries in 1977. It was considered so efficient that it had been designated the official model payroll system to be used by the entire Department of Defense, with an annual civilian payroll of fifteen billion dollars!

The system's luster quickly began to tarnish when the U.S. General Accounting Office reported on an audit of the system. Among their actual findings: of just eighty-seven employee records subjected to thorough scrutiny, auditors discovered that seventy-three were incorrect. Of those records selected for examination, an astounding 83.9% contained errors! They discovered that "a few" employees had two active records on the computer masterfile, causing the system to issue them duplicate paychecks each payday. GAO auditors also expressed dismay at the careless handling of blank documents by the computer staff. They reportedly found more than 13,000 blank U.S. Treasury checks unprotected and unsecured, waiting for the imprinting of names and amounts. Nearby they also discovered U.S. Savings Bonds valued at nearly a half-million dollars, only waiting for the imprint of names.

Auditors also expressed amazement at how lacking or inadequate the system's controls and safeguards were. Auditors tested the system by providing simulated records and observing how the computer dealt with them. They reported that it accepted without question one employee's pay record that indicated 300 hours of overtime pay within a two-week period. It also accepted test records containing more than eighty hours of regular pay for two weeks. Auditors introduced test records reflecting far greater hourly pay rates than employees should earn based on their pay grades. The system accepted the inflated hourly rates and computed pay accordingly--often paying clerical employees at hourly rates earned by top managers. The system failed to restrict employee pay levels to the limits of the annual payscales then in effect. For example, auditors were able to generate bi-weekly paychecks of $9,999.99 (an annual salary of nearly $260,000--more than three times the amount payable to those receiving the maximum federal pay).

Auditors expressed their gravest concern over the fact that a single payroll clerk could manipulate all system functions required to generate paychecks. The same person could create fictitious employee records, enter phony pay data for each pay period, and instruct the computer to issue paychecks for the nonexistent employees--all with little chance of detection.

The General Accounting Office told Congress that the Army's civilian payroll system definitely should not be used as a model for the entire Department of Defense.

More recently military payrolls have continued to demonstrate the unexpected. For example, in 1994, Gen. John Shalikashvili, after becoming chairman of the Joint Chiefs of Staff, received extra housing allowances to which he was not entitled. Even though the perks of his position provided a house at Fort Myer, Virginia, the payroll computer included a basic housing allowance in his gross pay. After Shalikashvili alerted finance officials to the erroneous payments, they stopped. The computer then deducted the amount overpaid from future payments due the general.

In September 1995, the Defense Finance and Accounting Service in Denver reported that the computer system had underpaid nearly 5,000 Air Force members. Affected were approximately 3,600 promoted on September 1, and an additional 1,200 with other changes to their pay status. The data change was transmitted to a communications link in Denver, which inexplicably failed to transfer it to the payroll system. The problem was discovered too late to correct for the current payroll processing cycle, so all monies due were paid the following payday.

In a subsequent foul-up, when several computer files failed to interact as expected, the Army ended fiscal year 1996 with nearly 4,000 fewer soldiers than intended. Their files of recruiting data, training base reservations, and medical/entrance processing data apparently were not properly synchronized. This oversight led to their use of invalid computer models to determine the number of service members to recruit, promote, retain, and separate. The result: the Army ended the year with 491,203 soldiers instead of the 495,000 authorized by Congress. A military spokesperson explained that in the Army's rush to automate as many personnel management functions as possible, the data had not been properly integrated, meaning that recruiting data was not being compared with that from other personnel programs.

Even though another computer processing error at the Defense Finance and Accounting Service in Denver did not affect actual pay, it did cause erroneous Leave and Earning Statements to be issued to 44,449 active-duty Air Force members at the end of December 1996. Corrected statements were issued early in January.

Yet another computer glitch at the same organization caused 50,000 inaccurate W-2 forms to be sent to defense employees in California and New Mexico in January 1997. Officials publicly blamed a "failed computer hard drive" for "scrambling" the earnings information.

In a later computer snafu, officials said that service personnel returning from assignments in areas that qualified them for hostile-fire pay and combat-zone tax exclusions (such as Bosnia), continued to receive such extra pay upon return to America. They explained that the payroll computer system simply had not been informed of the members' status change.

Computer goofs occasionally cause actions that military commanders are reluctant to reverse. Such was the case in 1997, when a computer at the Air Force Personnel Center erred in creating a list of members eligible for promotion. Members whose names appeared above a designated selection line were promoted. A short time later someone discovered that the computer had received faulty instructions. When a new list of eligibles was created, seven of those already promoted no longer qualified. Rather than cancel the already publicly-announced promotions, personnel officials petitioned the Board for Correction of Military Records to let the promotions stand. The board agreed.

Another snafu resulted in more than 7,000 military personnel being paid $50 more than they were entitled to receive when computers failed to deduct Montgomery GI Bill allowances from paychecks dated October 1, 1997. The overpayments resulted from an error in software, newly installed to correct GI Bill accounting inconsistencies, that directed the computer to discontinue the deduction one month earlier than intended.

Twenty sailors died when the 3,500-ton British frigate *HMS Sheffield*, equipped with a state-of-the-art computerized air defense system, sunk after being torpedoed in the South Pacific in 1982. Details of this tragedy can be found in the chapter titled *Do Computers Really Kill People?*

Following an August 30, 1983 deadly international incident, investigators concluded that human error in operating computerized navigational equipment aboard Korean Air Lines flight 007 caused the jumbo jet to stray into Soviet airspace. Soviet fighters blasted the civilian airliner from the sky, killing 269 aboard. The chapter titled *Are Travelers Well-Served By Computers?* chronicles this deadly encounter.

Stunned authorities in Lehigh County, Pennsylvania found it difficult to believe that the nuclear attack that citizens had feared for decades had finally commenced! Nonetheless, it had just become official! On January 4, 1984, many feared that the world as they knew it would cease to exist.

Teletypes in police radio rooms and Civil Defense headquarters across Pennsylvania spewed out the dreaded message of doom, "This is an attack warning. Supplemental information will be provided when available. Take appropriate action." Even though it provided no information about what had happened or might happen later, the hair-raising message triggered those trained for nuclear emergencies to rush to their tasks. The Wednesday morning's calm was shattered by the unprecedented broadcast at 11:15 a.m. What a way to start a New Year--or end a civilization!

In Lehigh County, fire-alarm sirens, radio calls and telephones conveyed the devastating news to bewildered citizens. Emergency personnel rushed to their assigned duty stations.

Five minutes after the computerized emergency warning system message alerted police and Civil Defense officials in forty-one of Pennsylvania's sixty-seven counties to the nuclear threat, minutes in which many envisioned their version of the end of the world, the system transmitted a second notice. It offered no details, no explanation, no assurances--simply advised that the earlier warning should be ignored!

Enraged citizens did not know whether to believe the first message or the second. They wanted to know exactly what had happened. Embarrassed state officials eventually explained that a computer at the Pennsylvania Emergency Management Agency (PEMA), that was supposed to copy pre-recorded emergency messages from a floppy disk into its memory, instead transmitted the harrowing message that terrified so many Pennsylvanians. The

PEMA computer, not fully on-line at the time of the incident, was being readied to serve the entire state.

Officials were able to prevent state-wide panic because they recognized in time that the doomsday warning was a goof and prevented its broadcast over the Emergency Broadcast System.

It seemed a great idea when, in 1974, the U.S. Air Force, carrying hundreds of thousands of spare parts in various inventories, implemented a computer system designed to dispose of those no longer required. The automated system issued orders to scrap the entire inventory of all items not requested in the preceding twelve months. The computer selections were not reviewed by humans. The items simply were declared surplus and sold for whatever price they would bring in the surplus equipment market. In numerous instances requests came in for items shortly after they had been scrapped, necessitating the purchase of replacements. The Air Force frequently repurchased items they had sold as scrap; of course, the Air Force paid top dollar, usually about the same as newly manufactured goods.

When Congress became aware of the procedures (and the attendant waste) in 1984 and demanded an explanation, Air Force officials said that two "pressures" fueled the quick disposal policy. One was Congressional insistence that the military services not build and maintain costly inventories of equipment and spare parts. The other was the budgetary concerns that attempted to minimize the costs of both inventories and warehouses.

Aircraft maintenance personnel reported that the computer-controlled parts disposal system made their jobs unnecessarily difficult. They insisted that as long as the Air Force had a particular aircraft in service, a reasonable supply of all parts for it should be retained in inventory. They claimed to have experienced too many instances in which a part was readily available one month, then totally unavailable the next--simply because a computer had detected that none had been issued during the previous twelve months.

Without announcing a definitive figure, government officials did concede that the automated decision-making system was forcing the Air Force to spend "several million dollars" a year in "unnecessary procurements" to replace scrapped inventory items.

In a subsequent incident, Pentagon procurement officials announced on September 10, 1984, that they had stopped accepting shipments of military equipment containing Texas Instrument microchips because they had learned that the company had not been rigorously testing 100% of its chips as Pentagon contracts required. Manufacture of such sophisticated microchips is a most exact and difficult business. Many of the chips coming off assembly lines can be defective even under excellent manufacturing conditions. Most contracts specify rigid testing procedures to identify and reject all less-than-perfect chips to ensure they won't be used in some critical electronic device. Department of Defense contracts reportedly required testing of *every* chip used in any device procured by the Pentagon.

Texas Instruments reportedly manufactured 4,700 different versions of the suspect chip. Their situation involved a testing issue rather than a quality issue. Industry observers speculated that when Texas Instrument determined that its factories were turning out a very high percentage of top-quality chips, they relaxed their individual testing. According to one estimate, untested chips may have been used over an eight-year span in 15,000,000 military and commercial devices.

Numerous Texas Instrument microchips had been used in AWACS radar surveillance airplanes, B-52 bombers, F-15 and F-111 fighters, as well as in A-6 and A-7 attack aircraft. They also figured prominently in the B-1B nuclear bomber and the Lamps MK III anti-submarine warfare system. Because most newer weapons systems rely on sophisticated electronics, the suspect chip could have been installed in almost any recent military system.

An editorial in the *Los Angeles Times*, September 17, 1984, succinctly noted "...an obvious likelihood that bad chips are finding their way into weapons systems that may consequently fail--at grave peril to national security and the servicemen and women whose lives depend upon the equipment."

The problem reportedly surfaced when IBM complained that their tests revealed potential problems with a batch of chips purchased from Texas Instruments. After Texas Instruments conducted their own tests, they concluded that the chips might cause problems for their customers.

Within a week of learning of the inadequate chip testing at Texas Instruments, Pentagon officials announced their refusal to accept equipment or parts containing the potentially defective chip. A Pentagon spokesman advised all military contractors to return any Texas Instrument chip inventories to the firm for testing and certification.

Even so, officials at Todd Shipyards Corporation in San Pedro, California were stunned when the U.S. Navy refused to accept scheduled delivery of *The Gary*, a newly-built $300-million frigate, Friday, October 26, 1984. After all, this was the twenty-second guided missile ship of its class that Todd had built. How could the Navy refuse to accept their 3,585-ton creation? And who would pay the docking fees of more than $10,000 a day until the stalemate could be resolved?

A Navy spokesman explained that equipment on the vessel had not been "properly tested". He was referring, of course, to the numerous ship's systems containing inadequately tested Texas Instrument semiconductor chips. The Pentagon's blanket policy of refusing any equipment containing Texas Instrument chips included even this massive vessel.

Navy procurement officials reportedly originally told Todd that the company had to agree either to provide a special warranty on the components containing Texas Instrument chips or to replace them with new, test-certified devices. Todd officials replied that they held the manufacturer responsible for the quality and reliability of the chips.

Negotiators reached a compromise under which Todd officials reportedly agreed to extend by six months the warranty on all devices containing the suspect chip. Navy agreed to pay the docking fees caused by the delayed handover of the warship. One week later than originally anticipated, the Navy officially accepted delivery of *The Gary*.

Earlier the same year, another microchip manufacturer, National Semiconductor Corporation, had pleaded guilty to criminal charges involving that firm's failure to properly test chips delivered to the Pentagon. They paid a $1.7 million fine.

The federal government's direct deposit turned out to be a disappointment for thousands of civilian Navy employees in the Washington, D.C. area. Payroll funds were unavailable at their banks on Friday, December 16, 1986.

When officials at the Federal Reserve Bank of Richmond, Virginia became aware of the problem the following Monday morning, they blamed "a glitch" in a computer tape for the failure of the direct-deposit transfer of the payroll funds. Bank employees moved quickly to rectify the situation and many banks received the expected deposits that afternoon. A few institutions reported the funds were transferred to them the next morning.

Understanding banks promised not to charge their affected customers any penalty for the Federal Reserve Bank's computer screw-up. Any customer charges for overdrawn accounts, bounced checks, or late payments would be excused.

On May 17, 1987, an American ship's sophisticated electronic warfare equipment failed to detect incoming missiles fired by an Iraqi Mirage pilot. Thirty-seven American crewmen died in that attack. Details of the incident are included in the chapter titled *Do Computers Really Kill People?*

A Strategic Air Command spokesman reported in October 1987 that a computer had malfunctioned earlier, indicating to the crew of a Minuteman silo that one of their nuclear missiles was about to launch itself. Security police reportedly had responded to the January 10, 1984, crisis at Warren Air Force Base, Wyoming, by parking an armored car on top of the silo in an attempt to prevent it from opening.

The sixty-foot missile, with a range of more than 6.000 miles, was equipped with nuclear warheads which would have been armed in flight (after launch). Although base officials knew, at least in theory, that the missile could not launch itself, when the computer indicated that a launch was imminent, security police attempted to prevent a launch-by-mistake. Officials, for security reasons, declined to reveal what triggered the unusual incident.

In 1988, an automated system aboard the *Vincennes* led crew members to mistakenly conclude that an F-14 was attacking their ship. When they sought to defend their vessel, they inadvertently shot down a civilian airliner, killing 290 people. The chapter titled *Do Computers Really Kill People?* contains details of this tragic incident.

During the Gulf War, American surveillance satellites detected the launch of a Scud missile from a site in Iraq on February 25, 1991. After analyzing its speed and direction, the satellite identified the Scud's target as Dharan, Saudi Arabia. This critical intelligence was flashed immediately to the U.S. Space Command near Colorado Springs for evaluation and action. Before any warning was issued to American troops in the target area, the Scud impacted a corrugated metal warehouse serving as a temporary military barracks, killing twenty-eight American servicemen and wounding ninety-seven. This was the deadliest Iraqi attack on Americans during the Persian Gulf War.

Even though a Patriot missile launcher's radar on the ground in Dharan reportedly detected the incoming Scud, computer software problems prevented the Patriot from firing at it. Defense officials later claimed this to be the only incident during the entire Persian Gulf conflict in which a Patriot failed to fire at an incoming Scud. A spokesman explained that a deadly combination of "six to ten abnormal variables" kept the Patriot system from recognizing the threat as a Scud.

Canada and the United States in the 1950s jointly created an electronic early warning system to detect any Soviet missile launch against North America. This most hush-hush of organizations was designed to alert officials in both Washington and Ottawa of any serious threat in sufficient time to order appropriate retaliatory and defensive actions.

During the very early years, the computer system erroneously interpreted a flock of geese flying near the Canadian border as incoming Soviet missiles. Luckily, humans decided to verify the intrusion before reacting, thereby averting the possible start of a nuclear war.

In October 1960 Norad again triggered an alert when a computer interpreted data from the Distant Early Warning (DEW) line of sensors near Thule, Greenland as being Soviet missiles rushing toward North America. This time, when humans sought to verify the threat, they concluded that an unusually bright rising moon had misled the sensors.

Gradually the two nations installed numerous sophisticated interconnected systems that officials hoped could detect within seconds any Soviet missile launches. Infrared satellites were employed to detect exhaust from missiles. Near the Arctic Circle, ground radar was installed. Another radar installation on the New England coast was supposed to spot any missiles launched from Soviet submarines. All sensors automatically relayed data to military computers in several strategic locations, including the underground Cheyenne Mountain complex near Colorado Springs, the Strategic Air Command in Omaha, Nebraska, the Pentagon's National Military Command Center, and an ultra-secret underground military command bunker located fifty miles outside Washington, D.C. to which key government officials would be evacuated in the event of a nuclear attack.

Early Norad officials assumed that Soviet land-based missiles could reach North America within thirty minutes and that those launched by submarine could reach their targets within fifteen minutes. Even with these short warnings, officials thought that much could be done to defend against the incoming weapons as well as to launch a counterattack. As time passed Norad became a fact of life on the North American continent. Virtually everyone knew what Norad meant, even though few knew anything at all about its systems.

During the autumn of 1979, computer technicians replaced an antiquated Philco 2000 computer controlling the top-secret missile launch system with a modern, specially-built Honeywell 427-M. Close-mouthed officials refused to divulge any details about the Honeywell equipment, even the size of its memory. During a November 6 test of the new computer, the system interpreted a simulated attack as an actual Soviet missile attack requiring a military response. The Norad computer in Colorado Springs automatically notified three Air Force bases to immediately launch response aircraft. Two F-106 intercept planes lifted off from Kingsley Field, Oregon while two more were quickly launched from Sawyer Air Force Base in Michigan. Six F-101s flew from a Canadian base in British Columbia to counter the threat.

Within approximately five minutes Norad officials in Colorado reportedly had discovered that the warning was in error. Although the intercept planes were already aloft, Norad officials were able to stop the departure of nearly 100 B-52 bombers carrying weapons of mass destruction.

News media around the globe reported the nerve-racking incident. The Soviet news agency *Tass* said that such incidents potentially posed "irreparable consequences" to many nations.

Norad officials, quick to blame the Honeywell equipment, said that the government would conduct a thorough investigation of the incident, but warned that, because of the sensitive national security issues involved, the findings probably would never be made public. Authorities later explained that an employee had mistakenly loaded a tape containing test data into the computer system, triggering the crisis.

Less than a year later, *Tass* reported that for "...several minutes the world was on the brink of nuclear war" on Tuesday, June 3, 1980, when in the pre-dawn hours the Norad system activated both audio and visual signals indicating that the Soviets had launched intercontinental and submarine-launched missiles aimed at North American targets.

Without knowing whether they were responding to an actual threat or participating in another false alarm, Strategic Air Command crews again rushed to 100 B-2 bombers armed with nuclear weapons and awaiting takeoff instructions. An electronic control plane immediately zoomed into the sky from its base in Hawaii. Crews on board ballistic missile submarines and at silo-base missile sites were alerted. At Andrews Air Force Base in Maryland, the modified 747 designated as the Presidential airborne command center was readied for immediate take-off awaiting the arrival of the President via helicopter from the White House.

When the alarm sounded in the Pentagon's National Military Command Center, officers suspected that the warning was an error and decided not to advise Secretary of Defense Harold Brown or President Carter until they knew more about the situation.

Within three minutes, defense officials learned that radar, satellite, and other sensors not controlled by the Norad computer had indicated no warnings of missiles in flight. Without such collaboration, it was concluded that the computer had issued another false alarm. Officials canceled the alert.

Three days later, Norad computers triggered a nearly identical scenario. The June 6 incident also was judged a false alarm within three minutes and the alert canceled again. Immediately following the second incident within a week, Secretary Brown asked a team of computer experts from the private sector to search for problems in the automated early-warning command and control system.

Assistant Secretary of Defense Gerald Dinneen announced in Washington on June 17 that investigators had concluded that the incidents of June 3 and June 6 were caused by failure of a dime-sized electronic component costing less than fifty cents. The faulty chip reportedly caused failure of an integrated circuit within a communications device.

In the wake of these highly-publicized computer malfunctions, the (Norfolk) *Virginian-Pilot* reported that a former Department of Defense computer-testing specialist charged that he had been fired for warning military officials of major problems in the Norad computer system in 1973. Many of the same problems reportedly persisted into the next decade.

The Senate Armed Services Committee released a report in October 1980 stating that, between January 1979 and June 1980, Norad experienced 151 "relatively serious" alarms. One was triggered on October 3, 1979, when a tracking device sensed the wreckage of a decaying space rocket falling near the northwestern coast of the United States. Another occurred in March 1980 when a Soviet submarine, participating in a training exercise in the Pacific north of Japan, fired four missiles. Lesser alarms reportedly had been prompted by sensors detecting sun flares, forest fires, and even plane crashes.

Commercial electric service to Norad failed in December 1980, knocking out a relay switch and causing failure of two diesel-powered generators which were supposed to run constantly, even while commercial power was being used. The simultaneous, unexpected loss of both electric power options shut down Norad computers for an hour, until other generators could be started. Although the equipment suffered no damage, officials said that some lost data had to be restored.

Even though most of the system's major problems appeared to have been solved, the Norad System became obsolete. In 1984, the government awarded a competitive $202 million contract to General Telephone to create a replacement system. The new system was scheduled for completion in 1986.

On December 15, 1988, the U.S. General Accounting Office issued a scathing appraisal of Defense Department modernization efforts. Auditors charged that the equipment was behind schedule, over budget, and incompatible with other electronics in the comprehensive Norad system. GAO said that the cost of the new system had soared to $281 million and the completion date, which had been delayed four years, was rescheduled for 1990.

GAO further claimed that the software was unstable and that engineers had been unable to correct the problems. Although the contract specifications required the ability to restart the Norad system within two minutes following an electric power failure, auditors said that some restarts took half an hour. More shocking was the allegation by GAO that, when the contractor determined that the new system's wiring was incompatible with existing electronics, Air Force officials decided to change the wiring on all the old equipment rather than rewire the new! GAO condemned this decision, saying it would require two years to complete and cost $5 million.

During the September 1995 NATO air offensive against the Bosnian Serbs, commanders ordered the guided-missile cruiser *Monterey* to launch a Tomahawk cruise missile attack on Serb positions. The *Monterey* crew could not comply. Investigators later reported that a sailor, entering data into the Tomahawk's guidance computer, had inadvertently hit a button activating an unintended system update. When they discovered that the update had corrupted the system on the *Monterey*, creating technological problems that prevented the missiles' launch, commanders ordered the nearby *Normandy* to fire its Tomahawks. The *Normandy*'s crew, without apparent problems, fired its missile barrage at the Serb targets.

The military had reported numerous earlier problems with the sophisticated Tomahawk missiles. Six of those launched during the Gulf War unexplainedly fell into the sea. In nine reported incidents, launch attempts simply failed.

Similar problems were reported in June 1993, when the United States launched twenty-three Tomahawk missiles against Iraqi positions in retaliation for that country's plot to kill former President Bush. A military analyst estimated that problems had arisen with approximately 5% of the Navy's Tomahawk launch attempts.

In an unrelated incident, investigators concluded that after maintenance personnel aboard the aircraft carrier *Lincoln* ignored a computer warning and certified an F/A-18 safe-for-flight, it crashed into the Pacific Ocean on January 28, 1995. After catapulting from the *Lincoln*, pilot Lt. Glennon Kersgeiter was killed while attempting to eject from his Hornet.

In addition to ignoring the computer warning, investigators charged that maintenance personnel neglected to remove a serial number plate from a newly-installed device on the doomed jet. During the catapult shot the plate apparently detached, jamming a sensor used to fly the plane off the carrier, thus triggering the disaster. They concluded that, in response to the computer warning, maintenance personnel should have grounded the plane.

For at least three decades scientists and engineers have been aware of the calamitous devastation that electromagnetic pulses (EMP) can inflict upon solid-state electronics. Before the 1980s, defense experts had concluded that atomic bombs exploded high above the earth would create intense waves of invisible energy, disrupting electric power networks and communications systems, rendering computers unusable. Most modern weapons systems rely on computers; these would not be usable either defensively or offensively. If radio and telephone communications were disrupted military commanders could not even talk with each other. What a way to fight a war!

Although such an atomic attack would kill or injure no citizens, cause no physical damage to property, buildings, or facility, it could still, nevertheless render an entire nation defenseless in today's world of solid-state technology.

For at least fifteen years certain telephone and utility companies have installed limited protective equipment against the EMP threat. Many critical computer centers have been enclosed in electronically-protected shelters which should protect them from EMPs. Protection has also been built into some critical computer equipment operated by the federal government; however, because of national security implications, these endeavors are not publicly discussed.

The Navy, with vessels constantly in service around the globe, announced the formation, in October 1995, of the Fleet Information Warfare Center (FIWC), at Little Creek Naval Amphibious Base in Virginia. Fearing that an enemy could electronically neutralize an entire battle group, the Navy created FIWC for the development of equipment and tactics to prevent adversaries corrupting American information systems. They also wanted to learn how to attack and disable enemy information systems. Navy officials allocated $389 million to FIWC for its first year of operation. For obvious reasons, the specific offensive capabilities developed at FIWC remain classified.

3

WHAT HAPPENS WHEN
COMPUTERS CAN'T COMMUNICATE?

Computers, installed to modernize communications systems and corporate operations, frequently fail, creating widespread chaos.

On Sunday, May 28, 1978, an early morning power failure at a telephone company's office in downtown Washington, D.C. caused a computer to malfunction. The computer, which normally handled collect, person-to-person, and credit-card calls as well as those billed to a third number, was put out of service. The outage affected operator-assisted calls for the entire day. Only long-distance calls that customers dialed direct were unaffected by the computer failure.

In Abilene, Texas, data entry errors were blamed for misplacement of yellow pages listings in the spring 1980 telephone directories. For example, the foul-up, at Southwestern Bell Telephone Company, placed Elliott Insurance Company under the "Funeral Homes" classification. It also positioned the Elliott-Hamil Funeral Home under "Frozen Foods--Wholesale."

Construction workers severed an AT&T trunk line carrying communications between a Rockwell International site and the company's computer in Dallas. This incident from the 1980s shut down all telecommunications for twenty-four hours. A Rockwell spokesman estimated that the outage cost Rockwell about $25,000 in lost programmer productivity.

When fire destroyed a major Tokyo telephone exchange on November 16, 1984, more than a million Japanese lost telephone service. Numerous companies complained that their computers could not communicate with other computers or automated devices because of the damage inflicted by the sixteen-hour blaze. Police said they suspected that a worker's welding torch had accidentally started the fire by igniting one of the cables in an under-ground utility tunnel.

In its June 6, 1985 issue *Computerworld* reported that James Vinick of Springfield, Massachusetts had received 246 telephone credit cards from AT&T--even though he had not requested even one. Vinick said that when he called the AT&T 800 number printed on the cards, nobody could explain why the computer had issued him so many cards. However, Vinick said that the AT&T employee with whom he spoke warned him to expect an additional 725 cards which the computer indicated were being issued by the National Data Corporation in Atlanta! Sure enough, within a few days the postal service delivered three large mail sacks from Atlanta to the Vinick residence, containing 725 more cards.

In February 1986, police in Hackensack, New Jersey noticed the sudden, unexplained popularity of certain New Jersey Bell public telephones. They asked the phone company to explain why, even in extremely bad weather, customers waited in long lines at some telephones, while other, nearby phones remained unused.

Phone company officials told the police in April that they had learned the secret to the mysterious preference customers appeared to have for certain telephones. An error in a computer program at New Jersey Bell allowed callers from several Hackensack public phones to place international calls without paying for them. Telephones offering free calls attract more customers every time!

When GTE's Sprint combined with United Telecommunications in the summer of 1986, Charles M. Skibo was named president of the new entity, called US Sprint.

Although highly respected for his marketing savvy, many stockholders reportedly blamed Skibo for failing to correct computer problems which reportedly caused US Sprint to lose $76 million in the second quarter of 1987. They elected a new president.

A spokesman told reporters that the newly created company experienced great difficulty in combining computer billing systems from the two original companies. He explained that a substantial number of calls made the previous August, September, and October were not billed to customers until the following June. By then, customers disputed the charges and refused to pay. In addition to numerous problems of under-billing and delayed-billing, US Sprint reportedly sent more than 13,000 duplicate bills to customers.

ATT had different problems when it merged two computer billing systems, near the end of 1987. A corporate computer reportedly double-billed between one and two million customers. After paying the original bills, customers balked at the subsequent duplicates. Consequently, before AT&T identified and corrected the error, some accounts were referred to collection agencies; the computer indicated the customers owed past-due, outstanding balances.

Thousands of customers in Chicago's western suburbs lost all telephone communications when a fire burned cables and computer switching equipment in Hinsdale, Illinois. The service disruption, which affected both voice and data communications, began on Mother's Day, May 8, 1988. Investigators told reporters that the unmanned Hinsdale switching facility had no fire suppression system to protect its computers.

Illinois Bell reported that 118,000 long-distance lines and 30,000 data lines had been destroyed in the blaze. More than

35,000 local service voice lines were damaged. The company assigned 400 workers to rebuild the switching station and replace computers and fiber-optic communications lines destroyed by the fire. Although technicians restored service to most customers within two weeks, a few remained without service for almost a month.

After receiving numerous complaints from customers claiming they had not received requested telephone credit cards, AT&T employees in Piscataway, New Jersey created a list of 7,000 names and addresses they thought would clear up the backlog. In late December 1988, when they entered the list into the computer, the cards were printed and mailed to the customers. This undertaking should have solved the problem.

Unfortunately, nobody removed the special list from the computer after the cards were sent. So, each time the computer was instructed to print and mail customer cards, it created cards for everyone on that day's list--plus the special backlog list of 7,000 customers.

Because the goof remained undetected in the computer center for eleven processing days, all customers on the backlog list received eleven phone cards, instead of the single one they had requested!

After calls from customers alerted AT&T employees to the situation, the company sent out apology letters urging customers to destroy their extra cards. The letter also promised each customer another card with a different account number, in case the numbers on the earlier cards had been compromised.

Less than half of the long-distance calls placed with AT&T on January 15, 1990, were successfully completed. The fact that the service outage occurred on Martin Luther King's birthday, a holiday for most high-volume customers, lessened its impact.

A software flaw in an AT&T signaling processor serving New York, caused the switch to suspend operations for a few seconds. The system automatically transmitted a message informing other AT&T switches that New York was briefly out of service. The cascading problem prevented tens of millions of phone calls from being successfully completed. Toll-free 800 services were especially affected.

During the service disruption, which lasted from 2:00 p.m. to 11:30 p.m. (EST), AT&T reported that only 42% of attempted calls were completed. AT&T's typical completion rate, according to a spokesman, was 77.2%.

On Tuesday, January 16, AT&T's chairman apologized for the temporary loss of service. The problem was officially attributed to "a flaw in the software."

AT&T garnered worldwide favorable publicity during the autumn of 1990 when the company offered free phone calls home to U.S. military personnel in Saudi Arabia as part of Operation Desert Shield. Service personnel made more than 130,000 calls to the United States in October alone. During Thanksgiving week they placed 140,000 more. Even though AT&T asked the soldiers to limit each call to three minutes, some callers talked up to one hour.

Favorable publicity quickly turned sour in December, when phone bills sent to some 25,000 of the service personnel's families in the United States included normal charges for the supposedly free calls. A few families told reporters their phone bills for the month exceeded a thousand dollars.

An AT&T official hastened to tell reporters that "errors in a computer program" had caused improper billing of calls intended to be free. He explained that the computer was supposed to list the free calls, then suppress the charges when it created the bills for long-distance service. The suppression feature had not worked as planned.

On Christmas Eve a spokesman for AT&T apologized for the foul-up and announced that the communications giant was taking steps to ensure that customers did not pay for calls that American military personnel had expected to be free.

A broken fiber-optic cable disrupted air travel at New York City's three area airports on the morning of January 4, 1991. Because computers could not communicate, numerous flights were delayed and some were canceled.

The *New York Times* reported that air traffic controllers diverted flights destined for New York, forcing some to return to their points of origin.

A spokesman initially reported that an AT&T crew, removing antiquated underground cable near the New Jersey Turnpike, inadvertently snared and snapped an active fiber-optic cable at 9:35 a.m. The severed line reportedly was AT&T's primary communications link connecting New York City and Newark, New Jersey with the rest of the world.

Because water from the Passaic River had flooded the twenty-foot-deep manhole where the break occurred, repair crews had to pump it out before technicians could splice the micro-thin fibers and restore communications.

Although AT&T was able to meet service demands by 5:00 p.m., repairs were not completed until 8:00 p.m. Technicians continued working Friday night and Saturday to replace the temporary repairs with permanent fixes.

On Saturday, an AT&T spokesman announced that the cable had been mistakenly cut by an employee using wire cutters to remove old cable. He said that the earlier version of the accident had been in error. This was the same cable that a construction worker, using a backhoe, had accidentally severed on November 18, 1988, approximately twenty miles south of the current break. That service outage lasted nine hours.

It should have been a rather private, minor, sad event--a farmer burying a dead cow in February 1991. In digging the bovine's grave, he inadvertently damaged an underground fiber-optic cable connecting Birmingham, Alabama and Farmington, Tennessee. The cable break disrupted AT&T telephone service for four hours bringing grief to thousands of customers before the computer rerouted area phone traffic to bypass the fault.

On September 17, 1991, power equipment at AT&T's central facility in Manhattan, New York, failed at 10:00 a.m. The station switched to battery backup power and continued to function. Although the system generated both auditory and visual warnings that the system was operating on battery power, operators ignored the warnings, neglecting to switch the system to internal diesel-generated power as corporate procedures required. When the batteries finally failed at 4:50 p.m., the center lost its ability to switch two million calls per hour.

The major outage disrupted inter-airport traffic controller communications, shutting down all regional airport operations. It shut down the Federal Reserve network (Fedwire), making it unavailable for settling end-of-day banking balances. The batch transfers of the day's stock transactions from brokerage houses were delayed.

By 8:30 p.m. technicians had the AT&T switching station working at 65% capacity. They restored full service by midnight.

In a headline extending across the entire front page, the *Washington Post* for June 27, 1991, announced: "Computer Failure Paralyzes Region's Phone Service." How eerie, Washington incommunicado! Well, almost--long distance calls continued to go through, and federal government employees could dial other federal offices. However, the public, for the most part, could not complete either business or residential local calls.

The outage began about 11:30 a.m., Wednesday, June 26, when a computer system in Baltimore malfunctioned. After erroneously sensing that the system was overloaded, the computer shut itself down. This move caused a chain reaction which knocked out three other regional computers, disrupting phone service to approximately six million homes in Virginia, Maryland, West Virginia, and the District of Columbia.

The Chesapeake and Potomac Telephone Company temporarily had linked the four computers, enabling each to provide backup in the event that problems arose while new, call-routing, computer software was being installed. During the service disruption customers could dial only local calls handled by their own switching computers because the new software could only switch local calls passing through a second switching center,. They could also dial long-distance calls which the software did not switch. Savvy callers discovered that they could call within the affected area by dialing each call as if it were long-distance, prefaced by the area code.

C&P officials quickly announced they had ruled out mischief by computer hackers, software viruses, and sabotage as possible causes of their computer problems.

Technicians gathered data about the outage and designed a repair strategy which they began at 2:15 p.m. Computers in Washington and Baltimore had been disconnected from the temporary linkage, reprogrammed, and restarted by early evening. By 8:00 p.m. service to all of Maryland had been restored. At 9:30 p.m. C&P announced that virtually the entire system was again up and running.

Coincidentally, Pacific Bell Telephone, while installing the same new computer software in California, experienced identical problems on that same day! Affecting southern California customers in area codes 213, 818 and 805, the Pacific Bell outage began about 11:00 a.m. The California snafu affected an estimated three million customers who were unable to place local calls and experienced difficulty with incoming long-distance calls.

After a Pacific Bell spokesperson reported four computer failures, technicians quickly determined that the California problem was nearly identical to the one affecting Washington and Baltimore. Most California service was restored by 2:00 p.m.

The combined outages in the eastern and western portions of the country removed more than nine million telephones from service. This number accounted for 4.5% of all phones in American, or 1.5% of all phones on earth.

Pittsburgh suffered a similar loss of local phone service when computer software overloaded two computers on Monday, July 1, 1991. The Pennsylvania system failure affected almost a million customers in the western part of the state. The problem was discovered about 11:00 a.m.; operations were back to normal shortly after 5:00 p.m.

On the same day, San Francisco experienced similar, but very brief, local phone service overloading problems that officials attributed to software problems.

All four jurisdictions were among the one hundred communications companies using the same computer switches and software provided by DSC Communications Corporation of Plano, Texas. Technicians investigating the four similar system failures reported to the Federal Communications Commission in November 1991, that the disruptions had been caused by a single mis-typed character in one of the program's more than two million lines of code! The error had been distributed to DSC customers when the company issued a program patch (programming code designed to fix a problem in an existing computer program). In keying the patch code, a DSC employee inadvertently keyed a "6" instead of a "d". Magnetic tapes containing the program patch were distributed to communications companies using the DSC system. When they introduced the change into their switching programs, that simple keying error caused their computers to malfunction, resulting in unprecedented loss of local telephone service.

A complaint to MCI about an overcharge of less than twenty-five cents led to the discovery of overcharges of tens of millions of dollars. After a customer complained of being overcharged for a collect call, the company investigators reportedly discovered that a computer programming error had overcharged millions of customers--for more than two years! A spokesman said that faulty software installed in mid-1993 had overcharged customers an average of eighteen cents per call. To set things right, MCI promised to mail certificates worth $2.50 to customers who had used the company's automated-operator-collect service while the faulty software was in use. Announced in March 1996, the refunds to customers nationwide were expected to exceed $44 million.

4

CAN BANKERS BANK
ON COMPUTER TECHNOLOGY?

"Federal Reserve States Computer Error Caused Its Puzzling Money-Market Steps," reported the *Wall Street Journal*, February 18, 1972.

An unspecified computer error caused the Federal Reserve System to confound the money market by buying large quantities of U.S. Government securities in the early part of the week, then, when the error was discovered, selling huge quantities of Treasury bills on Thursday. An official explained that the error had caused officials to believe the banking system reserves were lower than they actually were, resulting in the Federal Reserve's orders to buy Treasury bills. The computer error's discovery led to corrective action, the selling-off of T-bills that should never have been bought. Experts estimated that the unusual computer glitch led the Federal Reserve to make excess purchases of about $270 million, thus disrupting the market.

In Washington, D.C., a less serious fault the weekend of January 22, 1977, caused an ATM at the National Bank of Washington's Dupont Circle Branch to mysteriously stop printing details of withdrawals. Although the computer continued to record the account number for each withdrawal, it ceased recording the amounts. The bank at that time limited withdrawals for each account to $100 per week.

The bank staff discovered the problem on Monday. Although they knew that two hundred customers had withdrawn money, they had no records indicating the specific amounts. The bank sent letters to each customer indicating that their withdrawal had been the maximum amount, $100. Upon receiving the letter, approximately 180 of the customers reported the actual amounts they had withdrawn. The bank accepted the customers' reports and entered the data into the computer. Even if the remaining twenty customers each kept $100, the bank's loss totaled only $2,000.

Although bank officials refused to disclose the exact cause of the snafu, they said that minor internal soldering fixed the problem with the receipt printer attached to the ATM.

During the late 1970s, California Federal Savings and Loan Association of Los Angeles installed about 300 ATMs in grocery stores and supermarkets. Problems of unexplained arithmetic errors, lost data regarding transactions, and ATM equipment breakdowns, plagued the new remote banking system.

After bank technicians investigated and ruled out numerous possible causes, an employee reported that customers often complained that a certain machine always shocked them when they used it. When technicians measured the amount of static generated by foot traffic on the carpeted floor near the ATMs, they found it was strong enough to erase computer data and, over time, even destroy sensitive electronic components.

When the bank placed anti-static mats in front of their ATMs, all of the mysterious problems ceased immediately.

In 1980, a reporter at *The Sentinel* in Montgomery County, Maryland, heard that a local bank was experiencing major computer problems. According to "informed sources" the bank's statements were unreliable.

When the reporter sought to investigate the situation, the bank's chairman candidly admitted that the bank's May conversion of its checking accounts to computer processing had resulted in incorrect customer account balances. He asked the newspaper to refrain from publicizing the problems until the bank staff could correct the computer programs. He further explained that when customers withdrew money, bank employees had to manually verify their account balances.

At the end of September, the bank chairman informed the reporter, that the programs had been corrected, and *The Sentinel* broke the story. The chairman declined to reveal what specifically had caused the numerous errors on the bank statements.

In the spring of 1981, a Washington, D.C. clothing store employee noticed huge stacks of computer paper waiting to be hauled away as trash from a loading dock belonging to the District of Columbia National Bank. Deciding that the paper could be recycled and used to stuff display merchandise in his store, the employee took several stacks of the computer printouts to his stockroom. His own employees crumpled the paper and stuffed it into purses and canvas bags displayed in the store.

When a curious customer, who had purchased one of the purses, smoothed out the computer pages, she discovered a listing of bank balances of prominent Washingtonians, including former Attorney General Benjamin Civiletti.

A bank spokesman told reporters that bank policy required such printouts to be shredded rather than discarded as trash. On that specific day, someone had carted the printouts to the loading dock and placed them with the trash rather than stacking them beside the shredder.

When the clothing store staff became aware of the sensitive nature of the snafu, they quickly removed the computer printouts from all remaining bags in the store.

On Saturday afternoon, September 26, 1981, Deborah Hall of Phoenix inserted her bank card and directed an ATM to dispense $40 from her First Interstate Bank of Arizona account. After complying with her request, the machine spewed out an additional 255 twenty-dollar bills ($5,100)! The bewildered bank customer rushed home and spread her loot so she could admire the wonderful collection of green and white.

Of course, she realized that she could not keep the money. However, because it was Saturday, there was no one at the bank to answer her telephone call. Fearful that she might land in trouble over the unusual incident, Hall called the local newspaper, seeking advice. After a newspaper employee contacted a bank manager at home, he dispatched a courier to Hall's residence to retrieve the mysterious computer windfall.

A spokesman told reporters that bank officials planned to reward Hall's honesty by treating her to lunch in a posh restaurant.

Murphy's Law exhibited itself "...at the worst possible time" when, on Christmas Eve, 1981, Security Pacific Bank's ATMs ceased to function throughout California.

Bank officials admitted receiving "a heavy volume" of telephone calls from irate customers prevented by the computer from withdrawing money to buy their final Christmas gifts. A bank spokesman told reporters that the huge computer in Glendale, which controlled the bank's 235 ATMs, for reasons unknown kept turning the devices off and on periodically throughout that memorable day.

Many federal government employees, for reasons of security and convenience, participate in a direct deposit program in which the government uses electronic funds transfers to send their pay to designated bank accounts.

Treasury Department officials in Washington revealed that something had gone wrong at the San Francisco Federal Reserve bank on February 13, 1984, causing the system to fail to process about 19,000 direct-deposit transfers! Although they declined to reveal details of the goof, officials promised that all of the missed deposits would be in designated bank accounts within forty-eight hours.

In Tokyo, after a fire in a utility tunnel destroyed a major telephone exchange, ATMs could not communicate with computers at Mitsubishi Bank, the Daiwa Bank, and several other financial institutions. Authorities suspected that a worker repairing a broken cable probably caused the sixteen-hour fire when his burning torch accidentally ignited one of the cables. The November 16, 1984, incident caused a major communications outage affecting more than a million homes and businesses.

Devastating earthquakes destroyed much of Mexico City on September 19 and 20, 1985. Although computers at Mexico's national bank, Banamex, survived, the killer quakes severed all communications links. Technicians eventually reestablished one critical link to the Society for Worldwide Interbank Financial Communications (SWIFT) in Madrid, Spain. For several weeks all Banamex communications with other financial institutions had to pass through this Madrid connection.

A computer software problem at the Bank of New York prevented the delivery of more than $20 billion in government securities to purchasers on November 21, 1985. The massive foul-up forced the bank to accept an emergency loan of $2 billion at 7.5% interest from the Federal Reserve Bank of New York--the largest loan ever made through the Reserve's discount "window".

Throughout the crisis the Bank of New York, one of the two largest clearers of U.S. Government securities, continued to receive Treasury notes and bonds from securities dealers and to immediately pay the sellers, as required by law. However, the bank was required to deliver the securities to purchasers prior to collecting payment. The computer failure prevented that delivery. By 8:30 p.m. the Bank of New York had amassed an overdraft with the Federal Reserve of nearly $30 billion.

As soon as the problem was discovered, the Bank of New York assigned fifty-five people to correct it. They created a temporary software patch to enable the computer to resume processing. Just after midnight the system crashed again. Additional systems modifications restarted the computer about 2:00 a.m. and by noon, November 22, the system was again operating normally.

Luckily, the Bank of New York's data processing department enjoyed an excellent reputation. When word of the technical problem spread through financial circles, no one rushed to the news media to declare it a crisis.

Before the close of business on November 22, the bank had repaid its $22.6 billion loan, plus approximately $5 million in overnight interest.

In December, the bank's chairman told the U.S. House of Representatives Subcommittee on Domestic Monetary Policy that the unprecedented failure was caused by flawed software that failed to instruct the computer how to store data when the number of securities issues exceeded 32,000. For the first time ever, on November 20, the number of issues being cleared by the Bank of New York, exceeded the 32,000 limit, causing the computer system to fail. Simply put, the computer stored the data incorrectly, thus corrupting its own data base.

In another Federal Reserve incident, employees in San Francisco, after testing modifications to the Bank's wire transfer net, January 17, 1986, neglected to delete a file of test data from the computer. When other employees activated the system after the holiday weekend, the computer transmitted more than $2 billion worth of erroneous electronic fund tranfers to nineteen banks!

The banks immediately reported receiving the enormous accidental cash transfers. Federal Reserve employees, upon discovering that their test data had been transmitted as actual cash transfers, quickly corrected the problem. No money was lost in this mixup. As punishment for their failure to remove the test data from the computer upon completion of the systems test, the Federal Reserve reportedly placed several employees on three days of unpaid leave.

San Francisco's Bank of America was once the largest in the world. In 1980, it reported profits in excess of $643 million.

During the 1950s, when computer technology was new, the institution became a world leader in bank automation. It is still recognized as the innovator of MICR (magnetic ink character recognition) which enables computers to read the codes on checks.

By 1980, the bank had started to lose its computer technology edge because of its reduced investments in state-of-the-art technology. Samuel Armacost became head of BankAmerica, the parent company, in 1981. He soon announced a $4 billion program to modernize the bank's computer system and develop the ultimate system for handling a bank's trust department.

Engineers, attempting to update the bank's existing system, reported in 1981 that an initial outlay of $6 million had produced unusable results. Following this embarrassing failure by its employees, bank officials began an exhaustive search to identify qualified outside experts to help create the desired system. They selected Premier Systems of Wayne, Pennsylvania for the task.

Bank of America persuaded three other banks to share in the development costs of the ambitious new project: Seattle First National, United Virginia, and Philadelphia National.

Premier's executives reportedly insisted that, in order to achieve the desired results, Bank of America replace existing IBM computers with new machines from Prime.

Bank of America officials approved funding for the new system in March 1984 and entered into a contract with Premier to create MasterNet. They announced the goal of implementing the TrustPlus portion of the unprecedented new system by the end of 1984.

December 31, 1984, passed without implementation. So did December 31, 1985. Even though the bank had invested $20 million, their new system was far from ready to use.

The software system had grown to 3,500,000 lines of code by the spring of 1986. Test runs had not been flawless, but technicians argued that they could resolve remaining problems after the system went into operation.

The Bank of America invited several dozen of their most important clients to an extravagant demonstration of "the industry's most sophisticated technology for handling trust accounts." The tab for the two-day affair, held in May at the Santa Barbara Biltmore, reportedly exceeded $75,000. A bank insider later told a reporter that he thought that the Biltmore bash was the only major part of the system's effort that turned out as planned.

Following the Santa Barbara unveiling of the new trust system, previously unknown technical problems appeared, sufficiently serious to further delay the system's implementation. The staff continued to run the old system to get their jobs done, while they ran the new one, struggling to make it work correctly.

Heavy financial losses in 1986 forced bank officials to sell portions of the bank's business and cut nearly 10,000 jobs.

Finally they announced the system's conversion date would be March 2, 1987.

Bank of America then unexpectedly announced that it had sold its consumer trust business to Wells Fargo Bank, with the deal scheduled to close on March 31, 1987.

Even so, through Herculean personal efforts, the new system was up and running on Monday, March 2. The sweet success lasted only five days. On Saturday, March 7, one of the system's twenty-four disk drives crashed, destroying much of the data base. Within a month, fifteen of the disk drives suffered similar fates. Much later investigators discovered that the disk drives were all part of a faulty batch manufactured by Control Data Corporation.

Information Week reported, in its issue dated November 16, 1987, that MasterNet's collapse had "scrambled data on $10 billion in transactions..."

Collectively, the widespread failure of so many critical pieces of equipment doomed the system. Although employees teamed with outside consultants in a struggle to resurrect the system, it was not to be.

Bank of America announced in July 1987 that it had set aside $25 million to cover anticipated MasterNet losses. The bank quietly attempted to sell the trust department but found no buyers.

How financial fortunes change! The bank reported losses of $955 million in 1987!

The bank announced in January 1988 that an additional $35 million had been set aside to correct problems with MasterNet.

With little fanfare, the bank soon began to transfer about 95% of its trust business to an affiliate, Seattle First National, that used a different computer system. A few accounts, deemed too complex for the system at SeaFirst, were transferred to State Street Bank in Boston.

In effect, the Bank of America invested $20 million to create the ultimate trust department system, then allocated an additional $60 million to make it function properly. After investing $80 million and six years of effort, the bank abandoned the whole system.

The Fedwire funds transfer system operated by the Federal Reserve Bank of New York crashed on September 29, 1987. On September 30 it crashed again. The two computer failures, on consecutive days, left numerous banks that did business with the New York Federal Reserve Bank ignorant of their own financial positions.

At the time the Federal Reserve Bank of New York electronically moved more than a trillion dollars a day over its portion of Fedwire. The total electronic traffic flow on the nationwide Fedwire system often exceeded 150,000 transactions a minute. Because of its tremendous financial importance, employees copied the Fedwire data base several times daily. A duplicate of each backup copy was sent to an off-site, backup computer facility.

Technicians concluded that the data base was contaminated after the September 30 system's crash. They successfully recovered and closed the bank's accounts just before 4:00 a.m. October 1.

An earthquake, measuring 6.1 on the Richter Scale, broke water pipes and shook loose ceiling tiles, causing a computer at California Federal Saving and Loan in Rosemead to crash on October 1, 1987. Technicians ran the institution's most critical computer work at a temporary site in San Diego until the damage could be repaired and the computer center reopened.

On February 22, 1989, the failure of a communications link, from a central computer to the ATMs it controlled, shut down 445 of Wells Fargo's 1,200 ATMs. The shutdown primarily affected bank machines in California's central valley; a few in southern California also were put out of service. Although the outage lasted several hours, a bank spokesman said that no customer records or transactions were lost. He said that the nature of the problem prevented the use of a backup computer.

A short time later, the computer system at Security Pacific National Bank took a partial holiday on May 31, 1989. At 2:00 a.m. the computer began to post transactions for the long Memorial Day weekend through Tuesday's close of business. Four hours into the process, the computer unexplainably ceased its updating of accounts. Among the items left unposted were the bank's direct deposits, affecting funds available to thousands of bank customers on the first day of the month.

Luckily the computer continued to provide accurate historical data about all accounts, thus enabling the bank to continue limited service to most customers. By mid-afternoon the problems had been identified and corrected, and the accounts had been correctly updated.

An accidentally severed fiber-optic cable in Newark, New Jersey, disabled ATMs across New York City on January 4, 1991. Twenty-three computers, controlling the NYCE Network's inter-bank transaction, were thrown out of service. Because the cable connected New York City with the rest of the world, ATMs could not process withdrawal requests by out-of-towners. Local residents could withdraw money only from their own banks. Complete service was restored in approximately five hours.

A monumental snow storm in the eastern United States was blamed by the *Dallas* (Texas) *Morning News* for the March 1993 shutdown of 5,200 ATMs in Texas. The paper said the storm caused "the most widespread failure of cash machines in U.S. history." Texans found it difficult to fathom that a roof collapsed by heavy snow in New Jersey could put ATMs in Texas out of service for nearly two weeks.

On Saturday, March 13, 1993, in Clifton, New Jersey, a blizzard piled snow so deeply on the roof of a building housing Electronic Data Systems' (EDS) data center that it caved in, causing the walls to buckle and the building to be condemned. Employees had sufficient warning of the impending disaster to perform a controlled shutdown of the system, saving all data and turning off all equipment before evacuating the building. Even though the equipment was not damaged, local authorities prohibited EDS employees from entering the damaged facility to recover it.

Thirteen ATM networks operated by EDS, serving 5,200 ATMs across the United States with heavy concentrations in Texas, California, and Illinois, were shut down by the incident.

EDS had always counted on being able to use an alternate site at North Bergen, New Jersey, in such emergency situations. However, firms forced to evacuate following the bombing of the World Trade Center in New York were occupying the intended site when EDS sorely needed it.

EDS quickly located a site near the ruined data center and began gathering computer and communications equipment from other EDS sites. The firm also struck temporary emergency deals with competing ATM networks to honor bank cards for customers of the downed networks. Even though EDS lacked such critical data as customer account balances, the temporary arrangements permitted customers to withdraw up to $100 a day during the emergency. On Friday, March 26, EDS announced that the thirteen-day crisis was over and that service on the ATM networks had returned to normal.

Bank Network News estimated that EDS spent $20 million in new equipment, emergency personnel, and interim operating costs during the emergency. The periodical estimated that the loss of ATM user fees over the two weeks exceeded $6 million.

A "computer error" at Chemical Bank in New York affected the accounts of 100,000 customers in February 1994. Newly inserted program code caused the computer to process every ATM withdrawal twice; for each dollar actually withdrawn, the computer subtracted two dollars from a customer's account balance. Auditors subsequently reported that 430 checks, actually legitimate, bounced because of the program logic error.

Although the faulty program only processed transactions for a single day, bank officials reported that the computer mistakenly deducted $15 million from customers' accounts! More than 4,000 people called customer service reps at the bank after discovering the errors on their accounts. Even though ATM withdrawals were charged twice, ATM deposits were only credited once. A bank spokesman later told reporters that a single line of code in the program had caused what was probably the most massive computer problem any bank had ever encountered.

A benevolent computer at First National Bank of Chicago, on May 16, 1996, converted customers with ordinary account balances into near-billionaires! More than $763,000,000,000 (yes, billion!) was unexplainedly credited to 800 customer accounts, enriching each by more than $900,000,000 (yes, million)!

Bank officials got their first hint of a possible problem when several customers called to verify their account balances. Each caller reported previously calling the bank's automated system to obtain their balance and being told by voice response that their current balance exceeded $925 million!

Upon learning that an unknown number of accounts had been erroneously credited with nearly a billion dollars each, the bank immediately froze all accounts in order to gain time for sorting out such an unbelievable problem.

Investigators soon discovered that a computer programming error, introduced as part of a recent software modification, had credited customer accounts with an amount more than six times the total assets of the bank's holding company!

In an anticipated case of the computer giveth and the computer taketh away, by Monday, May 20, the computer had changed all of the account balances of the near-billionaires back to actual numbers.

Computers at British Banks have also frequently gone awry! *The Times* of London reported that, on Saturday, November 4, 1989, a Barclays Bank ATM located in Kilburn High Road, London, dispensed more than £1,000 to astonished pedestrians. Bank officials offered no public explanation of what prompted the device's unexpected generosity.

Software changes undertaken in the quest for improvement often yield unexpected consequences. In the U.K., First Data Resources attempted to improve their banking software to enable it to better detect fraud.

In the summer of 1992, the new system overcharged 250,000 customers of the National Westminster Bank. It reportedly charged interest or levied late payment fees when none were due. Direct debits were also collected late. In addition, customer statements contained erroneous information about cash advances.

Embarrassed bank officials apologized to customers by letter and promised that "...correcting entries will be passed to your account shortly."

In 1992, it seemed as if an ATM "grinch" were attempting to steal Christmas from many Britons. Barclays Bank ATM network of 2,600 devices initially was operating normally, dispensing an incredible £2,000 per second on that busy Christmas Eve.

An electric power failure suddenly shut down about half of the ATMs in the Midlands and north of England, depriving frantic last-minute shoppers of access to their money. Quick-thinking bank officials helped alleviate the unexpected problem by keeping branch banks, that were scheduled to close at noon, open through the crisis to provide cash to desperate customers.

In November 1993 a technician mis-loaded an ATM at Cardiff University, causing the machine to dispense to delighted students twenty-pound notes instead of ten-pound ones.

An executive of National Westminster Bank admitted that the institution's computer had processed approximately 60,000 Visa charges twice. Somehow the transactions for May 26, 1994, mistakenly were entered into the computer for processing a second time, resulting in double charges for purchases made on that date. After apologizing to customers who were twice-charged, bank officials promised that any resulting overdrafts would be excused.

The following week red-faced officials of the same institution announced that they had discovered another instance in which their computer had overcharged the customers. Visa and Mastercard charge transactions turned in by Country Casual, May 13, 1994, had been processed "more than once." The *Times of London* reported that the computer overcharged approximately 1,300 National Westminster customers in this incident.

The same newspaper reported December 4, 1994, that at least one ATM in London's Marchmont area was behaving peculiarly. Customers who used the device received transaction printouts of other customers' accounts. The ATM receipt contained a customer account number, transaction listing, and current balance pertaining to an account other than that of the ATM cardholder.

The Royal Bank of Scotland, owner of the errant ATM, assured an inquiring reporter that the bank was aware of the problem, described it as mechanical, and claimed that no money had been debited from the wrong account.

"What's in a name?" In May 1995 a computer at Barclays Bank apparently liked the name "Fiona".

A newly-installed computer accounting system neglected to generate monthly statements for mortgage and loan payments due from customers named Fiona. The unusual problem became apparent to bank employees only after they had received several telephone calls from customers inquiring why their accounts were not collected as usual. All of the inquiries came from customers named Fiona.

Bank employees quickly corrected the computer system but refused to disclose what had caused the computer's favoritism for that name. A spokesman said the situation affected more than 100 accounts and blamed it on "a blip."

The Times of London reported, October 15, 1995, that Diane Burnett had been withdrawing cash from a TSB cash machine, in London, when a voice spoke to her from inside the ATM!

According to *The Times*, the branch manager and an assistant had accidentally locked themselves inside the ATM safe. Ms. Burnett heard the manager, pleading to be let out. He managed to pass the appropriate keys through the ATM to Burnett who then opened the door to free the embarrassed couple.

5

HOW DO ELECTRICAL FAILURES AFFECT COMPUTERS?

Computers enabled electrical power providers to link their generating capabilities into gigantic power grids, allowing utility companies to draw from the common pool to meet peak demands. Blocks of electricity could be freely traded back and forth as needed. By the mid-1960s one pool served all of New England, Pennsylvania, New York, Ontario, and Quebec.

America learned just how fragile such interconnected power grids could be on November 9, 1965, when a massive electrical failure darkened most of the Northeast. At approximately 5:30 p.m., lights flickered, then went out across the entire region. Workers departing for the day had to find their way in nearly total darkness. With elevators not operating, thousands had to feel their way down darkened stairwells.

Outside, the street lights were off and traffic signals had ceased to function. Pedestrians in the streets helped to turn the normally chaotic evening traffic into hopeless gridlock.

Subway systems could not operate without electricity. Approximately a million commuters were stranded in New York City alone. Electrically-powered trains that normally carried commuters to more distant destinations such as New Haven, Westchester, and Long Island, stopped on the tracks.

Computers shut down across the blackout area. Banks from New York to Boston to Hartford to Toronto simply could not balance their financial records for the day. An official at New York

Federal Reserve Bank said that at his bank alone, the blackout delayed the processing of some 2,700,000 checks valued at $1.5 billion.

Although the New York Stock Exchange had been closed long enough to complete processing of most of the seven million shares traded that day, brokerage houses reportedly had not finished processing that day's trades.

Computerized airline reservations systems were out of service, as were some hotel reservations systems and computers authorizing credit card approvals.

Investigators later reported that problems with an electrical switching center near Niagara Falls had caused the regional blackout. When that small center drew increasing amounts of electricity from the far-flung, interconnected portions of the power pool, it gradually drained the entire network, causing the massive outage.

In 1977, after lightning struck power transmission lines in upstate New York, a major electrical failure plunged New York City and Westchester County into darkness. Vandalism and looting cost New York City residents hundreds of millions of dollars. More than fifty firefighters were injured while dealing with over a thousand fires set by vandals. New York City police arrested nearly 4,000 lawbreakers during the power outage.

The July 13 blackout's impact on computers was catastrophic. Hotels could not perform even basic functions such as determining whether arriving guests had reservations. In some newer hotels computer-controlled electronic door locks prevented hotel guests from entering their rooms. Employees could not obtain from their computer files details required to prepare bills for departing guests.

Inoperable computers at area airports caused additional chaos, stranding thousands of passengers.

Because it was apparent that, without electricity needed to operate computers, banks could not open as usual, the governor declared July 14 a bank holiday.

Several larger organizations that earlier had installed uninterruptible power supply (UPS) systems reportedly experienced no computer processing interruptions. When their computers sensed the outage, they automatically switched to backup power from batteries or generators. The Federal Reserve Bank of New York's UPS system provided backup electricity to light offices and run air conditioning--but not to power the bank's IBM 370/155 computer!

Although the two-day outage created widespread inconvenience and extensive processing delays, it caused very little actual damage to computer files or equipment.

More than thirty lawsuits were filed, seeking $225 million in damages from Consolidated Edison before the three-year statute of limitation expired. New York City's suit sought $58 million to cover income losses from the transportation system, the Offtrack Betting Corporation, and overtime pay for police and firemen--plus $50 million in punitive damages.

Continued power fluctuations often pose greater problems to computer facilities than sporadic blackouts. Officials at the National Institutes of Health's computer facility in Bethesda, Maryland, estimated in the late 1970s that they had lost $500,000 annually from electric power fluctuations which ruined computer runs or lost computer data, forcing them to rerun the jobs.

The fluctuations also wreaked havoc with expensive electronic components. During one carefully monitored five-week period, NIH reportedly had to replace $90,000 worth of electronics damaged by power fluctuations. During the same time, data for 375 jobs in the computer center was contaminated or destroyed. Employees using remote terminals reported having lost data almost 2,000 times during the period monitored.

In New York, an explosion and fire at a Consolidated Edison power plant cut electricity to much of the city's financial district at 3:25 p.m., Wednesday, September 9, 1981. The power loss forced both the New York Stock Exchange and the American Stock Exchange to close early. Even though the exchanges' computers sensed the power fluctuation and switched to emergency backup power systems, the computer terminals at the exchanges went blank because *they were not connected to an auxiliary power source*.

The Federal Reserve Bank, which reportedly then handled almost $200 billion a day in cash and securities transactions, reported most of the day's computer work had been finished before the blackout occurred.

Morgan Guaranty and Trust Company announced that fuel pump problems affected their auxiliary generators, rendering their computers inoperable for fifteen hours.

Computers at Chemical Bank continued to run for fifteen minutes on emergency power, enabling employees to conduct an orderly system's shutdown.

Some computers, such as those at Citibank's Wall Street center, were unaffected by the sporadic outage.

ConEd reported that a short circuit in a transformer caused an electric arc, resulting in the fire and explosion. A spokesman said that all power was restored before 8:00 p.m.; the outage lasted less than five hours.

When South Florida recorded record cold temperatures, December 24-25, 1989, customer demand for electricity reached an all-time high.

Unable to generate, or buy from other utilities, sufficient electricity to meet the unprecedented demand, officials at Miami's Florida Power and Light Company initiated a wave of rotating blackouts, cutting power to half a million customers in various areas for periods ranging from fifteen to twenty-five minutes. Although the move avoided a potential total blackout, it thoroughly confused the company's computer, which could not distinguish between service cuts initiated by utility company employees and those that required service crews to respond!

Fortunately, most government and business organizations, whose managers normally would be concerned about the impact of such a rolling blackout on their facilities, were closed for Christmas.

Monday, August 13, 1990 started as a rather typical day in Manhattan. At 1:13 p.m. an electrical blackout darkened seventy square blocks of lower Manhattan. Trading ceased on the American Stock Exchange and the Commodity Exchange. Electrical service to nearly two hundred computer centers was disrupted.

Computerworld described the incident as "...one of the worst regional computer-related disasters in at least a decade."

The outage, which totally cut electricity to some buildings in the affected areas, continued to provide uninterrupted service to others, such as the Marine Midland Building and Chase Manhattan headquarters.

Approximately twenty financial services firms switched to temporary computer sites for support. Although ConEd had restored electrical service to about half of the affected area within five hours, at least sixty computer centers remained without power the entire week. Some of those data centers whose electricity was restored reported that the power level was inadequate to operate both computers and air conditioning.

The Federal Reserve Bank shifted its computer operations to a Pearl River, New York, backup computer center.

Manufacturers Hanover Corporation relocated its computer operations to another site for the entire week.

Citibank reportedly suffered most from this blackout. Unscathed in a similar 1977 incident, officials expected to weather the current crisis by continuing to operate their computer systems with batteries and generators. Their generators' unexpected failure forced the computer operations staff to relocate to an alternate site outside the blacked-out area.

According to a ConEd spokesman the massive blackout which deprived many businesses of reliable electrical service for a week, was caused by a fire at an electrical substation.

Nature constantly belies conventional human wisdom. For example, lightning does strike twice in the same location. It also sometimes bypasses surge protectors installed on electrical lines, knocking out computer communications lines or coaxial cables connecting local-area-networks. Such was the case in Fort Myers, Florida at Erwin Consulting Ecologists, where lighting inflicted major equipment damage twice during July 1991. An official estimated that the two days of computer network downtime, coupled with the cost to replace destroyed equipment, totaled more than $40,000.

A construction accident darkened Newark International Airport on January 9, 1995. Workmen driving steel beams into the ground severed three power cables serving three of the airport's terminals. Airline reservations systems immediately shut down, forcing airlines to divert passengers to other airports. An FAA spokesman told reporters that 616 flights had to be canceled or rerouted because of the electrical problem.

Investigators later reported that, although the airport maintained auxiliary power source lines that should have provided electricity during the emergency, because the auxiliary lines had been installed in the same conduit as the primary line. The construction accident severed both.

6

ARE COMPUTERS ESPECIALLY SUSCEPTIBLE TO FIRE?

When fire destroyed a computer room in a top-secret area of the Pentagon, July 2, 1959, the event garnered worldwide attention. Centered in the U.S. Air Force Statistical Center on the first floor, the blaze buckled the floor of the Pentagon's main concourse, one floor above. Officials initially told reporters that the fire, discovered at 11:00 a.m., destroyed computer equipment valued at $30 million, plus 7,000 computer tapes containing classified Air Force information, before firemen brought it under control five hours later.

The day after the historic fire, Air Force officials revised downward their damage estimate. They said that IBM owned the three computers melted by the fire, and that they were fully insured. The value of the lost machines was put at $6 million; damage to the building was estimated at $200,000. The number of destroyed computer tapes was revised to 5,200.

Fire-fighting efforts became extremely hazardous because no one could reach the main electrical switch to turn off electricity to the burning computer room!

On August 3, 1959 the General Services Administration (GSA) reported that workmen moving tape storage racks had pushed a 300-watt light bulb against the ceiling tile. Heat from the bulb eventually ignited the tile, starting the devastating inferno.

At Eglin Air Force Base, Florida the wedge-shaped building was so new that it had not yet been used. As long as a football field and pie-shaped, the steel structure housed a satellite-tracking station. With state-of-the-art computers and experimental radar equipment, the windowless building being constructed by the Bendix Corporation contained an advanced system capable of simultaneously tracking several satellites at different altitudes.

Despite the fact that experts considered the building noncombustible, a major fire erupted in mid-afternoon January 5, 1965, inflicting heavy damage on the structure. Firefighters could not effectively combat the blaze because insufficient water pressure would not reach the upper floors of the eleven-story building. Millions of dollars worth of computers and other electronic equipment were destroyed. Total loss from the incident was officially put at $30 million.

In autumn of the same year, a fire in a top-secret American military communications center in Japan killed eleven military personnel. When an electrical power cable malfunctioned on September 24, 1965, it set ablaze a highly-combustible wood-frame building. Security restrictions reportedly delayed firefighters being granted access to such a sensitive area. Authorities said that computers and communications equipment valued at more than $1 million were destroyed in the deadly incident.

In Florida, "an improper cable connection" was cited as the cause of a fire in a computer manufacturing facility on April 12, 1969. Firefighters had to don protective breathing apparatus because smoke from poly-vinyl chloride (PVC) cable insulation had filled the facility. A spokesman said that two computer systems were heavily damaged in the fire while another fifty suffered minor damage. He estimated the damage at more than $4 million.

Less than a week later, a computerized pilot-training simulator in Denver was destroyed by fire. A resistor on a miniaturized circuit board failed, igniting the April 18 fire. Officials, seeking to discover why no fire alarm sounded, discovered that the flow of cool air in the area was so strong that sensors failed to detect the fire. Damage to the equipment was estimated at $850,000.

In 1969 a small airplane crashed into a New Jersey building housing Applied Data Research, Inc. The resulting fire extensively damaged the company's computer center, disrupting operations for several days.

When fire destroyed Volkswagen South-Central Distributors' computer room in San Antonio, Texas, on Friday, February 26, 1971, the magnetic tapes containing critical company records survived intact in a fireproof vault in the burned facility. An IBM 360/40 computer was totally destroyed.

Because seventy Volkswagen dealers in Oklahoma, Texas, Colorado, New Mexico, and Wyoming depended upon the San Antonio computer, it was imperative that a replacement be rushed into service as quickly as possible. IBM employees in Poughkeepsie, New York, tested a replacement model and dispatched it by truck on an 1,800-mile journey to Texas. Employees in Endicott, New York shipped the peripheral devices. Replacement disk drives were located in Texas. Disk packs were shipped from San Jose, California.

By early Tuesday morning, March 2, technicians had installed and tested a duplicate of the destroyed data processing system. Since the computer tapes had suffered no damage, Volkswagen returned to business as usual in less than 100 hours.

Before being extinguished, fire raged in an IBM building in Hawthorne, New York for thirteen hours, September 10, 1972. Investigators reported that the blaze, which started in a basement room where computer tapes and manuals were stored, spread to the floor above, causing extensive damage to offices and computers. An IBM spokesman later estimated the financial loss at more than one million dollars.

Quick-thinking employees kept the U.S. Military Personnel Records Center fire in Overland, Kansas from being remembered as a major computer fire. When that fire of September 12, 1973, destroyed millions of paper military records, it reached none of the computer-readable records. Employees in the Federal Data Processing Center first covered essential computer equipment with plastic sheeting, then removed the master programs and disk packs before the fire could reach the computer center.

In February 1977, a predawn fire in Braintree, Massachusetts destroyed the headquarters building and computer center belonging to Campanelli, Inc. A broken fuel line to an oil burner was identified as the cause of the disaster. A Basic Four computer system, used for accounts payable, general ledger, and management of trust properties, was lost. Six disk packs containing crucial data were rescued before they could be damaged. Employees said they expected to be able to re-create any missing data by using partially-burned, water-soaked, paper documents. Basic Four announced that it was making an inhouse computer system available to Campanelli as needed until the firm could return to business as usual.

Eighty-four people were killed when fire ravaged the MGM Grand Hotel in Las Vegas, November 21, 1980. The fire caused the floor of the computer center to collapse, dumping equipment and computer files into the inferno. In the aftermath, recovery teams found two badly battered computer disk packs that appeared beyond salvage. However, those two disks held the only hope for recovery of the hotel's critical financial records. The backup copies, as well as the original paper transactions, had been destroyed in the flames.

Anxious to retrieve what appeared to be irretrievable, MGM Grand executives turned to David Brown, a California consultant specializing in such challenges. For a reported $1,200 fee, he carefully hand-cleaned the contaminated disks and successfully read them once--recovering and copying the hotel's accounts receivable, accounts payable, and guest registration files.

On Thanksgiving Day, 1982, fire totally consumed the Norwest National Bank Building in Minneapolis. Although Norwest's main computer center was located in a building six blocks away, the fire destroyed the bank's online networks, some computer equipment, several controllers, and more than 150 terminals and ATMs.

After a 1973 fire destroyed the Anthony Hotel, Norwest executives had decided to decentralize their computer processing capabilities. The bank's computer center, then adjacent to the Anthony Hotel, was moved. Norwest later relocated approximately half of its data processing operations to a new computer center. This earlier precautionary maneuver enabled the company to resume relatively normal operations much more quickly after the 1982 disaster.

Much of the computer equipment recovered from the Norwest Building had been damaged, mainly by smoke and soot. Technicians recovered all of the data stored on the hard disks in the burned computer center. Fortunately, recovered floppy disks containing Wednesday's business transactions were readable. Within forty-eight hours the computer center staff had resumed near-normal operations at a temporary site. Officials estimated total damage from the blaze at $75 million.

The *Wall Street Journal* briefly noted in March 1982, that a computer used by the Senate Budget Committee in Washington, D.C. had been damaged by fire.

Although the May 15, 1983 power transformer explosion at Del Monte Corporate Headquarters in San Francisco caused no damage to the firm's computer center, or injury to any employee, it did shut down the entire headquarters facility for one business day.

On Sunday, a power transformer located in the basement of a fourteen-story building exploded, producing a fire that vaporized the polychlorinated biphenyl (PCB) used as the transformer's coolant. Toxic chemical fumes resulted. Sensing smoke, the air circulation systems turned themselves off, preventing the PCB vapors from entering the building's air ducts.

On Monday, public health officials, citing the PCB hazard, refused entry to 1,200 employees arriving for work. They did permit data-processing employees to enter the computer center long enough to shut down the auxiliary power system. Those workers reported that Del Monte's IBM 3083 computer was unscathed.

For the remainder of the week health officials sporadically permitted computer room employees to enter the facility. One week after the explosion a Del Monte spokesman reported that operations in the computer facility were back to normal. Ten days after the incident health authorities announced that Del Monte's data entry support personnel could return to their work areas.

The 150 members of the Information Resources Department, temporarily housed in six locations, were not permitted to return to their regular workplace until the following April--eleven months after the explosion.

The October 12, 1983 fire that destroyed two wings of an eight-wing state office building in Olympia, Washington, temporarily closed down two computer centers. Fire on the third floor of the northwest wing of the Washington Department of Social and Health Services was reported at 5:45 a.m. An excited employee shut down an IBM 3043 in the west wing, causing some file damage in the panic. A more orderly shutdown of the Univac 1100/83 in the east wing averted any damage to files. Employees also covered the Univac equipment with sheets of plastic to protect it from water damage. Several computer terminals scattered throughout the building reportedly were damaged or destroyed by the fire.

By 2:00 p.m. firefighters had extinguished the fire and the Univac computer was functioning normally. Before the close of business the following day, employees had reconstructed the entire IBM file from backup copies, and that system was also back in service.

Washington D.C.'s second-largest fire, first reported at 11:23 p.m., October 15, 1984, started on the ninth floor of the U.S. Postal Service Headquarters at L'Enfant Plaza. The blaze spread to the tenth and eleventh floors before firefighters announced it had been extinguished.

Postal Service officials announced that water, mixed with soot, ashes, and debris, had cascaded to numerous lower floor offices not directly affected by the flames. On the third floor a DEC PDP 11/70 belonging to the U.S. Postal Service Federal Credit Union was saturated.

When a Credit Union official contacted the local Digital Equipment Corporation representative the next day, the two worked out an arrangement for the credit union to use a compatible DEC computer in nearby Maryland during the emergency. Computer tapes containing credit union members' accounts were taken from the L'Enfant Plaza building to the Maryland site.

Payday for Postal Service employees fell on the Thursday following the Monday fire. The Postal Service Credit Union set up a heavily-guarded temporary office in a trailer at L'Enfant Plaza; security concerns limited the trailer service to one day. Managers arranged to have other financial institutions process deposits and withdrawals for members until normal operations could be resumed.

By mid-December technicians began testing the contaminated credit union system. After overcoming several hurdles, officials announced in February that the system was operating as it had before the fire.

Postal Service officials declined to place a dollar value on the loss of backup computer and word processing files stored in "fireproof" vaults that proved otherwise. They reported total destruction of approximately fifty personal computers and numerous word processing work stations. Technicians cleaned and restored to service more than 500 keyboards, 650 disk drives, 325 terminals,

400 printers and 400 typewriters. A spokesman estimated total equipment damage at $20 million.

Japanese workers in Tokyo, repairing a broken cable in an underground utility tunnel, reportedly started a fire just before noon on Friday, November 16, 1984. During the next sixteen hours, the fire destroyed a major telephone exchange, disrupting service to about a million customers. ATMs, unable to communicate with their computers at the Mitsubishi Bank, the Daiwa Bank and several smaller institutions, were put out of service. Japan's post office, where many citizens maintain checking accounts, reported that nearly fifty branches were similarly affected by the communications outage.

Police speculated that a worker probably had left a burning welding torch near a cable, starting the fire.

Experts in Japan eventually estimated direct and indirect business losses from the Tokyo incident at more than twelve billion yen ($45 million).

After U.S. Administrators, Inc. reported that, on June 14, 1985, fire had destroyed two communications controllers, a high-speed printer, and twenty-eight computer terminals, the company announced that within forty-eight hours they had replaced the equipment and were operating normally in an alternate site.

The fire apparently had started in a photo lab beneath the Calabasas, California regional office of U.S. Administrators, then spread to the floor above.

On the day of the fire Pacific Bell workers rerouted voice and data lines to a nearby vacant warehouse selected to house a replacement facility. The following morning furniture was delivered and set up. Replacement computer equipment arrived shortly after noon. Before the day ended, the telephone link for the new facility was successfully reestablished.

Following a 1986 fire in a Silver Spring, Maryland support facility belonging to the Chesapeake and Potomac Telephone

Company, officials announced that their main computer in an adjacent building had suffered no damage. However, an undisclosed number of peripheral devices, computer terminals and personal computers were damaged or destroyed. The facility, housing programmers and systems development staff in addition to the records and payroll departments, reportedly contained 1,200 personal computers, 4,000 computer terminals, and 200 printers.

Although the company declined comment about lost data, a disaster-recovery contractor told reporters that C&P had lost "untold amounts" in the disaster. He estimated that more than 300 personal computers had been totally destroyed. A company spokesman estimated total damage at $8 million.

The discovery of three different fires in the same facility at Chicago's O'Hare International Airport on the same night looked suspicious. The first two were discovered and extinguished before causing serious damage. The third, near United Airlines' baggage handling facility, remained undetected until it had burned through 5,000 voice and data circuits, knocking out connections to most United computer terminals in the airport.

When reservations and passenger check-in employees were forced to revert to manual operations, they simply could not manage the workload normally handled by the computer system. The third fire of December 3, 1987, forced United to cancel 175 flights, stranding an estimated 10,000 passengers.

California's tallest building was burning! To combat the worst high-rise fire in the city's history, Los Angeles fire officials committed 270 firefighters and four helicopters. First reported at 10.38 p.m. Wednesday, May 4, 1988, the fire started on the twelfth floor and quickly devastated the twelfth through the fifteenth floors of the sixty-two story First Interstate Bank Building.

A fire department spokesman told reporters that officials initially feared the blaze would race beyond the reach of firefighters, who attempted to stop it on the fifteenth floor. After being forced to retreat to the seventeenth floor, they successfully confined the flames below.

Approximately fifty people were inside the threatened skyscraper when the fire alarm sounded. Many of the janitorial crew, understanding little or no English, did not initially comprehend the fire warnings broadcast throughout the building. Most of them eventually climbed the stairs to reach the roof, where they were rescued by helicopter.

One man, trapped on the fiftieth floor, waved draperies to attract the attention of helicopter rescuers. Fire rescue teams rappelled down the side of the building but were prevented by dense smoke from reaching him. Firefighters finally descended through the smoke-clogged stairwell to rescue the trapped man. A helicopter plucked him from the roof and flew him to a hospital, where he was treated for smoke inhalation and released. Of the forty people injured, a dozen were hospitalized. A maintenance worker reportedly died when the elevator car in which he was trapped burned on the twelfth floor.

By dawn the fire had destroyed the bank's personal trust, foreign exchange, asset management, and bond-trading departments.

First Interstate reported that a DEC Vax computer, several minicomputers, and approximately sixty personal computers were destroyed in the fire. The bank's main computers, two IBM 3090s that handled checking and savings accounts as well as customer loans, were housed in another building and not affected by the disaster. The institution also maintained backup computer equipment at another site, enabling employees to immediately switch the bond department's processing to an almost identical DEC Vax computer.

Ironically, the fire was first reported by a team of workers installing sprinklers in the skyscraper. The building had been built in 1973, before the Los Angeles building code required sprinklers.

Had the fire not interrupted the project, the sprinkler system installation would have been completed throughout the building within two weeks!

Los Angeles authorities announced the First Interstate fire caused $450 million damage, making it the most costly high-rise fire in the city's history.

On Mother's Day, May 8, 1988, fire burned cables and destroyed computer equipment at Illinois Bell's Hinsdale switching station, interrupting voice and data communications for thousands of customers west of Chicago.

When communications to the computer used by Florists' Transworld Union ceased, thousands of florists across the country were unable to transmit orders for flowers by wire. A nearby Holiday Inn reservation computer that normally processed 35,000 calls a day was unable to receive customers' calls. Flight delays at O'Hare Airport were attributed to the loss of communications links between FAA computers.

Dominicks Finer Foods, a supermarket chain, reported they were unable to connect computer terminals at forty-three of their eighty-nine stores with host mainframes.

Investigators reported that the Hinsdale switches were essentially computers, monitored over telephone lines from Springfield, 200 miles away. The unmanned Hinsdale facility reportedly contained no fire suppression system. An Illinois Bell spokesman explained to reporters that a Springfield technician noted the fire alarm in Hinsdale but his phone call to the Hinsdale fire department could not go through--because the fire had already damaged the phone lines required to complete his call.

Illinois Bell assigned 400 repair workers to rebuild the interior of the switching station and replace the computer equipment and fiber optic communications lines destroyed in the fire. They revealed that 118,000 long-distance lines and 30,000 data lines had been destroyed. More than 35,000 local service voice lines had been damaged. The company also set up more than 100 temporary telephones around the area to help customers cope during the communications emergency.

Two-and-a-half weeks after the fire Illinois Bell announced that a new system was in place. Although technicians continued to clear up remaining obstacles, some Hinsdale area customers were plagued by difficulties well into June.

On Saturday, June 29, 1991, at approximately 2:00 a.m., fire was detected inside a computer room at the National Oceanographic and Atmospheric Administration in Suitland, Maryland. Firefighters successfully contained the blaze, preventing its feared spread to U.S. Census Bureau offices housed in the same building. The four NOAA employees working in the computer center at the time of the fire escaped without injury. The initial damage estimate was $1.75 million.

Measures intended to prevent and control fires have caused extensive damage to computer facilities. So have ruptured water pipes.

The accidental activation of a fire-control sprinkler system on August 8, 1979, flooded the Census Bureau's main computer center, causing a "total loss of all inhouse (computer) capacity." Two Univac 1108s were completely destroyed, while a third was damaged but repairable. A Univac 1110, damaged by the water, was also repaired and returned to service, as was most of the peripheral equipment in the computer center.

Bureau officials credited quick-thinking employees with saving so much of the sensitive electronic equipment operating when the deluge struck. Soon after the water was turned off, employees rushed to several nearby stores and bought their entire stock of hand-held hair dryers, which they used to dry the sensitive circuit boards! On-site engineers immediately treated many of the boards with an anti-corrosive solution.

With the 1980 Decennial Census scheduled to start in April, observers expressed concern that the devastating damage to its computer center had imperiled the Bureau's ability to tabulate the upcoming census. After all, computers such as those destroyed could not be purchased from existing inventory; they were usually manufactured only after contracts were accepted, with delivery as much as two years later.

Luckily the Census Bureau had a unique relationship with the Sperry Corporation: Census had installed the first general-purpose electronic computer (Univac I, serial number 001) in June 1951, and subsequently had purchased several other mainframe Univacs. Given the pressing needs of such an important and high-profile customer, the manufacturer gave top priority to providing a replacement computer as quickly as possible. To the amazement of industry watchers, a $7 million Univac 1100/83 arrived at the Bureau early in October, just two months after the disaster.

Tabulations for the 1980 Decennial Census of Population and Housing were not adversely affected by the $20 million catastrophe.

At Riverside Hospital in Newport News, Virginia, a first-floor laboratory routinely used salt water to clean blood-analysis equipment. A drain ran beneath the lab's floor. In the basement directly underneath the laboratory sat the hospital's computer equipment.

On June 23, 1980, data processing employees arrived to discover that corrosive salt water had leaked from ruptured plumbing, had penetrated the computer room ceiling, and had been sprayed by the air conditioner onto the computer equipment. The hospital's DEC PDP 11/70 was declared a total loss.

The destroyed computer normally supported patient registration and treatment monitoring, as well as functions for the emergency room, pharmacy, laboratory and clinic. Riverside Hospital, was one of twenty-three health care facilities connected to the Hospital Data Center of Virginia in nearby Norfolk, almost immediately opened a dozen communications lines allowing Riverside employees to run critical computer jobs remotely.

Within a week, Digital Equipment Corporation had delivered, installed, and tested a replacement computer system.

The H. C. Prange Company, headquartered in Sheboygan, Wisconsin, operated forty-two department stores in sixteen cities in 1983. On May 4, a broken water main eroded the soil beneath the building housing Prange's computer center, causing one of the building's support columns to sink. Authorities ordered an immediate evacuation of the premises.

After company officials persuaded local government authorities to permit an employee inside the building to retrieve the company's payroll files, they used a county-owned computer to generate paychecks for employees.

After locating and renting a vacant building previously used as a data center, Prange trucked their NCR mainframe computer fifty miles to Green Bay. Within a week officials reported their computer systems were again operating normally.

Even though a fire that roared through a Montreal, Quebec office building October 26, 1986, was stopped before it reached Steinberg, Inc.'s computer center, the building's sprinkler system extensively damaged the equipment.

Under the company's contingency plan, data-processing personnel were dispatched to set up operations at two prearranged alternative sites. Twenty-five employees hauled 10,000 computer tapes to a leased computer hot-site in New Jersey. Seventy employees moved to a temporary Montreal facility already equipped with computer terminals and remote communications systems.

Two days after the fire, company officials reported that Steinberg had reestablished normal computer links with all of their retail stores. Four days after the incident, officials reported that the company had processed and distributed 28,000 employee paychecks. They considered the crisis concluded.

During the wee hours of July 23, 1987, an iron pipe ruptured above the ninth floor of a building known as 95 Wall Street, spilling thousands of gallons of water and turning ceiling tiles into a mess resembling white mud. The space immediately beneath the broken pipe housed the computer room for Goldman, Sachs & Company. A spokesman told reporters that the computer center contained several IBM mainframes, two Wang systems, and numerous Unisys peripheral devices. He declined to identify the specific models or to estimate damages.

Even though *Computerworld* reported the value of ruined equipment as "millions of dollars," the article described business interruptions attributable to the incident as "modest."

By borrowing computer equipment from another Wall Street company and quickly acquiring replacements from computer manufacturers, the firm reopened its computer facility in less than a week.

In August 1987, workers installing a power cable at Houston's Johnson Space Center accidentally broke a fitting on an air conditioner's water pipe. When water started to spew across the computer room, employees immediately suspended a space shuttle reentry simulation and powered down the computer equipment. Their quick action in covering the IBM 3083 computers with sheets of plastic averted damage to the computers. However, the water damaged some of the peripheral devices.

While briefing reporters about the incident, a Space Center spokesman cited two reasons why a similar accident could not affect an actual shuttle mission. He said that such wiring jobs would never be undertaken during a mission. He added that the Goddard Space Flight Center in Maryland served as backup for shuttle missions. If anything ever impaired the Johnson Space Center's computer system during a mission, the Goddard computer would assume control.

7

DO COMPUTERS COMPROMISE
AIR TRAFFIC SAFETY?

In the wake of two deadly air collisions (one near Las Vegas, Nevada, the other near Brunswick, Maryland) in 1958, Congress and President Eisenhower rushed to create a new, independent federal agency to police and enforce air traffic safety rules. They agreed to combine functions of several existing government entities: authority over air traffic research and modernization, airport construction, safety regulations, and air traffic control would merge to a single agency called the Federal Aviation Administration (FAA).

Federal executives reasoned that, by absorbing all of the Civil Aeronautics Administration and the Airways Modernization Board, and part of the Civil Aeronautics Board, FAA could begin operation soon after the president signed the bill into law on August 23, 1958.

With the goal of quickly improving air safety, FAA created twenty control centers to direct air traffic across the United States. Pilots flying across certain portions of the country were required to file flight plans with FAA, then fly under the guidance of air traffic controllers. As controllers monitored and analyzed flight data displayed on radar scopes, they communicated specific instructions to each aircraft, advising its crew how to move safely through each designated area.

Although this simple system was a vast improvement over prior air safety efforts, FAA officials soon decided to ask Congress to fund computerization of much of the air traffic control function. Winning such approval was a slow and arduous process but, in March 1974, the FAA installed a new computerized radar data processing system in Los Angeles and Kansas City. Within a year, similar systems were in operation in seventeen of the twenty air traffic centers. A computer displayed the whereabouts of airplanes on television screens, replacing traditional radar screens that used a sweep-hand and blips to communicate the location of each aircraft.

Even though, at least in theory, the old radar systems were maintained for backup use when computers failed, newer controllers generally never learned how to use them. Veteran controllers, who earlier had used the older system, became so accustomed to the new computer system that they found it extremely difficult to revert to obsolete methods.

The Log, journal of the British Airline Pilots Association, charged in its April 1975 issue that the new American air traffic control system was unsafe. The article claimed that the computer had shown planes' positions to be twenty miles from their actual locations. British pilots reported several near-collisions and identified more than 125 "hazardous situations."

In Washington, an FAA spokesman denied that such problems still existed, claiming they were resolved before the system went into operational use. He told reporters that the agency had received "...no reports of any hazardous conditions or near-misses attributable to malfunctions or inadequacy of the system."

In its issue of January 6, 1978, the *Washington Post* reported that on December 15, 1977, two U.S. Air Force planes had passed within seventy-five feet of each other near Richmond, Virginia. The incident reportedly occurred during a two-and-a-half hour failure of the air traffic control computer at Leesburg, Virginia.

O'Hare International Airport came to a virtual halt on October 25, 1978, when a speck of dirt too small for the human eye to detect somehow attached itself to a wiring connector inside a computer's memory. At the same time, a second computer system at O'Hare's control tower also failed.

The double computer failure, which began about 9:00 a.m., soon created a backup of nearly 100 planes waiting to depart O'Hare. The waiting planes created such a traffic jam on the runways that soon there was no room at the airport to accommodate arriving planes. Luckily the world's busiest airport survived that day of computer failures, heavy air traffic, and foul weather conditions without an accident. One official shrugged, explaining that computer problems were nothing new to O'Hare, where computer systems reportedly had failed on forty-six occasions in 1977.

Shortly after the 1978 government deregulation of the airline industry, new carriers, increased flights, and lower fares attracted millions of new fliers. Within ten years the number of air passengers would almost double.

In the New York City area, the failure of a computer storage element on November 15, 1978, forced controllers to revert to voice contact with pilots to elicit information usually displayed automatically on their computer screens. They had to request flight identification, speed, and altitude by radio as they worked with backup radar displays. During the computer failure, seventy-five flights departing J.F. Kennedy, LaGuardia, and Newark airports recorded delays of up to one hour.

Shortly after a Frontier Airlines plane carrying fifty passengers departed Denver's Stapleton Airport on March 17, 1979, the pilot reported engine trouble and requested permission to return to Stapleton. As the plane approached the airport, the air traffic control computer failed. A controller quickly cleared other aircraft from the approach pattern and the Frontier plane, its engine shut down, landed safely.

An airport employee reported that flights were further disrupted during that two-and-a-half hour computer failure because planes, which could fly one-and-a-half miles apart under the computer control system, required at least five miles separation under the old radar system. The increased distance required between planes reduced the normal take-off rate from seventy planes an hour to only fifteen.

After a Leesburg, Virginia air traffic control computer failed for six minutes on October 31, 1979, then returned to service, controllers discovered they had "lost" a civilian passenger plane somewhere over North Carolina. Controllers said that an Air Florida flight carrying ninety-three people from Miami to New York simply failed to appear on the screen when the computer resumed operation.

Meanwhile, Delta Flight 1061, enroute from New York to Fort Lauderdale with 115 passengers, requested a course change because of turbulent weather. A few minutes after permission was granted, the pilots of both the Air Florida and Delta flights reported they had been forced to take evasive action to avoid colliding. They estimated the planes flew within 300 feet of each other before crew members spotted an approaching plane in the same airspace.

Within a month of the near-collision over North Carolina, the House Ways and Means Subcommittee on Oversight conducted aviation safety hearings in Washington, D.C. One of the most widely-reported items from the hearing was a partial list of computer outages at nine of the FAA air traffic control centers during 1979, submitted by Congressman Bob Whittaker. Albuquerque, New Mexico had computer outages of one hour and fifteen minutes on September 1, one hour and thirty-three minutes on September 19, and two hours on November 6. Atlanta, Georgia reported forty-six computer failures lasting longer than one minute each--during the week of August 28 alone. During a six-hour period on August 7, the computer failed twenty-four times. Cleveland, Ohio reported 143 computer failures lasting longer than one minute between May and October. Denver reported a ten-minute computer shut-down on October 13. In Houston, Texas, a June 13 computer malfunction lasted more than fourteen hours. During the month of October Houston reported nineteen outages lasting longer than one minute.

Indianapolis, Indiana reported twenty-four computer failures during August, twenty-seven during September and sixty-eight during October. Miami reported thirty computer failures in September and forty-nine in October. New York City experienced a major headache when computers were entirely inoperable for more than forty-eight hours from November 21 to 23. Washington, D.C. reported a total of 143 computer failures between April 3 and October 22, 1979.

John Leyden, president of the Professional Air Traffic Controllers Organization (PATCO), testified that the numerous computer failures constituted "a serious menace." He pleaded for replacement of the obsolete IBM 360-based systems.

On November 17, one day after the Congressional hearings, two American Airlines planes flew dangerously close to each other over Texarkana, Texas. Original reports indicated that the aircraft passed vertically within 600 feet of each other.

Investigators reported that when the air traffic control computer had "gone down" for several minutes, controllers had switched to their radarscopes and established radio contact with pilots. The computer then resumed operation briefly and shut down a second time.

Weeks after the Texarkana incident, an FAA spokesman said that the computer failures contributed to, but did not cause, the American Airlines near-collision. He blamed the dangerous proximity of the planes on both chaos and controller disorientation, which he said were created by switching back and forth between the two, very different air traffic control systems. He also told reporters that the first computer problem had been traced to a "storage element malfunction." An unspecified "program problem" reportedly caused the second system's failure that day.

On October 30, 1979, two F-15 fighters reportedly flew within fifteen feet of a Concorde supersonic airliner over the Atlantic Ocean, approximately fifty miles from the New Jersey coast. Investigators reported that civilian controllers of the Concorde flight had not received adequate information about the F-15s from Air

Force controllers. This absence of information prevented the Air Force computer's "conflict alert" feature from warning the fighter planes that they were too close to the Concorde. The Air Force also admitted that the F-15s had dropped below their assigned altitude.

Computerworld reported, in its February 11, 1980 issue, that controllers in Tampa often referred to their system as "Track-a-truck." The name derived from the fact that the system, less than a year old, tracked more than aircraft. It frequently also tracked large, fast-moving objects on the ground, such as trucks or trains!

The controllers' major complaint about Tampa's experimental system, however, was its unreliability. During its first six months of use, the system reportedly was out of service fifty-seven times. Although the system was intentionally shut down twenty-seven times for modifications and maintenance, the other thirty outages resulted from system failures.

In Fremont, California a malfunctioning program card in a computer memory unit shut down an air traffic control computer, June 22, 1980. Similar problems with that system three times the preceding month reportedly slowed air traffic over northern California and Nevada.

July wasn't much better. On Thursday, July 10, the computer shut down and had to be restarted ten times between 8:00 a.m. and 9:30 a.m. California airports at San Francisco, Oakland, Sacramento, Fresno, San Jose, and Monterrey, as well as at Reno, Nevada, were affected. Officials reported that sixty-six flights were delayed, some for as long as one hour.

The next day a computer failure of seventy-four minutes again delayed area air traffic. Two days later, a thirty-six-minute computer outage delayed Sunday's air traffic across the area. Perplexed technicians could not pinpoint the problems' cause.

The computer monitoring air traffic at Chicago's O'Hare International Airport failed on June 20, 1980. Twelve technicians were dispatched to the scene to identify the problem and restore service. Officials reported that controllers, using the old radar system, coped well during this emergency. Fewer flight delays were recorded than in earlier emergencies, even though the outage lasted ten days. Investigators later reported that the extensive failure had been caused by a software problem that prevented the system from accepting all of the data the computer generated about each flight.

Just prior to a July 2, 1980, system failure that affected flights to and from three major airports serving New York City, the computer reportedly provided erroneous information to controllers. Controllers cited one instance in which the computer displayed incorrect information about a small plane, which flew through the paths of several huge passenger planes before controllers became aware of the problem. None of the close encounters triggered accidents.

A Boston controller reported that two passenger jets flew within 200 feet of each other on an August morning in 1980. He expressed outrage that the computer system's conflict alert feature failed to warn of the near-collision. When controllers noticed that the screen display indicated that the two planes were dangerously close to each other, the Eastern Airlines L-1011 had commenced to climb toward the position of the Delta 727. Controllers instructed the Delta plane to climb also to avoid a collision.

Much of Cleveland, Ohio was blacked out by an electrical power failure starting at 8:01 p.m., November 11, 1980. When the Cleveland Air Traffic Control Center attempted to switch to generator power, that system also failed. They cut over to battery power, which lasted long enough to transfer, to two adjacent control centers, control for the flights the Cleveland center normally handled. Both the electricity and the computer system were back in service by 9:00 p.m.

New York controller Donald Zimmerman probably prevented an Argentine Boeing 707 from crashing into the World Trade Center in early March 1981. As the plane made its final approach for landing at JFK, Zimmerman noticed that the plane was flying so low that it would collide with the 1,749-foot steel television antenna atop the north tower of the World Trade Center. The plane was only ninety seconds away from the antenna when Zimmerman received both audible and visual warnings on his radarscope. The computer system, comparing data about all possible obstructions in each plane's flight path, determined the antenna posed a danger and triggered the alarms to Zimmerman's scope. He quickly radioed the airplane, directing the pilot to veer sharply to the south and climb rapidly.

After more than 11,000 controllers nationwide went on strike in August 1981, President Reagan fired them. Supervisory personnel and military controllers kept the system running while replacement controllers were hired and trained. Most control centers were operating with fewer controllers, each working a greater number of hours each week than previously.

A four-hour computer failure at Leesburg, Virginia air traffic control center the morning of February 28, 1983, forced controllers in the Washington, D.C. area to resort to telephones for exchanging flight data and handing off flights between controller facilities. Electronic links that normally transferred such data automatically were out of service that morning.

When a Falcon corporate jet reportedly took off from Morristown, New Jersey nineteen minutes earlier than scheduled, it bypassed a computerized flight strip system. The computer should have sent a controller strip showing the plane's identify and its intention to land at Teterboro, but no such strip was received at Teterboro that evening in November 1985.

Investigators later charged that the controller, busy with five other planes when the Falcon unexpectedly arrived in Teterboro airspace, failed to properly inform the small jet's pilot about other aircraft in the immediate area. They reported that the controller also gave erroneous information to the jet's pilot by twice informing him that a nearby single-engine Piper Archer plane was flying west when in fact it was flying east.

The two planes collided, plunging into the communities of Cliffside Park and Fairview. All five people aboard the two planes and one person on the ground were killed; eight others on the ground were injured.

Hundreds of Chicago flights were delayed August 5, 1986, when a computer failed and remained out of service for two hours. A less sophisticated backup computer system was used during the crisis. The malfunction of an element providing computer radar information to the system was identified as the cause of the failure.

When NTSB investigators looked for causes of a deadly collision in southern California on August 31, 1986, they noted a crucial factor: the absence in FAA computers of a feature to automatically track aircraft outside FAA control and to alert controllers of possible collisions. They pointedly cited inadequacies of the air control system, rather than human error, as the primary cause of the fatal collision near Los Angeles.

An Aeromexico DC-9 carrying sixty-four people from Tijuana to Los Angeles International Airport, under guidance from air traffic controllers, was struck by a single-engine Piper Archer not under control of the air traffic system. At an altitude of 6,500 feet, the Piper reportedly clipped the tail of the DC-9, sending both planes crashing into the suburbs of Cerritos, spraying flaming fuel as they fell. Damage on the ground was extensive, including the total destruction of ten houses. Body parts were scattered across many blocks. All sixty-four people aboard the DC-9 died, along with three on the Piper and fifteen on the ground.

Investigators concluded that, although the small plane probably showed up as a tiny blip on radar, its altitude could not have appeared on a controller's screen because the plane carried no altitude-reporting device. Such devices were required for planes entering the highly restricted area near Los Angeles International.

The captain of a Northwest Airlines Boeing 727 reported that, if he had not disengaged his automatic pilot, abruptly veered left, and descended, his plane would have collided with an Air Force plane over South Dakota June 2, 1987. The Northwest flight, enroute from San Francisco to Minneapolis, carried fifty-five passengers and eight crew members. Investigators blamed the near-collision on "miscommunication" between the air traffic controller and the pilot of the military plane. Approximately 1,000 feet separated the two aircraft when the Northwest pilot spotted the military plane and took evasive action.

Both Saturday and Sunday, June 13 and 14, 1987, were plagued with computer breakdowns at Chicago's air traffic control center. The FAA reported that 131 flights were delayed, some for as long as ninety minutes. They explained that the backup system was capable of handling only about two-thirds of the traffic volume that the primary system normally handled.

The Jacksonville, Florida Air Route Traffic Control Center reported that more than 800 flights across the southeastern United States were delayed February 12, 1988, when the flight control computer failed. Officials later reported that "a severed cable" had caused the three-hour outage, forcing controllers to rely on telephone and teletype lines to convey flight information among airport control towers.

Record high temperatures in the San Francisco Bay area pushed the temperature inside Oakland Airport's radar control facility past 100 degrees on July 17, 1988. Air conditioning units proved inadequate. Although radar continued to function normally, three computers shut down, halting all air traffic for two hours.

At Chicago's O'Hare Airport, technicians attempting to increase the capacity of an eighteen-year-old radar tracking system on August 1, 1988, caused the airport's air traffic control system to crash. The boost in capacity for older systems was part of FAA's year-long effort to enhance antiquated systems scheduled to remain in place for at least six more years. Technicians encountered problems when they attempted to load new software into the system. Nearly twenty hours later, after they had finally identified and replaced a faulty circuit board, they returned the computer to service.

On August 5, 1988, technicians at the Boston Center (actually located in Nashua, New Hampshire), installed a software upgrade that directed flight-path reports to the wrong printers. The early morning snafu forced controllers to revert to manual procedures for directing regional air traffic. Three hours later employees restarted their computer using the old version of the software. Control operations and air traffic flow both had returned to normal by 9:30 a.m.

The National Transportation Safety Board (NTSB) reported that Air Force One, carrying President Reagan from Philadelphia to Newark on October 12, 1988, passed within 1.58 miles of a Bar Harbor commuter plane over New Jersey. To ensure that an accompanying airplane, ferrying reporters, landed in Newark ahead of the President's plane, Air Force One was pursuing non-standard routing to Newark at an altitude of 11,000 feet.

NTSB investigators cited several factors that they said contributed to the troubling incident: First, they faulted the Washington Center for failure to hold all flights to Newark until Air Force One had landed. Washington Center had allowed the Bar Harbor plane to proceed. Next, NTSB charged that a Philadelphia controller, who was supposed to change Air Force One's flight plan in the computer, had failed to do so. The third factor cited was that a controller in New York misidentified the air sector he was in charge of controlling. A supervisor at the New York center reportedly neglected to assign a controller to the Bar Harbor commuter plane, even though he had accepted a computerized transfer of control responsibility. Finally, NTSB reported that, even though controllers in Washington Center reportedly noticed that Air Force One and the Bar Harbor commuter flight appeared to be converging, they took no action--assuming that controllers for the New Jersey sector would separate the two planes. The incident raised worrisome questions about the safety of a president in flight.

The FAA reported twenty-four mid-air collisions in 1987. The agency counted 1,059 near-collisions for that year. Both statistics improved for 1988, when FAA reported nineteen collisions and 706 near-collisions. Most of the accidents involved non-commercial flights.

Air traffic controllers in the New York area complained in the 1980s of frequent computer lapses, during which the identities of hundreds of planes simply vanished from their radar screens. Each plane's image was still depicted--but without any identification. Controllers referred to printed lists of planes in the area and, after positioning a cursor near a plane, depended upon their memory to key each plane's identification into the computer. Such identity-retagging operations required several minutes to complete and were successful only because the controllers correctly remembered the planes' locations. Official stressed that no near-collisions resulted from this particular computer anomaly.

After regional air traffic controllers lost contact with 150 aircraft, controllers in Washington, D.C., using a newly installed computer system, on the evening of September 28, 1988, assumed control of air traffic stretching from Indianapolis to Denver. Heavy rain flooded a Southwestern Bell Telephone Company's repeater station in Shawnee, Kansas, knocking out communications. Some of the backup radio systems, which controllers would have used to communicate with planes in the air at the time, also failed. Controllers had to radio officials in Washington and ask them to take over air traffic control until local communications were restored.

On May 7, 1989, an Air New Zealand jumbo jet, descending toward Los Angeles International Airport, suddenly swerved to avoid hitting a small plane in its path. The computer system failed to warn of the impending collision. The sudden evasive maneuver, twenty miles off the California coast, caused no damage to either plane or injury to any of the jumbo jet's 350 passengers.

The same month, a Pan American World Airways jet, taking off from Washington, D.C.'s Dulles International Airport, reportedly passed within 500 feet of a Navy T-38 jet piloted by astronaut David Walker.

July 1989 was a terrible month for air traffic controllers across the United States. On July 6, around 8:30 a.m., shortly after technicians loaded some software changes into a computer at Chicago's air traffic control center, all terminal screens mysteriously went blank. That hour-and-a-half outage delayed traffic across the entire country for most of the day.

On July 7, severe thunderstorms disrupted telephone communications linking the air traffic control system with Boston's Logan International Airport flight control tower.

Traffic at southern California airports was disrupted July 8 because the computer system overheated and reset itself more than 100 times, erasing all data from controllers' screens each time. The problem was traced to broken wires in three computer memories in Santa Ana.

Controllers, attempting to enter flight information into an air traffic control computer at Leesburg, Virginia around 4:25 p.m., November 3, 1989, were unable to do so--the computer's keyboard had mysteriously locked up. However, the system continued to display information about the planes then in the area. Because controllers could not enter or update flight data, they asked other control centers to delay airplanes destined for the Washington, D.C. area. They also redirected nearly 150 flights around the problem area. Departures from Washington-area's three airports were delayed for up to two hours. Finally, a replacement keyboard was installed and operations returned to normal by 8:00 p.m.

Leesburg reported computer failures of a very different nature on November 7. A crack in a telephone company fiber-optic cable, linking Leesburg's computer with those in the Federal Aviation Administration, prevented any exchange of flight data. The computer actually failed three times that day: at 4:49 a.m., at 7:36 a.m., and again at two minutes before noon.

The Leesburg facility had been using a greatly-improved $3.5 million Host computer system for two years when these two outages occurred. The new system, though nearly ten times faster than their older equipment, still was subject to outages. Failure of the two systems caused numerous Washington-area flight delays and cancellations.

An NTSB investigator reported that a Los Angeles International Airport controller's log entry indicated that the air traffic controllers screen for the ground radar was "out of service" starting at midnight, January 31, 1991. Information from the radar antenna was not being communicated to the controllers because their scopes, intended to permit them to see aircraft positions on runways, were out of service. The system was still inoperative eighteen hours later, when an arriving USAir Boeing 737 with 89 people aboard struck a SkyWest commuter plane carrying twelve.

The investigator said that the USAir plane struck the rear of the commuter plane, almost obliterating it, before dragging it more than 1,800 feet. After crossing a gravel median, a taxiway, and a service road, both planes stopped abruptly when they crashed into an abandoned fire station. The larger plane came to rest on top of the commuter plane.

The inferno killed everyone on the SkyWest Swearingen Metroliner commuter plane, which was about to depart for Palmdale. Of the eight-nine passengers aboard USAir flight 1493, which had flown a Syracuse-Washington-Columbus-Los Angeles route, twenty-two died.

Two months earlier, a similar accident occurred at Detroit Metropolitan Airport. On December 3, 1990, a Northwest Airlines DC-9, waiting to take off, was hit by a Northwest Boeing 727. Investigators blamed the eight deaths aboard the DC-9 on the lack of a collision warning system at the Detroit airport.

Soon after the two incidents, FAA officials told reporters that United Technologies' Norden Systems Division was developing a new automated system intended to warn controllers of impending collisions on airport runways and taxiways. The new setup, with its ability to track planes and vehicles, would employ a computer program to calculate whether a collision might occur. If the system sensed imminent danger, it would alert controller by both a computer-generated warning and a flashing screen display. The new collision warning system, intended to prevent tragic accidents like those at Detroit and LAX, was said to be about three years away from installation.

On April 8, 1992, an IBM 3083 computer temporarily removed all aircraft identification labels from radar screens across southern California, thereby snarling hundreds of flights. The problem, which persisted from 8:18 a.m. to 10:30 a.m. at the Fremont FAA center, was attributed to "a software error."

Numerous other computer outages have been reported at air traffic control centers around the country, prompting the FAA in 1995 to award contracts for up-to-date systems in all twenty regional control centers, to be completely operational in the year 2000. A skeptical editorial in the *New York Times*, July 29, 1995 cautioned, "But contracts for this work have been signed before and not completed."

In the spring of 1995, faulty computer equipment in San Juan, Puerto Rico, reportedly generated erroneous information that caused a controller to direct two American Airlines planes into paths that would have resulted in a head-on collision! Fortunately, American had installed on-board collision-avoidance computers. When these devices alerted the pilots to the impending danger, they took evasive action.

In Aurora, Illinois computer screens began to flicker badly at 8:30 a.m., May 17, 1995. Controllers' screens indicated that the portion of the system that assisted them in controlling airplanes across the region were continuing to operate normally when in fact they were not! Although controllers assumed the computer commands they entered (by pointing and clicking a mouse) were routinely handing off planes to other controllers, the computer was not performing hand-offs!

Thousands of passengers were stranded on May 25, 1995 when a power failure knocked out air traffic control computers serving New York City's three major airports. The tripping of one of the center's three master circuit breakers, for no apparent reason, caused the 6:00 a.m. outage. Controllers were unable to "see" some of the thirty-seven planes in the area at the time. Radio contact to some of them was also impossible during the electrical failure. Approximately 200 departures from Kennedy, LaGuardia and Newark airports were delayed during the six-hour loss of computer systems. Dozens of planes destined for the area were diverted to Boston, Washington, and Baltimore airports.

Widespread adverse publicity prompted the FAA to announce in June the addition of fifteen technicians to the New York Center for better maintenance of the air traffic control system's equipment.

Three failures in a single week of the computer relied upon by nearly 400 Chicago controllers snarled traffic in mid-July 1995. Each time the controllers reverted to their much slower backup system as they directed the movements of the more than 9,000 daily flights they routinely handled. A spokesman told reporters that "equipment problems" had caused the failures of computers connecting the FAA's radar system with the controllers' console displays.

The *New York Times* published a special report titled "Flying Blind" in its August 20, 1995 issue. The report indicated that no crashes had yet resulted from failures of air traffic control computers. It went on to describe some of the FAA equipment as being so old that no one else in the world still used it. The article added that no spare parts were available and that neither the equipment manufacturer nor third-party maintenance firms would agree to service or maintain the ancient hardware. According to the report, "FAA is still dealing with equipment with vacuum tubes, dense webs of wiring, thousands of circuit boards and other components that are as extinct outside the FAA as punch-card readers and core memories."

Soon after the widely-publicized computer breakdowns at New York City in May and at Chicago in July, the government bowed to public pressure and announced an interim solution to the persistent problem. FAA announced August 1, 1995, that it planned to spend $65 million for new IBM 9121 computers to be installed as soon as possible at five of the most heavily-traveled air traffic control centers: Chicago, Cleveland, Dallas-Fort Worth, New York, and Washington.

Critics quickly pointed out that the tortoise-pace of government procurement procedures, followed by the time a winning vendor would need to create the special purpose software, would delay the interim solution well into 1997. New York and Chicago were already scheduled to receive replacement computer equipment in 1998 under the system-wide modernization effort.

Electronic "ghosts" caused locations for both real and phantom flights to appear on controller screens in Illinois the afternoon of July 28, 1995. After integrating data from eight radar stations, the computer displayed plane images accompanied by a text-block transmitted by each plane's transponder, followed by a radar blip. The false readings consisted only of the text-blocks. In some instances the locations of the actual and phantom images appeared to be nearly 100 miles apart. Controllers not only had to remember which images were real, but also which locations were genuine. Imagine the embarrassment if they had warned a pilot to swerve to avoid an on-coming plane which didn't exist!

Even backup systems for backup systems fail--and usually at the worst possible time. While a power supply system in Oakland, California was taken out of service for testing, August 9, 1995, both the primary supply and its backup system failed. Then the emergency generators would not start. The electrical failure knocked out operations at the air traffic control center, severing radar and radio contact with dozens of airplanes in the vicinity. The short-lived blackout, which began at 7:17 a.m., disrupted air traffic control for two hours.

On August 17, the air route traffic control center in Auburn, Washington lost all ground-to-air communications because of a malfunctioning part in the new Harris Corporation's Voice Switching and Control System, installed in June. Controllers, who switched to a backup system, later reported that they experienced no significant problems from the incident.

After being taken out of service for repairs during the night, Chicago's primary air traffic control computer, which normally handled nearly 10,000 flights a day across the mid-west, could not be restarted the morning of September 12, 1995. When controllers attempted to switch to a secondary computer, it too failed, significantly delaying more than 200 flights. During the outage a passenger plane, climbing from 19,000 feet, encountered an unexpected private plane at 20,000 feet near Ottumwa, Iowa. When an onboard computer in the passenger plane sensed the presence of the second plane and sounded an alarm, its pilot put the plane into a dive to avoid a potential collision.

In the New York City area, hundreds of flights were delayed when an air traffic control computer failed twice on the evening of May 20, 1996. The controllers' radar screens continued to function; however, they were unable to display each plane's route during the two computer outages. Some flights were delayed for more than an hour. Several controllers, who had used the computer keyboard or printer just prior to the computer failure, told investigators they had suffered mild electrical shocks from contact with the equipment.

Over the difficult years, FAA officials have attempted two major system modernization efforts. Their first, unveiled in 1981, was dubbed the National Airspace System Plan. By replacing all computer equipment within ten years, it intended to increase the control system's efficiency and reduce the number of human controllers. Officials estimated the cost of such an ambitious undertaking at $12 billion.

The federal government asked contractors to submit proposals and, after reviewing them, contracted with two of the vendors to build demonstration models of their proposed systems. The government paid IBM and Hughes Electronics more than $450 million to create the two prototypes.

On May 17, 1987, FAA began to use a small part of the systems modernization system, enabling air traffic managers in Washington, D.C. to see every airplane flying under FAA jurisdiction within U.S. borders. The new system provided managers with several options: they could focus on air traffic in any one of the twenty zones into which the forty-eight contiguous states were divided; they could observe traffic in a narrow corridor such as that using a single airport; or they could identify individual aircraft and monitor their altitude and speed.

On June 3, FAA dedicated the first of twenty IBM computers in Auburn, Washington's air traffic control center near Seattle. Officials announced that the replacement computers had five times the capacity and ten times the speed of the old devices. The interim computers were scheduled to be installed at all twenty air traffic control centers by the summer of 1988.

These systems fragments provided badly-needed interim solutions and helped the agency gain time to install the ultimate system, by then estimated by FAA to cost $15.3 billion. The GAO warned Congress in April 1988 that this system would actually cost far more than FAA had estimated. GAO projected the system's cost at more than $24 billion, making it the second most expensive civilian technology program ever undertaken in the United States. Only the Apollo manned spacecraft race to the moon had cost more.

Despite the warning, FAA proceeded. On Monday, July 25, 1988, the agency announced that it had awarded IBM a $3.6 billion contract to replace air traffic computers and radar screen across America. IBM acknowledged that the contract was the largest the firm had ever negotiated. Dubbed the Advanced Automation System, this phase of the modernization effort would replace FAA's existing air traffic control systems with new equipment, software, and enhanced color work-stations expected to provide controllers with easy-to-read current weather, radar, and flight data. The ambitious undertaking was scheduled for completion in February 1998. FAA officials expressed confidence that new computers, radar scopes, and communications links would greatly improve air traffic control quality and reduce systems failures.

Almost immediately after the contract award announcement, Hughes Aircraft Company of El Segundo, California filed a protest and asked that the federal government overturn the contract awarded to IBM. Hughes claimed that the government had given IBM unfair advantage in the procurement process. Pending a hearing, the General Services Administration's Board of Contract Appeals suspended FAA's contract with IBM.

On October 28, a Board of Contract Appeals law judge concluded that FAA had not given unfair advantage to IBM but had acted reasonably in deciding that the unproven technology proposed by Hughes was not worth $700 million more than the more conventional solution IBM had proposed. He denied Hughes' protest and reinstated the contract with IBM.

A month later, GAO published a highly critical report regarding the FAA's system modernization effort, charging that the agency had "...underestimated the complexity of these systems, the time needed to develop software and the interdependency among systems." GAO said that the project was already years behind schedule and revised its cost estimate upward to $27 billion. An FAA spokesman explained that writing the program of two million lines in Ada language was taking much longer than anticipated.

In May 1990 the GAO reported that nearly 70% of the nation's sixty-three largest airports had reported problems involving computer screens that either flickered or went totally dark. GAO concluded that the volume of air traffic simply overloaded the fifteen-year-old computers, described as vacuum tube machines with archaic core memories.

FAA officials continued to enter into contracts in support of their National Airspace System. On January 1, 1992, the agency announced that it had awarded a $1.66 billion contract for a computer-controlled communications system, to link controllers within air traffic control centers as well as controllers with flight crews. Harris Corporation of Melbourne, Florida said the sophisticated radio and telephone voice-switching system would be installed at all FAA air route traffic control centers as well as at several other sites.

On February 4, FAA entered into a $508 million contract with Electronic Data Systems to provide computer services.

The FAA announced on March 15, 1992, the signing of a $558 million agreement with MCI Communications for the Leased Interfacility National Airspace Communications Systems, commonly referred to as "Lincs." Carrying air traffic controller-to-pilot communications, as well as radar information and computer data, the upgraded system would replace an existing AT&T service. An MCI vice-president said that, if FAA exercised all of the options contained in the ten-year contract, MCI could be paid nearly one billion dollars.

By the end of 1992, FAA officials were clearly unhappy with IBM's performance on the Advanced Automation System. In December they went public, threatening to withhold payments to IBM for work performed, unless the computer giant submitted an acceptable plan to create software for the computer work-station-- work which FAA charged was almost three years behind schedule. Fearing outright cancellation of the multi-billion-dollar contract, IBM tightened management control of the project and agreed to have TRW audit the software.

Software development was more difficult than usual due to constantly changing specifications. FAA requested substantial modifications to the work-in-progress based on feedback from controllers who had tested a prototype of the system for several months. The agency also asked that the system be changed to enable controllers to use their work-stations while data was being updated. All together FAA's requests for systems changes resulted in nearly 300 contract modifications. By December 1993, the cost overrun estimates reportedly exceeded one billion dollars.

Concern about the future of the Advanced Automation System was heightened when IBM announced on December 13, 1993, the sale to Loral Corporation of its Federal Systems unit, responsible for developing the FAA system.

In early March 1994, FAA Administrator David Hinson revealed that the federal government had paid a half-billion dollars for software that would never be used! He said that a new internal FAA study indicated that the Advanced Automation System, projected in 1988 to cost $4.3 billion, currently was estimated to cost between $6.5 and $7.3 billion. The study also concluded that the first installation in Seattle, originally scheduled for completion by August 1993, had been rescheduled for June 1998. Hinson announced that he was replacing the project's management team and changing the specifications to create a less-ambitious system-- one that contractors were more likely to be able to build.

A government-ordered independent study of the project by CNA Corporation reported that much of the IBM-developed software was flawed. The report estimated that 6,000 programmer-workdays would be required just to eliminate the more than 3,000 program bugs detected during the evaluation.

The CNA report indicated that the major problem was FAA officials' inability to decide what they wanted the replacement system to do. According to the report, officials had "reached for the sky" when they planned to consolidate the work of 254 terminal radar approach control operations into the agency's twenty air traffic control centers.

The report also concluded that FAA officials had insisted upon a system's performance level that many engineers said simply was not attainable. Their requirement for a reliability of "seven nines" (99.99999%) was deemed unrealistic. Simply put, it required the system to perform correctly for all but 3.15 seconds each year! The FAA was also faulted for not changing its specifications to incorporate new global-positioning satellite technology into their modernization system.

Early in June 1994 the FAA announced that it was scaling back and restructuring major portions of its Advanced Automation System contract, originally awarded to IBM, now held by Loral. The contract, by then valued at $7 billion, was the core of FAA's total modernization effort, whose cost estimates had risen to $18 billion. An FAA spokesman said that MIT's Lincoln Laboratory and Carnegie Mellon University's Software Engineering Institute had been asked to evaluate the software being developed for the controllers' work-stations. Within a few months both evaluators concluded that the software's underlying structure was sound. However, both faulted its documentation and implementation.

In October 1994, FAA announced that the agency had decided to retain Loral Corporation as its prime contractor for development of its drastically scaled-down version of the Advanced Automation System.

FAA awarded Loral contract additions valued at $955 million in April 1995. A spokesman explained that $898 million was slated for automated controllers' work-stations and new display screens. The remaining $57 million was intended for airport-tower control computer systems.

The *New York Times* reported, October 6, 1995, that an FAA internal report had recommended that the agency delay the implementation of its long-awaited new equipment at the New York air traffic control center because controllers could not be spared from their jobs long enough to be trained to use the new technology! The new equipment, though installed, sat idle. Despite the fact that a new computer system, designed to display the positions of planes over the Atlantic Ocean, was in place and ready to go, controllers had not been taught to use it. They continued to write the same information with grease pencils onto plastic-covered maps.

The implementation efforts were further complicated by the unavailability of instructors qualified to conduct the specialized training.

In Washington an FAA spokesman said that any substantial slippage in the New York implementation schedule would result in similar implementation delays at all other locations because they were scheduled to follow New York.

Under a headline reading "Ambitious Update of Air Navigation Becomes a Fiasco," the *New York Times*, on January 29, 1996, charged that FAA's management had "squandered" a half-billion dollars on an air traffic control system that would be obsolete before its installation. A retired admiral, brought in by FAA to evaluate the agency's systems modernization efforts to date, concluded that "they needed some adult supervision."

When FAA officials scaled back their computer modernization efforts in 1994, they dropped the portion of their system that controlled planes within fifty miles of airports and concentrated their efforts instead on the agency's twenty air traffic control centers handling long-distance flights. On September 16, 1996, FAA announced that they had entered into an agreement with Raytheon Company of Marlborough, Massachusetts, starting at Boston in 1998, to install new computers and software at civilian and military air traffic control offices across the country. Initially funded for $80 million, the contract provided FAA options to extend coverage to the year 2007 and to convert up to 172 civilian sites and 192 military ones, thus raising the value of the Raytheon contract to $1 billion.

Raytheon announced that it planned to use off-the-shelf computers rather than custom-designed machines. The company also expected to use many computer programs they had written for air traffic control systems in other countries.

Life goes on. Millions of flyers, blissfully unaware of the system's fragility, entrust their lives to air-traffic control computers.

8

ARE TRAVELERS WELL-SERVED BY COMPUTERS?

Travel industry executives quickly recognized the almost unlimited uses to which they could apply computer power. Airline companies built world-wide reservations systems, listing not just one airline's flights, but those of most carriers. They created extensive ticket information and reservations networks. Aircraft maintenance, personnel scheduling, and the traditional business data processing tasks quickly were automated.

Hotel chains installed reservations systems that could book, confirm, and bill customers. Car rental companies quickly did the same, even while cruise ship companies were creating similar computer systems.

As the travel industry increased its degree of automation, executives also probably unknowingly raised the likelihood that critical computer systems upon which they had come to rely, would fail--usually at the worst time. Such breakdowns caused operations either to slow dramatically or shut down completely. For most computer-dependent users, there was no reverting to the ways of yesteryear.

Computers have more recently assumed an almost irreplaceable presence in the cockpits of airliners. Newer planes often are so heavily automated that the computer controls the take-off, an auto-pilot controls the flight, and a computer lands the aircraft. Humans in the cockpit often appear to do little more than monitor the actions of various computer systems.

During its rush to automate, the industry has encountered a variety of problems, ranging from amusing to annoying to deadly.

After being dedicated with great hoopla on Friday, April 20, 1973, a computer-controlled system to advise motorists on the Santa Monica Freeway failed to perform as expected on its first day of service. Designed to flash detailed traffic advisory messages to thirty-five electronic signs between Santa Monica and the Harbor Freeway, the system could instantly retrieve from its memory any of 100 warning and informational messages and display them at appropriate locations. Technicians, attempting to communicate details of a collision and advise motorists how best to cope with the resulting traffic impediments the following Monday morning, discovered that the computer had malfunctioned over the weekend and could not display the messages needed.

A computer-controlled subway train, carrying 115 morning commuters, ran amok under the streets of Washington, D.C. on October 8, 1979, after the train's operator stepped off the train and it departed without him. The harrowing runaway ride began at Brentwood Station and proceeded to the heart of downtown.

The operator-less Red Line train departed Brentwood Station and proceeded to Union Station, where it stopped but its doors failed to open. Next, it stopped at Judiciary Square; again the doors did not open. It zoomed right through Gallery Place without even stopping.

Passengers throughout the train had become aware that something was amiss. Only those in the front car could clearly see that there was no operator in the control booth.

Kilena Loveless became an instant celebrity that morning when she calmly used a barrette from her purse to pick the door lock to the control booth, stepped inside, and pushed an emergency stop button. When the runaway train halted at Metro Center, she pressed another button which opened all of the train's doors and allowed the relieved passengers to exit.

Predictably, Metro officials told reporters that the passengers were perfectly safe throughout their extraordinary ride, because the train remained under computer control. However, unidentified Metro employees told reporters that the computer lacked the ability to detect obstructions on the track and halt the train to avoid hitting them. He also said that those in charge were not even aware that the Red Line train was speeding under the city streets without an operator--until Loveless stopped the train at Metro Center!

In explaining the incident, Metro officials reported that Metro's central control had contacted the Red Line's operator, asking whether he could see another train that was supposed to be leaving the Brentwood Station at about the same time. Because he could not see the other train from his control booth, the operator reportedly stopped his train at a red signal light, set its controls to automatic mode, and descended to the roadbed. As he walked away from the train, officials said that the red signal light changed to green and the computer sent a signal instructing the train to proceed. Even though Metro trains could run without an engineer aboard, the train's doors could be opened only by a human operator in the control booth.

Two days after the incident, an editorial in the *Evening Star* paid tribute to Loveless as the woman with "...the barrette, the brains and the initiative." A *Washington Post* editorial praised her initiative and her ability "...to find the right button."

At Amtrak a newly-installed computer information and ticketing system reportedly sold more than 5,000 sleeping compartments--each to multiple customers! When employees became aware of the computer's double-booking of sleepers and attempted to book accommodations for the duplicate customers, the computer indicated that absolutely no sleepers were available. An Amtrak spokesman admitted that the computer system indicated that all sleeping compartments on all trains were sold out from November 27 to December 9, 1981.

In its December 21, 1981 issue, *Computerworld* reported that thousands of passengers had been refused tickets because Amtrak's computers had erroneously reported that all trains were booked to capacity when in fact some were totally empty. Amtrak said that "programming problems" created the confusing situation. A spokesman declined to speculate on the amount of business Amtrak lost because of the incident.

Officials of Air Canada said that an "erroneous computation" involving jet fuel requirements forced an emergency landing of a Boeing 767 in Gimli, Manitoba on July 23, 1983. The plane's electronic fuel measurement system reportedly was not working properly. It appeared that the plane had taken on 22,300 *pounds* of jet fuel instead of the 22,300 kilograms it actually needed. The Montreal-to-Edmonton flight, carrying seventy-three people, ran out of fuel over Manitoba and went into a powerless glide at 36,000 feet. It made a rough but safe landing without damage or injuries.

Every aspect of United Flight 310 appeared normal as the Boeing 767 jet began a computer-controlled, gradual descent for a landing at Denver's Stapleton Airport on Friday, August 10, 1983. As its computer guided the airplane through a descent from 41,000 feet to 24,000 feet, it maintained the rate of descent at 1,000 feet per minute, maximizing fuel efficiency. Suddenly both engines overheated to the point that the pilot was forced to turn them off, putting the powerless airliner into a long glide.

The loss of normal electrical power knocked out computer displays in the cockpit. However, navigational instruments operated under emergency power. By the time the plane had descended to 14,000 feet, the crew had restarted both engines. They safely landed the jet without further problems.

NTSB investigators said they believed that, when the onboard computer slowed the plane's engines to gain fuel efficiency, the engines were not moving fast enough to generate sufficient heat to prevent ice from forming on them. As ice formed, it reduced the air flow, causing both engines to overheat.

An odyssey of death began at 11:00 p.m., Tuesday, August 30, 1983, when Korean Air Lines Flight 007 departed New York's J. F. Kennedy Airport, bound for Seoul, South Korea. After a scheduled refueling stop in Anchorage, Alaska, the flight departed Wednesday at 10:00 a.m. Less than five hours later the Boeing 747 jumbo jet vanished from Japanese radar screens.

American officials charged that Soviet military planes tracked the civilian airliner, which had strayed into Soviet airspace, for two-and-a-half hours, then fired a missile, destroying the plane over the Sea of Japan. Search ships and planes reported finding only traces of fuel where they assumed the jumbo jet's wreckage had fallen into the water.

Airline officials reported that 269 people died in the incident. Passengers included seventy-two Koreans, thirty-four Taiwanese, thirty Americans, and twenty-two Japanese, plus more than eighty additional passengers representing numerous other nationalities. The jumbo jet carried a crew of twenty-nine.

The Soviets initially refused to admit that the plane had been shot down. They also refused to release recordings of Soviet conversations involved in tracking the doomed flight.

The Soviets sent an armada of forty ships to search for the flight data and cockpit recorders. American vessels searched for the recorders until November 5. When they abandoned their unproductive efforts, the world assumed that the plane's flight data and cockpit recorders would never be recovered from the depths of the Sea of Japan.

News reports included several theories about what caused the downed airliner to stray so far off course. Some speculated that the U.S. Government had arranged the intrusion into Soviet airspace to test reaction of the Soviet radar defense systems.

Others suggested that the flight crew purposely chose to fly through Soviet airspace to save fuel--a feat which would earn the crew a bonus from their employer.

Most aviation experts who have spoken publicly about the incident express the opinion that KAL Flight 007's crew members misprogrammed the airplane's inertial navigation system. The doomed flight's onboard system consisted of three computers: one connected to the pilot's autopilot, another to the co-pilot's autopilot, and the third to monitor the other two. In the event the third computer sensed any disagreement between the two autopilot systems, it would alert the crew of the discrepancy.

Prior to each takeoff, the pilot had to manually enter numbers into a keypad resembling a touch-tone telephone. These numbers communicated to the computers the latitude and longitude coordinates of the flight's originating point, various way-points, and destination. The system displayed all keyed data on a screen for visual verification before actually entering it into the computer. The same data had to be similarly entered into each of the plane's three computers. The probability was deemed low of a human making the same mistake in entering the same data three different times. Not true, claimed crew members who appeared to have done precisely that on other flights. They said that it was easy to select a wrong coordinate, enter it, and verify its correctness three times.

A study by the International Civil Aviation Organization (ICAO) concluded, in December 1983, that human error in operating the computerized navigational equipment was the most probable cause of KAL 007 straying into Soviet airspace. The study also charged that the Soviets failed to make "exhaustive efforts" to identify the Korean airliner prior to blasting it from the sky.

An ICAO spokesman told reporters that Soviet officials still refused to turn over various recordings that might have aided the investigation.

Several years passed before some of the relevant facts were finally revealed. In a deposition taken in Seoul in September 1987, the pilot of Korean Air Lines Flight 015 said that he departed Anchorage, enroute to Seoul, just fourteen minutes behind Flight 007. Both flights were slated to fly North Pacific route R20.

Flight 007 had begun to stray off-course before it flew out of range of American civilian radar. Officials later reported that on several occasions air traffic controllers were unable to establish normal communications with the airliner. They said that the crew of Flight 015 relayed routine checkpoint reports from Flight 007 to controllers during that loss of direct communications.

The pilot of Flight 015 testified that the pilot of Flight 007 had told him by radio that he was flying through strong winds; Flight 015 reportedly never encountered the turbulence.

Flight 015's pilot told the court he suspected that the crew of Flight 007, even after realizing they had a major problem, decided not to dump fuel and return to Anchorage because they feared that their employer would punish them. An aviation expert said that, in order to be granted permission to return, the flight would have had to jettison more than 20,000 gallons of fuel, then valued at about $20,000. Court documents confirmed that in some previous fuel-dumping incidents KAL had "disciplined" pilots.

Lawyers representing families of the victims contended that KAL was at fault because an error in the plane's navigation system allegedly caused the airliner to wander into Soviet airspace. They also told the jury that the KAL crew probably knew of the error but did not choose to turn back. The court ended with a finding of willful misconduct by the airline company and ordered KAL to pay punitive damages of $50 million.

An appeals court in Washington, by a vote of 3-0, upheld the finding of willful misconduct, but reversed the jury's $50 million award. By upholding the willful misconduct finding, the appeals court in effect allowed the families to sue for damages based on each victim's potential lifetime earnings.

The U.S. Supreme Court, in December 1991, refused to reinstate the $50 million punitive damage award.

The Russian newspaper *Izvestia* surprised the world when, on October 15, 1992, it published what it claimed to be transcripts from KAL Flight 007's cockpit recorder. The report indicated that one voice yelled "Smoke!" just before another commanded "Get up!", probably during the pilot's attempt to pull up the plane's nose. A pilot told Tokyo air traffic control that the plane had experienced rapid decompression and was descending to a lower altitude. The last voice on the tape was a Japanese air controller informing the pilot "I can't read you. Move to one-zero..." The tape abruptly ended there.

After studying the transcript, aviation experts concluded that the crew received no radio warnings prior to the attack. Further, if the Soviet plane had fired warning shots as claimed, the Korean airliner's crew failed to detect them. It appeared that the plane continued to fly for ninety seconds after the Soviet missile struck it.

Although the recovery of the black boxes had been kept secret until *Izvestia* published the transcript, the Soviets had recovered them on October 20, 1983, from a depth of 594 feet, approximately four miles off the Soviet coast.

On November 19, 1992, while on a state visit in South Korea, Russian President Boris Yeltsin surprised his hosts by presenting President Roh Tae Woo with a case containing KAL's flight recorders. This gesture of good will might have been in response to recent diplomatic changes between the two former enemies. After they established full diplomatic relations in 1990, South Korea loaned several billion dollars to Russia.

After Yeltsin returned to Russia, South Korea's Vice Minister of Transportation announced that the flight data recorder from

Yeltsin did not contain the expected tape. He said that Korean diplomats in Moscow would attempt to obtain the missing tape.

The ICAO announced in Montreal on December 18, 1992, that it was resuming its fact-finding inquiry after the Russian Government promised to provide copies of the tapes as well as numerous previously unavailable documents.

ICAO's final report, June 14, 1993, concluded that Soviet military officers had assumed that the Korean air liner was a U.S. reconnaissance plane intruding into Soviet airspace. The report also said that Flight 007 was more than 300 miles off course because the crew had switched to a constant magnetic heading of about 245 degrees, instead of relying on a computerized setting.

Delta Airlines implemented a new computerized system, designed to provide passengers with boarding passes when they bought their tickets, at midnight, Friday, September 16, 1983, . The system did not perform as expected. On both Saturday and Sunday the malfunctioning system delayed numerous flights departing Atlanta, Boston, Newark, Washington, Los Angeles, and San Francisco, with other airports reporting fewer and shorter departure delays.

Computerworld reported in its issue dated October 14, 1985, that, due to a human procedural foul-up during routine computer file maintenance, American Airlines employees had written new reservations data over existing records, thereby obliterating them. The corruption of the computer data caused a seven-hour shut down of the Saber system. Reservations agents responding to more than 30,000 calls had to handwrite tickets-- something that most American Air agents had not done since the late 1960s. Employees reportedly recovered from the data disaster by copying the lost data from backup tapes, then rerunning the computer file maintenance operation.

Eighty-two people died on August 31, 1986, when a Piper Archer struck an Aeromexico DC-9, causing both planes to crash near Los Angeles International Airport. The Piper reportedly was not equipped with an automatic altitude reporting device, required for planes entering the busy LAX corridor. Details of this deadly crash appear in the preceding chapter.

At Delta Airlines computer errors reportedly caused 700 frequent fliers to receive free or reduced-fare trips which they had not earned. Some 2,000 customers who deserved such awards received nothing. A Delta spokesman announced in January 1988, that the company had decided to compensate for the computer's "goofs" by sending appropriate coupons to those frequent fliers who should have received them, but did not. He also announced that Delta would honor the unearned rewards the computer had erroneously issued.

At O'Hare International Airport, authorities said that the flight delays on Mother's Day, May 8, 1988, had been caused by their computers' inability to communicate with each other. A fire had destroyed vital computer equipment at Illinois Bell's switching station in Hinsdale, Illinois.

When puzzled analysts at American Airlines investigated lagging sales for the second quarter of 1988, their analysis of load numbers revealed that sales of discount fare tickets were substantially below expectations. Seeking the reason, they discovered that their Saber reservation system had indicated that flights were sold out of discount seats when, in fact, such seats were still available. The glitch was attributed to an error in the logic of a recently changed computer program. AMR corporate president Robert Crandal announced that the error may have cost as much as $50 million in lost revenue when would-be American customers turned to United or Delta for discounted fares.

The following year American Airlines employees demonstrated that they could function near normally, without computer support. They operated the nationwide service for more than 2,000 flights during a twelve-hour period, on May 12, 1989, during which their normal computer support was unavailable. The computers continued to function but were unable to access critical data regarding reservations, fares, ticketing, seating, etc. Airline employees and travel agents across America had to refer to printed fares and schedules, then handwrite tickets as in times long past. Flight operations such as crew scheduling, weight loads, and fuel loads reportedly were unaffected by the computer problem.

In its May 22, 1989 issue, *Computerworld* reported that the problem had started when one program erroneously changed another, resulting in the stripping away of the computer-readable labels on more than 1,000 disks. Even though the computers continued to operate, without those disk labels they could not access any of the system's data stored on disks. Technicians reportedly identified the cause of the failure within an hour. Then more than 100 programmers and systems engineers worked more than ten hours to relabel the disk files, restore the system, and return Sabre to normal operational status.

An old discount fare, offering travelers round-trip tickets on American Airlines anywhere in the United States for $152, mysteriously reappeared in American's computerized Saber reservations system on July 20, 1989. The special fare required no advance purchase, however, it mandated a Saturday-night stay at the ticketed destination.

Although American personnel attempted to dismiss the incident as a human error in reloading the promotional fare, someone apparently had also extended the expiration date for the promotional fare in the computer to September 30. The airline refused to divulge how many deeply discounted tickets were issued before employees became aware of the error and deleted it from the Saber system.

European executives decided that they needed to introduce a gigantic aviation technological advantage to break the near-monopoly held by Boeing and McDonnell-Douglas for commercial aircraft sales around the world. They decided to form a four-nation consortium consisting of Britain, France, West Germany, and Spain to build aircraft in which they would substitute advanced computer technology for traditional solid pulley-and-wire equipment.

Their Airbus Industrie consortium developed the Airbus, described as the most computerized aircraft in civilian aviation. Because of the plane's extensive use of computer-controlled electronics to guide rudder movement while it also controlled flaps and hydraulic systems, the technology was dubbed "fly-by-wire". The plane's cockpit controls operated by electrical pulses rather than traditional mechanical methods. The cockpit crew worked with six computer screens displaying flight guidance and navigational information, engine parameters, maps, the aircraft's position, etc. Fly-by-wire technology made it possible to automate an entire flight, including engine-firing, take-off, and landing. Three fail-safe computers were incorporated into the Airbus design.

Even before the first planes rolled off the assembly line, Airbus Industries announced that the revolutionary aircraft had already become the world's best selling twin-engine jet ever, judged by the number of firm orders received.

On June 26, 1988, in anticipation of an exhilarating experience, more than 125 invited passengers boarded an A-320 near Mulhouse, France, for a demonstration flight at a nearby airshow. France's chief instructor of Airbus pilots, Captain Michael Hasseline, was piloting the plane.

After taking off from Mulhouse and flying a few miles to Habsheim Airport, the plane descended so it could be clearly seen by the 30,000 spectators gathered for the airshow. TV cameras transmitted images of the plane's descent to millions of enthralled viewers. With its landing gear down, the A-320 reportedly flew across the airfield at a height of about sixty feet, to provide a very close-up view to those on the ground. Observers noted that the plane did not appear to be rising as it cleared the outer edges of the airport. They watched in horror as the low-flying plane struck a line of trees and crashed into a dense forest. The trees cushioned the plane's fall, causing it to settle back on its tail instead of nose-diving into the ground. Survivors scrambled from the plane as flames began to appear within the wreckage. Because of its proximity to the airport, fire fighters quickly reached the crash site and were able to douse or control the fires. Even so, rescuers reported that three passengers died in the crash. Twenty more remained hospitalized for several days following the incident.

Critics rushed to blame the A-320's computer for the crash, especially after the *Times of London* reported that Captain Hasseline had said, immediately after the crash, that when he attempted to boost power to rise safely above the trees, the plane failed to respond.

In the wake of the crash, both Air France, with four A-320s in service, and British Airways, with two in service, announced suspension of all A-320 flights pending preliminary investigations into the cause of the Habsheim crash.

Investigators studying the downed plane's "black box" flight recorder revealed that the A-320 was flying at an altitude of fifty feet and a speed of 119 knots (137 miles per hour) as it approached the runway at Habsheim. They said that the plane had dropped to an altitude of thirty feet by the time it reached the middle of the runway's length. The investigators told reporters that when an A-320 flew at a height of at least 100 feet, the plane's throttles would automatically open if the computer sensed the plane was about to stall. However, in situations where the altitude was less than 100 feet, they said the computer system would react as if a pilot were landing the aircraft.

When the first of the Airbus 320s were about to be delivered to Indian Airlines in 1988, their pilots had reportedly threatened to refuse to fly them, claiming that such sophisticated aircraft could not be properly maintained in India. Some also voiced concerns that the Airbus's advanced computer system took away a pilot's ability to respond quickly in emergency situations.

Still others, considered aviation experts, insisted that the Airbus 320 was the safest aircraft ever built.

An Indian Airlines Airbus 320, favored with clear skies for its midday landing at Bangalore on February 14, 1990, crashed about 1,000 feet short of the intended runway, killing ninety-seven of the 146 people on board. The pilot and copilot were among the dead. At the time of the Bangalore tragedy Indian Airlines had fifteen A-320s in service and sixteen more on order.

Four days after the crash, Indian Government officials ordered the remaining fourteen Airbus 320s grounded, pending an investigation into the craft's safety. The chairman of Indian Airlines announced that he accepted "moral responsibility" for the crash, then resigned.

In France, the Indian crash ignited a smoldering dispute over whether the Airbus was too over-complicated to fly safely. The French pilots union called for the grounding of the Airbus in France. Safety officials conducted a brief investigation, then pronounced the A-320 safe to fly.

In May 1990, investigators told a court of inquiry convened in New Delhi that both the pilot and copilot had keyed into the automated system a number that was lower than the plane's actual altitude. They reportedly also had failed to disengage a manual override of the plane's computerized control system. The court also was told that the plane's black boxes indicated that either the pilot or copilot attempted, in the final few seconds, to accelerate the plane's speed so it could gain altitude and go around to make another landing approach. The engines, apparently too near idling speed, reportedly failed to provide the power required for such a maneuver. The plane touched the ground short of the runway, bounced, tore off its engines, and burst into flames.

In yet another incident, investigators speculated whether a fatal computer programming error caused the January 20, 1992, deadly crash of an A-320 near Strasbourg, France.

Airport authorities announced that they had lost radar and radio contact with Air Inter flight 5148 from Lyons to Strasbourg around 7:45 p.m. At the time of last contact, the A-320 was over Mont Saint Odile in the Vosges Mountains. When an excited inhabitant of the mountain village of Barr contacted authorities to report that he had heard a huge explosion at approximately the same time, authorities began a massive ground and air search for the plane they presumed was down.

Despite heavy clouds, dense fog, and temperatures hovering near freezing, helicopters and a Mirage fighter began overflying the mountains, in a search for the missing plane. On the ground, more than 500 troops, police, and emergency medical teams scoured the pine forests.

Shortly before midnight, French authorities announced that searchers had reached the wreckage and found few survivors. The doomed plane reportedly carried ninety passengers and a crew of six. The death toll eventually was confirmed as eighty-seven.

Aviation investigators revealed that navigational maps for the crash area define the minimum safe altitude as 4,700 feet. They said that the plane had crashed into a mountain only 2,500 feet high.

Because altitude reporting was not automatically controlled by computers onboard the A-320, investigators speculated that the computer had been instructed to descend at a designated angle, rather than at a specified number of feet per minute. If the person programming the computer selected vertical speed mode and dialed 1,500, the plane would descend at the constant rate of 1,500 feet per minute as it approached the airport. If the person selected flight path angle mode and dialed fifteen degrees, the plane would descend at a constant angle of fifteen degrees from level flight.

Flight investigators indicated that it would be extremely easy to confuse the options because the same dial (in the center of the instrument panel) was used for both options. They strongly suggested that Airbus Industries immediately change the manner in which the crew instructed the plane's automatic vertical guidance system.

At the time France did not require all passenger planes to have ground proximity warning systems to alert pilots when the aircraft flew too low. Nonetheless, investigators urged that such devices be installed immediately in all A-320s in use.

At the time of the accident Air Inter had twenty-seven A-320s in service flying domestic routes within France. Worldwide, more than two hundred and fifty A-320s were in regular use. Air Industries had confirmed orders for more than four hundred more.

Boeing introduced their 747-400, a new long-range version of the firm's very successful jumbo jet, in 1989. Almost immediately rumors began to circulate that the massive plane had serious computer problems.

British Airways reported that on six separate occasions, between October 1989 and February 1990, the computer closed the throttle on all four engines, effectively shutting them down. In all instances, British Airways said, pilots saw the throttles closing and overrode the autopilot to restore full power to the engines.

Investigators reportedly determined that a printed circuit card in the autopilot was giving out spurious information, causing the system to mistakenly sense that leading edge slats in the plane's wings had been deployed. This erroneous reading resulted in automatic cutting of power. In April 1990, spokesmen for Boeing and British Airways announced that new software, extensively tested through actual use for several weeks, apparently had corrected the problem.

Speculation persists whether computers were responsible for the crash of a Lauda Air jet in Thailand, May 23, 1991, that killed all 223 people aboard. While enroute from Bangkok to Vienna, one of the Boeing 767 jetliner's engine thrust reversers, intended for use as a braking mechanism after the plane landed, mysteriously deployed in flight. FAA officials investigating the crash site confirmed that the thrust reverser on the plane's number one engine was found in a fully deployed position.

Thai investigators released a partial transcript of the cockpit voice recorder in which the pilot and copilot appeared to have received warnings that an engine thrust reverser had inadvertently deployed--but they had decided the warning signal was false.

In August, both the FAA in the United States and the Civil Aviation Authority in Britain ordered airlines to insert pins in all Boeing 767s to disable thrust reversers until investigators could determine whether the planes were safe to fly.

Computerworld, in its issue dated September 16, 1991, reported that the FAA was carefully examining the computer simulations used in the airline safety program. They hoped to determine if any flaws in that program might have played a role in the deadly crash.

In October 1993, the NTSB announced the discovery that autopilots on some Boeing 757s and 767s had mysteriously engaged and disengaged on their own, causing the planes to change direction for no apparent reason. The FAA was asked to notify pilots of the anomaly and to suggest that they cut power to their autopilots when the systems were not in use.

NTSB officials said that they had learned of the problem while investigating a June 1993 incident in which a United Airlines 767 landing in Frankfurt, Germany, skidded off the runway. The crew reported that as the plane touched down, its rudder moved on its own. After investigators ran extensive tests on the plane's equipment, they reported that the autopilot display panel did in fact change on its own without any human intervention. Further, the plane turned in response to the unintended changes. A "component failure" was cited as the cause of this autopilot malfunction.

In 1994, Northwest Airlines installed computerized interactive video systems on nine of their planes, enabling passengers to watch movies, shop, or play video games. Dependent upon individual computers at each passenger's seat, the system reportedly achieved a reliability rate of about 90% for most flights. Even so, on a jumbo jet this often meant that as many as three dozen customers could not use the system, creating three dozen new "emergencies" for flight attendants to deal with. By September 1994, Northwest Airlines announced the removal of the interactive system, which had cost about $1.5 million to install on each plane, and the return to a non-interactive system providing only movies and music. The *New York Times* described the termination of the interactive system as "...the equivalent of an aborted takeoff."

9

HOW RELIABLE ARE COMPUTERS IN THE SECURITIES INDUSTRY?

Computers have been used in stock exchanges since 1964. The exchanges' employees suffered through the same early uncertainties, goofs, errors and unexplained phenomena that plagued most organizations learning to cope with the new technology.

The computer driving the New York Stock Exchange's stock ticker broke down on Thursday, February 24, 1972, halting trading for twenty-four minutes. Data losses forced the exchange to publish incomplete volume and price-index figures for the day.

When the computer controlling the stock ticker crashed at 10:58 a.m., a backup computer was supposed to intercede and take over the task. When it became clear to exchange officials that the backup system had also failed, they halted trading from 11:01 until 11:25. Officials reported that the data lost during the computer failure had been recorded on magnetic tape and they promised it would be restored and available by the start of the next trading day.

Another computer malfunction, on February 28, 1972, briefly put the ticker out of operation. This three-minute incident did not result in any loss of data or halt in trading.

Years later, commodities-trading abruptly halted at 11:30 a.m., November 19, 1979, when all electrical power to the computers at the Chicago Board of Trade was lost.

Traders could not use their backup, chalk-board system because they could not transmit prices outside the building. The

Board of Trade remained closed for the remainder of the trading day.

Technicians reported that a switch in an uninterruptible power supply (UPS) had failed, forcing them to rewire the computer equipment, bypassing the UPS in order to restart the computer. No data was lost in the system's crash. The Board of Trade opened for business as usual the following day.

To encourage more universal investing, the Swedish Government instituted tax breaks for those investing in corporate shares in 1978 and 1980. By 1983, fully one-sixth of Sweden's citizens were investing in the stock market.

In May 1983 the surge of trading activity overwhelmed the stock market computer. Millions of transactions, being processed when the computer crashed, remained unsettled for several days, meaning that investors could obtain neither their stocks nor their money. Even though a small army of technicians worked around-the-clock to restore computer service, the Stockholm market remained closed for a week.

A few weeks later a computer at Merrill Lynch and Company, in mid-July 1983, turned some of the firm's modest investors into instant millionaires! In preparing monthly statements, the computer mysteriously moved the decimal point one, two, or more places to the right of its correct position. Some accounts, actually valued at only a few thousand dollars, suddenly appeared to be worth millions. After phone calls alerted Merrill Lynch to the situation, corrected monthly statements were quickly issued.

"Time is money." It normally took the Chicago Mercantile Exchange's computer system less than two seconds to post price changes on the futures market. When points on a contract fluctuated almost constantly, and each point was valued at up to $2.00, speedy posting was vital.

On March 16, 1984, the posting speed slowed so dramatically that officials decided to shut down the exchange until they could identify and correct the unknown problem. Although officials refused to reveal details about the cause of the computer system's slowdown, they described it as a "combination hardware and software failure." Users had complained of delays of as long as twenty seconds just prior to the shutdown. The system was returned to service after an outage lasting two-and-a-half hours.

Although futures trading continued at other U.S. mercantile exchanges, Chicago traders reportedly lost money, since they could not sell contacts which dropped in price while the computer system was down.

Before noon, October 19, 1987, the New York Stock Exchange traded more shares than on any previous day in history! By the close of business the Dow had plummeted 508 points--a record one-day drop. This misfortune followed a decline of 395 points over the preceding two weeks. For October alone, the Dow was off more than 900 points. A substantial number of companies found that their stock traded at less than half of its September value.

The Designated Order Turnaround (DOT) System, begun in 1976, electronically linked computer systems at brokerage houses to those at Securities Industry Automation Corporation (SIAC)--the stock markets' computers. This connection enabled traders to transmit multi-stock orders from their firms' computers directly to the stock exchange computer, where the trades could be executed within seconds.

Analysts were quick to blame computerized trading methods, which were designed to quickly sell off stocks when the market turned down and minimize losses to their huge institutional investors. They estimated that stocks valued in excess of $50 billion were protected by such trading programs at the time of the October '87 crash.

Senator John Heinz of Pennsylvania called for a suspension of program trading in which "mindless, computer-driven algorithms have driven the market." A Presidential task force reported that more than 20% of the stock sales of October 19 had been generated by the DOT system.

On the day following the crash, watchful stock market officials observed that DOT trading was causing some orders awaiting execution to back up as much as three hours. They asked program traders to discontinue using DOT until trading returned to a semblance of normality.

Following the October investors' nightmare, the New York Stock Exchange instituted a change in the DOT system that places individual orders ahead of institutional orders when the DOW advances or declines a specified number of points.

Officials of the Securities and Exchange Commission (SEC) concluded in Washington, during the spring of 1988, that computer trading added to the market's volatility and reduced investor confidence. They approved a limited experiment restricting the use of computerized trading whenever the Dow Jones Industrial average moves fifty points in a single day. This action seemed especially prudent at the time, as the Dow had dropped 101.46 points (4.82 percent), on January 8, creating yet another crisis of confidence in the stock market.

On October 16, 1989, an unusually heavy volume of trading in the first hour after the New York Stock Exchange opened, caused traders to closely watch their computer monitors. Some of those watching Quotron devices saw advances and declines unlike any they had ever experienced. The Dow plummeted ninety-nine points within seconds, then just as amazingly soared more than 125 points before again losing 113 points almost as quickly. Seasoned veterans decided that the market could not possibly be so erratic and therefore turned to other electronic quotation services.

Quotron officials blamed the early morning foul-up on a software timing problem. They maintained that only the average was wrong; they claimed that prices of the individual stocks had been correct throughout the see-sawing advance/decline displays. The company switched to a backup system while technicians worked to correct the software problem.

An electrical fire that erupted in a lower Manhattan computer center, Friday, November 10, 1989, forced both the New York Stock Exchange and the American Stock Exchange to close. The Securities Industry Automation Corporation (SIAC), owned jointly by the two exchanges, reported that the fire at 55 Water Street, which was discovered at approximately 8:00 a.m., apparently started in a basement electrical vault. When officials, as a precautionary move, decided to switch to emergency power, the computers were disrupted. Because SIAC lacked an emergency computer backup facility, the opening of both exchanges was delayed for one hour. The fire damaged none of the computer equipment.

Just over a year later, a fire that shot flames eight stories high, accompanied by a explosion that blew out windows on the lower three floors of the fifty-four story skyscraper, forced the hasty evacuation of the same building. The December 27, 1990, incident occurred in a Consolidated Edison transformer in the street adjacent to the building. Although electrical power to the building was not interrupted, officials feared that the fire might spread PCBs (polychlorinated biphenyls) into the building. They ordered all employees outside until engineers could determine whether PCBs were present inside the facility. The all-clear was given at 10:30, employees returned to their desks, and trading on the two stock exchanges opened only ninety minutes late.

This was the fourth trading interruption in just over a year. In addition to the November '89 incident, a fire in a Consolidated Edison substation had halted AMEX trading in August, but without affecting operation of the NYSE. Then, in November 1990, an equipment circuit failure at the New York Stock Exchange halted trading for an hour and a half.

Then, on January 4, 1991, an AT&T worker mistakenly cut a fiber-optic cable connecting New York City with the rest of the world forcing both the Commodity Exchange and the New York Mercantile Exchange to close. Both computer and human communications were disrupted for several hours.

In Chicago, workers driving pilings into the Chicago River accidentally breached a fifty-eight mile system of tunnels built a century earlier to deliver coal to downtown locations. On April 13, 1992, several million gallons of water raced through the ancient tunnels, flooding basements in some of Chicago's skyscrapers to depths as great as thirty-five feet!

City officials, in conference with Commonwealth Edison about the unusual situation, warned most large employers that electrical power to the affected buildings would be cut off within two hours. This warning proved sufficient for most organizations to power down computer systems and dismiss employees before electrical and telephone services were shut down.

The Chicago Board of Trade (CBOT), one of the largest commodity exchanges, reportedly lost billions of dollars worth of business because it was forced to close for the entire day. Warned of the impending flood and anticipated power loss around 6:30 a.m., employees systematically shut down CBOT's fifteen computer systems. By setting up terminals at another site, CBOT opened for portions of each day through the rest of the week.

Industry observers reported that approximately two dozen organizations temporarily moved their computer operations to alternate sites because of Chicago's Flood of '92.

The Times of London printed a rarely-used oversize headline to announce in its issue of Friday, March 12, 1993, "Chief of Stock Exchange quits in computer fiasco." Efforts to create a computerized, paperless stock transfer and registration system for the London Stock Exchange had been ordered stopped the preceding day. To date results of the 75 million pound ($115 million) effort were declared unusable. The costs required to make the system operational were deemed unacceptable. Consequently, the system was simply abandoned and the 350 people working on the system's development were dismissed.

The much-vaunted Taurus (Transfer and automated registration of uncertificated stock) reportedly was the victim of nearly constant changes in specifications that forced its developers to confront constantly changing goals. Politicians kept demanding modifications to satisfy various constituent groups. Brokers wanted a simpler, easier-to-use system. Banks, acting as registrars for investors, pushed for a system more compatible with their existing computer systems, seeking to avoid massive inhouse changes to make their systems compatible with Taurus.

As Taurus was being created at the Stock Exchange, stockbrokers, banks, pension funds, insurance companies and investment houses were modifying their inhouse computer systems for compatibility with Taurus. Experts estimated the cost of these developmental and modification efforts at an additional £100 million--money and effort wasted because Taurus would never be implemented.

In 1981, serious discussion took place concerning a single computerized register to cover all share dealings maintained by the Stock Exchange. When the registrars objected loudly, the original Taurus proposal was put on hold. In 1987, the project was partially revived when a committee was assembled to identify and coordinate the primary interests and concerns of all organizations that might use such a system. The committee promised that the new Taurus could be partially operational by the end of 1990. It was intended to link existing commercial databases maintained by brokers, registrars, bank nominees, and others into a cohesive computer network.

Peter Rawlins became chief executive of the London Stock Exchange in November 1989, with public expectation that he would modernize back office operations. Share certificates and stock transfer forms would be replaced by electronic registers. Computers would issue to shareholders periodic statements listing transactions. The task of transforming the Taurus concept into a reality was entrusted to Coopers and Lybrand.

After a series of delays, and expenditure of tens of millions of pounds, the Stock Exchange engaged Andersen Consulting to conduct practical tests of the Taurus system near the end of 1992. After Andersen pronounced the system "inoperable," Stock Exchange employees undertook a detailed review of their own. In addition to confirming the earlier verdict of Andersen Consulting, they announced the discovery of fundamental system flaws that would cost an additional seventy-five million pounds to correct. Experts concluded that modification and redesign work required to make Taurus perform as expected would also delay implementation still further--until 1996.

The projected doubling of the system's cost, coupled with yet another long implementation delay, convinced London Stock Market officials to cut their losses and abandon the project, a decision they made on March 11, 1993. Chief Executive Rawlins immediately resigned.

A spokesman told reporters that the Exchange's existing system continued to perform both efficiently and cheaply. The scrapping of the Taurus system, considered by many an embarrassingly severe blow to the City of London, would not impede the continued orderly business of the Exchange.

In a March 12, 1993, editorial titled "This Bull Called Taurus," *The Times* opined: "The biggest loss to the City will be counted not in time or money, but in reputation--a commodity which is supposed to be more valuable than either in the financial world."

In a letter to the *Times*, published March 19, Roger Johnson, president of the Chartered Engineering Institution for Information Systems Engineers, stated that "The public has a right to expect that those who commission major computer systems developments should ensure that the same standards of professionalism are sought and applied as they would require in any other branch of engineering. Anything else is, surely, negligent and irresponsible."

In the United States, Newbridge Networks, a Canadian manufacturer of computer network equipment, asked Nasdaq officials to halt trading of Newbridge stock on August 1, 1994, pending an important company announcement. Because of a delay in getting Nasdaq approval, the stock traded for the first two minutes of the trading day. The official ban was supposed to be effective at 9:32 a.m.

At 11:00 a.m. a Newbridge spokesman revealed quarterly earnings lower than expected.

At 11:32 a.m. Nasdaq announced that trading in Newbridge shares would resume at 11:45 and that brokers could begin posting quotes five minutes earlier. Through a human error, the computer opened for both quotes and trades at 11:40 a.m. Approximately 100 orders were executed within five minutes, at prices ranging from $37.25 to $38 per share. At 11:45, when trading should have resumed, the price stood at $33.50.

Nasdaq officials, upon learning that trading had started five minutes earlier than planned, announced at 12:40 p.m. that all trades in Newbridge shares executed between 9:32 a.m. and 11:45 a.m. were being canceled.

By retroactively canceling the millions of dollars in Newbridge trade, Nasdaq saved some investors from huge losses. The same maneuver also canceled corresponding profits for other investors. In that single trading day, Newbridge stock dropped 32%.

"The stock market for the next 100 years," as Nasdaq refers to itself, is probably the only major organization in the world to have had its computer service shut down by squirrels--twice! Even without a traditional trading floor, this nationwide network of computers and telephones was trading more than 300,000,000 shares on heavy trading days.

In December 1987, one of the furry critters interrupted trading on the Nasdaq stock exchange when it caused a computer in Trumbull, Connecticut to crash. That unlikely occurrence attracted wide media attention and endeared squirrels to many computer-haters.

Then, on August 1, 1994--different squirrel, same organization, same story: the primary computer crashed! When a backup electrical power system failed to switch on following a power failure, employees discovered that one of the animals had chewed through a power line. Computer service was restored after thirty-four minutes by switching to an alternate computer in Rockville, Maryland.

Computer security specialists had to add squirrels to their long lists of threats to computer stability and reliability.

In another incident, Nasdaq officials reported that a "trader's mistake" resulted in the transmission of incorrect last-sale prices for shares of more than two dozen large companies traded on that exchange, September 9, 1994. The erroneous figures were transmitted to a central computer system providing stock tables to be printed in major newspapers across the nation. The error was discovered too late to correct before its publication in the next editions.

When a computer system that posted prices of completed stock trades at the Chicago Board of Trade malfunctioned on September 14, 1994, officials halted trading for four hours. The shutdown, ordered minutes after the day's opening, closed the market for most of the day. Trading resumed a mere fifteen minutes before the market's closing time.

Some thought that it surely was a Canadian April Fool's joke when news spread that the Toronto Stock Exchange's computer system had crashed on April 1, 1997. After all, the same system had gone down just a few days earlier. Officials said that the heavy volume of trading activity had caused the outdated system to fail. Trading resumed two hours later.

10

IS MOTHER NATURE UNFAIRLY
HARSH WITH COMPUTERS?

Both hurricanes and tornados have caused extensive computer outages across the United States over the decades. Sometimes the disruptions resulted from power failures and communications lines being down. Often the winds themselves created havoc.

Warned that hurricane Frederic was headed for Alabama's Gulf coast, employees of Merchant Bank (Mobile's largest), spent Wednesday, September 12, 1979, frantically preparing for the storm's arrival. Although the bank's IBM mainframe computer as well as a fireproof vault containing the institution's current programs and data stored on reels of magnetic tape were located on the third-floor, well above harm's way, thousands of reels of tape containing backup and historical data were shelved in the basement. As it became more certain that Frederic was indeed headed for Mobile, cautious employees rushed to move copies of the bank's most critical tapes to another Merchant's building. They also carried all of the tapes from the basement to the third floor. Day's end found technicians making backup copies of current computer files and powering down the computer.

Labeled one of the century's most destructive storms, Frederic struck Mobile late Wednesday evening, September 12th.

A Merchant spokesman reported later that Frederic had disrupted both power and phone service at the bank, preventing some 150 terminals from communicating with their central computer.

At the Alabama Power Company, problems associated with computer controller units and modems were blamed for an electrical blackout that plagued much of the state for weeks. A company spokesman reported that Frederic had created such widespread communications and transportation difficulties that it took three days for technical support personnel to reach their computer room.

In fact, power and telephone outages caused far greater problems for area businesses than did flooding. Even after employees in numerous data processing shops set up generators to power their computers, dead telephone lines prevented widespread communication with them.

Computerworld reported that when Frederic hit Birmingham, employees at the First National Bank were in the process of converting their computer equipment from Burroughs to IBM mainframes. They interrupted their changeover to prepare for the hurricane, successfully shutting down all systems in time. Because of the continuing power outage, bank employees could not resume computer operations until Saturday, when they finally installed a generator.

So many computers were down because of Frederic that many Alabamians did not receive paychecks that week.

Power outages also plagued numerous computer installations in adjacent Mississippi. There Frederic toppled several power transmission towers, some of which had to be lifted back into place by helicopters.

In 1983, hurricane Alicia caused a Galveston County, Texas, building's upper floors to collapse and crash through the roof of the county's data processing center below. Starting shortly after 2:00 a.m., August 18, storm-driven rains pelted the Honeywell mainframe computer and peripheral equipment, causing extensive water damage. A spokesman told reporters that the water rendered all of the disk packs unusable. Fortunately, the spokesman added, magnetic copies existed of all data stored on the damaged disks-- tax appraisals, payroll, accounts payable and jury selection.

Data processing management exercised an in-place emergency agreement with U.S. Home Corporation in Houston, under which the county could use a similar computer facility there to process their most critical applications.

Even though Alicia caused widespread destruction across Galveston Island, many other nearby computer centers reported only minor problems. A number of computers remained inoperable for several days awaiting restoration of electrical service. Most equipment reportedly worked normally when reactivated.

Forecasters warned in 1985 that Hurricane Gloria, packing 130 mph winds, might prove to be one of the worst hurricanes of the century. They predicted a twelve-foot tidal surge for coastal portions of New York and Connecticut where much of the land lay only five or six feet above the high-tide mark.

For most threatened computer installations, September 27 had too few hours remaining in which to move their equipment to safer ground. Most organizations contented themselves with exercising more basic and realistic precautions such as moving copies of their critical computer programs and computer files to safer locations. A few data processing managers hastily negotiated emergency arrangements to run critical computer applications on compatible computers elsewhere, if the situation came to that.

In Milford, Connecticut, Gloria shut down Telecomp, Inc., a computer service bureau. Without electricity, telephone service, or its computer system, the bureau could not provide the services its customers expected. At least one customer reportedly resorted to hand writing checks to pay employees rather than leave them without funds during such a crisis. As most computer centers in the area, Telecomp remained inoperable for several days.

Another luckier Milford company, U.S. Electrical Motors, used the approaching storm threat as justification to replace the batteries for a diesel generator they counted on to power their computer during any electrical outage. This prudent move helped ensure that the firm's computer continued to support three manufacturing facilities in other parts of the country following Gloria's fury.

Such calamitous events seem to catch some organizations at the absolute worst possible time. On Long Island, the Dime Savings Bank computer center was in the midst of computing customer interest on accounts when they learned of Gloria's impending threat. They had to pause to make certain that all current computer files and programs were backed up and copies moved to a safe location. Officials feared that the predicted tidal surge could destroy their vulnerable computer facility.

Fortunately Gloria blew ashore at low tide with much lower velocity than expected. Although two of Dime's branches lost their computer communications link during the storm's fury, the bank's data center remained intact and continued to perform normally.

Four years later, when hurricane Hugo, with wind gusts of 140 mph, roared ashore in the Charleston, South Carolina area, Thursday, September 21, 1989, it caused little damage to computer systems. Despite the storm's $4 billion damage estimate, the loss of electrical power and downed phone lines were the biggest problems facing most data processing facilities.

First Federal Savings and Loan took the unusual precaution of making several copies of all critical computer programs and files and having employees take the copies to different locations in the immediate area. Although Hugo leveled more than two dozen major buildings in South Carolina, the storm inflicted no physical damage on First Federal's computer center.

On Sunday, because of the continuing power outage across 85% of Charleston, First Federal installed a generator to power their computer equipment. On Monday six of their seventeen branches were online and open for business.

Comdisco, Inc. reported that, although several subscribers had alerted them that they might need to use computer hot-sites because of Hugo, none actually relocated their computer operations to Comdisco sites because of the storm.

After destroying nearly all of the buildings on North Topsail Beach, near Wilmington, North Carolina, in August 1996, Hurricane Fran proceeded rapidly inland, toppling thousands of trees as far inland as Raleigh and Durham. Raleigh officials declared several thousand buildings unsafe for habitation. Downed power and telephone lines across the area shut down numerous computers.

In Durham, water damaged five computer systems belonging to the city, forcing employees to issue water bills based on customers' historical usage rather than current meter readings.

Hardee's Food Systems reported that a damaged fiber optic cable prevented their computer from automatically calling each of the company's 3,200 fast food outlets to obtain sales and financial data when the business day concluded.

Tornadoes usually produce even more devastating winds than hurricanes. Even though their strike zones threaten much smaller geographic areas than do hurricanes, tornadoes frequently inflict serious damage on computer installations.

In a part of the country unaccustomed to tornado activity, a twister caused nearly $200 million damage and hospitalized more than 100 citizens near Windsor Locks, Connecticut in October 1979. The freak storm tore the roof from a building belonging to United Technology Corporation. An electrical power failure forced the company's computer facility to shut down for more than twenty-four hours. Using an emergency generator, employees systematically powered down the IBM mainframe with no loss of data and no equipment damage.

Tornadoes are more common in North Carolina, where one descended near the small town of Washington on March 28, 1985, causing electric lights to blink several times, then go out completely. An IBM computer at the National Spinning Company abruptly stopped. For reasons engineers could not fathom, the sudden stop destroyed two hard disks, causing the loss of critical manufacturing and inventory data.

Rather than cease operations, employees resorted to recording inventory and shipping data with pencils and paper. Labels and packing slips were handwritten while technicians attempted to locate critical spare parts for the computer system. Once located, the parts were flown from nearby Greensboro and quickly installed. Within twenty-four hours the equipment damage had been repaired and employees were entering data from backup disks. Luckily they had copied data from the destroyed disks just two hours before the system crashed.

In Georgia, Basis Information Technologies, Inc., an Atlanta computer services company providing twenty-four hour service to 1,300 financial services clients, estimated its losses at more than $5 million after high winds and tornadoes whipped through their area at 6:00 a.m., Saturday, February 10, 1990.

The ferocious wind toppled a huge tree which fell on the power lines, then struck the roof of the computer center, tearing a fifty-foot hole. Employees immediately cut power to the computer room and cranked up a generator to provide sufficient emergency lighting to enable them to work in the shattered facility. Some workers rushed to the roof where they attempted to cover the gaping hole with plastic sheeting. Others removed the computer tapes to a dry place. Although more than an inch of water had already entered the room, employees, attempting to prevent further damage, covered the equipment with plastic. Technicians soon concluded that the waterlogged computer equipment was useless.

Basis quickly activated a disaster recovery team of nearly 200 people to concentrate on restoring data center operations to normal as quickly as humanly possible. Even though the company maintained a backup computer room less than a mile away, it did not contain adequate computer equipment to replace all the processing capabilities of the destroyed data center.

Unisys representatives quickly located two replacement mainframe computers, one in Illinois, the other in California. Both were crated and loaded on trucks enroute to Atlanta late Saturday, the day of the disaster.

Undamaged computers that handled ATM operations were reactivated on Sunday. The computer from Chicago arrived that day and engineers began its installation. Just before 6:00 a.m. Monday, only forty-eight hours after the storm struck, the computer from California arrived in Atlanta. By 8:00 a.m. Monday, basic service was again available to customers. By 10:00 a.m., full computer service had been restored for all Basis customers-- approximately fifty-two hours after the wind had inflicted $5 million damage on the facility.

The National Weather Service collects information about tornado activity and issues warnings for broadcast by radio and television stations in the affected areas.

On March 2, 1987 hundreds of stations received from the Weather Service wire reports that Rockport, Illinois had been destroyed by a tornado. Most stations interrupted their normal programming to announce the tragic event.

Five minutes later the wire carried a correction--Rockport was intact. In fact, no tornado had even been reported in the area!

The National Weather Service had distributed to their local offices special computer disks designed to speed the issuance of warnings of severe weather conditions. Local forecasters were supposed to insert the appropriate local area information into prepared messages stored on the disks, enabling them to issue any warning several minutes sooner than previously possible. Somehow the phrase "This is only a test" was omitted from some of the disks distributed.

In a similar incident on February 20, the Weather Service's New York office transmitted an unwarranted tornado warning. In that case, fifteen minutes passed before someone discovered the mistake and issued a correction over the weather wire.

Because early computers were huge and extremely heavy, organizations often created their computer centers in basements. Flood waters frequently spelled catastrophe for such facilities.

Torrential rains associated with tropical storm Agnes caused the Susquehanna River to overflow its banks and inundate the entire downtown area of Wilkes Barre, Pennsylvania, June 24, 1972. Some streets were covered in eight feet of water and sludge. In the Post Office Building, a computer center belonging to the U.S. Postal Service appeared to be doomed. After water flooded the entire basement where computer supplies were stored, it rose in the first floor computer center to a depth of only one foot, then stopped, sparing from ruin computer equipment valued at more than $8 million.

After the water receded, officials reported that the building, its backup power supply, communications lines, and equipment had suffered significant damage. Nearly 100 dump truck loads of mud and debris were removed from the building. Although most of the computer equipment was salvaged, all of the computer supplies had to be replaced.

Some 200 miles to the northwest, the Chemung River also rose rapidly, burst through protective dikes, and flooded Corning, New York. At Corning Glass Works, the computer center, several factories, and their world-class Museum of Glass were all inundated. Corning's mayor told federal officials that more than 40% of his city's homes had been ruined.

In 1977, Pikeville (Kentucky) National Bank and Trust Company's basement computer center was swamped by a summer storm. The institution had to shut down computer operations. Using disk packs that employees had safely removed before the water reached them, the bank set up a temporary computer system which they used until a new data center was created--on the third-floor.

On February 27, 1983, clogged drain pipes caused rain to form a 10,000-gallon lake on the roof of a Torrance, California building housing Mazda Motor's data center serving dealers in thirty-one states. The weight of the water collapsed the roof, dropping two huge air-conditioning units and all of the water onto the computer equipment below. A spokesman said that sixteen major pieces of equipment had been destroyed and estimated the loss at $1.5 million. Mazda reported two positive news items: no employees were injured in the incident, and backup copies of all critical programs and files survived the roof cave-in because they were routinely stored in a concrete vault.

Dealers who depended upon the Mazda computer facility, which controlled inventory, allocated vehicles, monitored parts distribution, and processed warranties, were forced to revert to manual methods of conducting business and keeping records.

Mazda managers moved decisively to restore full computer service within one week--a goal that many people thought unrealistic. The day after the disaster, contractors began working furiously to construct a replacement computer room. Orders for replacement equipment were placed Tuesday morning. By Thursday, the new computer facility had been built. The last of the replacement computer equipment, shipped from six different locations across the United States, arrived the same day. The new center was up and running normally over the weekend.

Numerous other organizations reported computer outages from the violent winter storm whose fury caused widespread flooding and mud slides in coastal California. The storm literally washed away a terrestrial communications link connecting McKesson Corporation's main computer facility with its nationwide network of a hundred distribution centers for the firm's drugs and chemical products.

Much of New Orleans was flooded Thursday, April 7, 1983, when eleven inches of torrential rain fell across southern Louisiana. The flood waters covered approaches to the bridges spanning the Mississippi River, making it practically impossible to cross.

The basement of South Central Bell's downtown sixteen-story building, housing their gigantic computer complex, was flooded. When, as a safety precaution, commercial power to the building was cut off at 5:00 a.m. Thursday, an emergency diesel generator kicked in automatically. About forty-five minutes later, sensing that its oil had overheated, the generator shut itself off. The company's secondary backup system, a collection of batteries housed on an upper floor, provided power until 9:30 a.m., when voltage began to drop rapidly.

Officials reluctantly decided to shut down the computer controlling long-distance service at 10:30 a.m. The 4ESS computer, installed in 1980, had never before been out of service. Officials said that during weekday business hours it typically handled 165,000 calls an hour. Without it, New Orleans lacked phone service with the rest of the world.

Officials quickly arranged a police escort to move a huge oil field generator from a western suburb. Before it could be pressed into service, technicians successfully restarted the building's emergency generator around 4:00 p.m. By 7:00 p.m. the massive communications computer was back in service, reconnecting New Orleans with the world after ten hours of isolation.

A South Central Bell spokesman later reported that a $2 electrical fuse no larger than a cigar had caused the building's generator to fail at such a crucial time.

The telephone outage across the area also played havoc with the New Orleans Police Department, where officers typically made more than 100,000 inquiries a day into computer files containing arrest warrants, stolen vehicles data, vehicle registrations, criminal histories, etc. Even though the Police Department's third-floor computer center escaped the floodwaters, their nearly 200 terminals could not communicate with the central computer system.

After a brief, early morning power outage, the police computer was restarted successfully. When some of the system's disk drives failed to restart properly, a customer service representative was unable to reach the facility because of flood waters. Using his telephone, he instructed a city employees how to reset specific switches thrown by the electrical failure. Shortly after the disk drives were brought back online and the staff began to think their problems were over--the ten-hour telephone service outage began.

In Illinois, small fish could be seen swimming through the two feet of water that flooded Household Financial Services' suburban Chicago computer center following a storm that dumped nine inches of rain on the area in less than twelve hours. A company spokesman reported that the flooding situation in their computer center arose because two adjacent corporate facilities had been granted city variances permitting them to drain their excess rainwater runoff across the grounds of Household Financial Services. The company reported that the deluge of August 13 and 14, 1987, had destroyed five IBM computers as well as many peripheral devices.

Because area electrical and telephone services were wiped out and numerous roads were under water, Household Financial Services officials declared a disaster situation and relocated to two emergency computer hot-sites. Within thirteen hours, HFS officials reported that their computer applications were up and running at the alternate location.

Within fifteen days after the flood, all four hundred data processing employees had returned to headquarters where the computer room had been decontaminated and refurbished. After new computer equipment had been installed and tested, computer processing capabilities and schedules quickly returned to normal.

Approximately ten miles away, in the suburb of Franklin Park, several inches of sewage-contaminated water covered the computer room floor at the headquarters of A.M. Castle and Company. The failure of their "uninterruptible" power supply, the contaminated water, and the absence of a pump to remove it, caused Castle's management to declare a computer room disaster. Because other clients had already filled the available computer hot-sites in the Chicago area, Castle temporarily relocated its computer operations to Carlstadt, New Jersey. Over the weekend technicians regenerated their computer data base, enabling employees at twenty-seven nationwide locations to track all inventory records and truck shipments.

The computer equipment damage at Castle was deemed minimal, primarily to communications controllers. On Wednesday they powered up the computers in Franklin Park in anticipation of moving all computer applications back to headquarters by the beginning of the following week.

Five years later, workers driving pilings into the Chicago River, accidentally breached a fifty-eight mile system of tunnels built a century earlier to deliver coal to downtown locations. Several hundred million gallons of water raced through the ancient tunnels, filling the basements of some of the city's skyscrapers with up to thirty-five feet of water!

City officials conferred with Commonwealth Edison and decided to contact larger employers to warn that commercial power would soon be cut to much of the commercial district. Their one-to-two-hour warnings proved sufficient for most organizations to power down computers and send employees home before their facilities lost electricity and telephone service.

The Chicago Board of Trade (CBOT), one of the largest commodity exchanges, reportedly lost business valued at billions of dollars because it was forced to close for the entire day. Warned of the impending flood and anticipated power loss around 6:30 a.m., employees systematically powered down CBOT's fifteen computer systems. After setting up terminals at another site, CBOT opened for portions of each day throughout the rest of the week.

Computer industry observers reported that approximately two dozen organizations temporarily moved their computer operations to alternate sites because of Chicago's Flood of April 13, 1992.

When severe storms hit New York City in mid-December 1992, water from New York harbor flooded basements of many downtown Manhattan buildings, crippling telecommunications and electrical service across the area.

Several companies weathered the flooding without relocating computer operations. The Depository Trust Company, with its data center on the twenty-first floor of 55 Water Street, used emergency generators to power its computers throughout the crisis.

Slightly less fortunate companies included Fahnestock, a government bond agency. When the building's manager cut off all electricity to the premises as a precautionary move, the company was forced to move its bond traders to other buildings. Generators kept their computer system humming normally.

Country West, a securities trading subsidiary of National Westminster Bank, moved its traders to a temporary Staten Island site over the weekend of December 12-13. After successfully linking terminals from the temporary site to the company's computer as well as to several online market data services maintained by other organizations, they began conducting trades as usual at 6:45 Monday morning.

Chemical Bank reportedly transferred numerous employees and part of its computer operations to another location because of the flooding.

When flooding forced the Commodities Exchange to start using a backup facility on Friday, that changeover went smoothly.

When back-to-back earthquakes devastated huge sections of Mexico City and three Mexican coastal states September 19 and 20, 1985, the death toll exceeded 25,000 and damage ran to billions of dollars.

Measuring 8.1 on the Richter scale, the killer quake destroyed several Mexican government computer installations. At the Ministry of Planning and Budget, the building housing the computer center was leveled, killing thirteen people. A leased Sperry 1100/80 computer was destroyed, along with 20,000 computer tapes containing vital Mexican population, housing, and economic census data dating from 1960. Officials voiced concern that backup copies for all of the destroyed tapes might not exist.

Computers serving the Ministry of Commerce and Industrial Development were also totally destroyed.

The computer center at Mexico's national bank, Banamex, survived almost intact because it was housed in an underground facility especially designed to withstand earthquakes and fire. However, Banamex could no longer communicate with other financial institutions because the powerful quake severed telephone lines and shut off electrical power, stopping all data transmission for an indefinite period. International banking ties were partially restored when Banamex reestablished a communications link with the Society for Worldwide Interbank Financial Communications (SWIFT) network in Madrid, Spain. During the crisis even communication with banks in the United States passed through the Madrid connection.

Four years later, most San Franciscans probably expected the big news story for Tuesday, October 17, 1989, to be about the third game of the World Series scheduled at Candlestick Park.

At 5:04 p.m. a powerful earthquake, centered in the Santa Cruz area seventy miles away, devastated much of the San Francisco Bay area. The Bay Bridge connecting San Francisco and Oakland was damaged and had to be closed. A mile-long section of the double-decked Nimitz Freeway in Oakland collapsed. The highly computerized Bay Area Rapid Transit (BART) system had to be shut down. Much of the area suddenly lacked essential water, gas, electricity, communications, and transportation services.

Nearly 60,000 people awaiting the start of the ball game in Candlestick Park fled into a changed world where countless bridges, ramps, and overpasses had been either damaged or destroyed. The situation was worsened because traffic signals were not working.

Power failures, caused by the most calamitous quake since "the big one" of 1906, shut down dozens of computers. While damage to buildings was extensive, damage to computer equipment was minimal for such an adversity. Most organizations weathered the crisis well, thanks in part to the uninterruptible power supplies included in their disaster recovery plans.

Officials at the University of California at Berkeley reported that the trembler, which scattered computer tapes all over the data center, failed to shut down their computer system. The less fortunate computer used by California's Police Information Network (PIN) was out of service for nearly thirty hours because of a quake-related circuit breaker problem. Police and court activities dependent upon that computer were unable to function normally during the outage.

Although the quake-induced power failures shut down computers and printing presses at the *San Francisco Chronicle* and the *San Francisco Examiner*, both newspapers printed smaller editions at alternate work sites the day after the earthquake.

Despite the fact that numerous ATMs were put out of service by the devastation, officials estimated that at least 80% of the bank machines remained operational throughout the crisis. Mainframe computer equipment at most banks suffered little damage.

Computerworld reported that the Bank of America used four airplane engines to provide backup power long enough to systematically shut down its fifteen computer systems without damage or loss of data.

Employees at Wells Fargo Bank reportedly kept four mainframe computers operating with auxiliary power throughout the night of the quake.

At Visa USA, Inc., a spokesman said that, even though the firm quickly shifted all credit card processing to their east coast computer center located in McLean, Virginia, the earthquake did not damage their San Mateo computer center.

Dozens of Bay area organizations exercised prearranged emergency options by declaring that a disaster had disabled their computer facility, then moving operations to alternate hot-sites-- compatible computer centers capable of running their work. Some dispatched employees laden with computer tapes and disks to Chicago, Philadelphia, Atlanta, San Diego--wherever compatible sites were available to run critical computer operations.

At San Francisco City Hall, which suffered severe structural damage, employees were permitted to reenter the computer center the morning after the quake. When they powered up the equipment, they discovered no damage.

The three computers at BART luckily also came through the incident unscathed. With damaged bridges and roadways preventing normal commutes, BART became the primary alternative. When engineers inspected the underground tubes they found no major damage. Employees reactivated the two computers that controlled the trains and service was resumed in less than two days.

In Silicone Valley, much nearer the quake's epicenter, many critical high-tech manufacturing facilities did not open Tuesday in order to assess their damage situations. Hewlett-Packard reported that two heavily-damaged buildings were declared off-limits to employees. However, a company spokesman said that the firm's main computer system continued to perform flawlessly. Apple Computer reportedly closed about two dozen buildings pending structural inspections. The engineers declared only one unsafe. Most valley manufacturers reported within forty-eight hours that their assembly lines were again running normally.

Eventually upgraded to 7.1 on the Richter scale, the California Quake of '89 damaged or destroyed more than 100,000 buildings. It injured 3,000 people and killed seventy. Although damage estimates varied greatly, experts generally agree that the losses ran to several billion dollars.

Earlier, less severe quakes had caused relatively minor damage in southern California. On October 1, 1987, one measuring 6.1 on the Richter scale inflicted extensive structural damage at California Federal Savings and Loan in Rosemead, only two miles from the quake's epicenter. The institution's mainframe computers suffered sufficient damage from broken water pipes and falling ceiling tiles to put the system out of service. Technicians carried computer tapes to an alternate San Diego site where they ran critical computer operations until service could be resumed in Rosemead. Computer industry experts reported that very few computer centers suffered significant damage in the Quake of '87.

Another earthquake hit the Pasadena, California area the morning of June 28, 1991. Despite early damage reports of crashed disks, damaged controllers, severed communications links, cracked walls, and broken windows, within two hours of the 6.0 quake, most Pasadena area computers were again operating normally.

The Blizzard of 1993 shut down hundreds of computer systems across the eastern United States from Florida to Canada. Accompanied by hurricane-force winds and surging coastal tides, the blizzard also spawned more than fifty tornadoes. Snow depths reached two feet in parts of Pennsylvania and New York. Snowdrifts of more than twenty feet were reported in the Great Smoky Mountains. Massive snow accumulations across the South collapsed thousands of roofs, damaging dozens of computers. Thousands of undamaged computers could not function because of power failures and/or downed telephone lines. Business remained at a virtual standstill for several days.

11

DO COMPUTERS REALLY KILL PEOPLE?

Hundreds of people have died because of flawed computer systems. Some incidents have killed dozens, while others have claimed victims one at a time. The following events are all documented in public records. It is probably reasonable to assume that hundreds of others have died because of defective computer systems, even though their deaths have been officially attributed to other causes.

Complex computer systems controlling airplanes in flight have caused crashes, killing those onboard. As aircraft become increasingly automated, pilots often appear to be on board merely to monitor computer systems. Only the Air New Zealand crash on Antarctica appears in this chapter. The chapter titled *Are Travelers Well-Served By Computers?* contains several deadly crashes of commercial airliners.

Major military systems, both offensive and defensive, have become so computerized that any fault or error endangers countless lives. Such systems frequently provide commanders with their greatest battlefield surprises! They sometimes kill, even when they aren't supposed to. They may fail to defend, even when they are the only defense for a particular threat.

Automated life-support and health-care systems have caused patients to die. In this area, incidents involving computers undoubtedly are under-reported. Death can easily be attributed to whatever other causes the medical circumstances will support.

As industry incorporates increasing numbers of robots into manufacturing, death-by-robot surely will become a relatively commonplace occurrence. This chapter reports two incidents in which robots have killed factory workers.

Law enforcement personnel, dependent upon computer systems for instantaneous information regarding the status of vehicles, individuals, and property, often have been misinformed. In numerous instances, an officer's over reaction has resulted in death for innocent citizens. Conversely, erroneous computer information has caused officers to permit wanted criminals to remain free.

Computers have been a contributing factor in the deaths of American astronauts and Russian cosmonauts. The chapter titled *How Adversely Have Computer Problems Impacted Space Exploration?* details these incidents.

The following are representative examples of incidents in which computers have contributed to multiple human deaths.

While on a sightseeing flight over Antarctica on November 28, 1979, an Air New Zealand DC-10 carrying 257 passengers crashed into Mount Erebus, killing all aboard.

In May 1981 a Royal Commission of Inquiry concluded that the tragedy resulted from careless reprogramming of the computer controlling the flight route. To correct existing software problems, unbeknownst to the plane's crew, software changes had been introduced just prior to the doomed excursion. The software sent the aircraft over the volcano and, when the pilot attempted to fly below the clouds seeking a clear view for his passengers, the plane slammed into the 11,300-foot mountain.

When Agentina unexpectedly attacked the Falkland Islands in the spring of 1982, the 3,500-ton British frigate *HMS Sheffield*, equipped with a state-of-the-art computerized air defense system, was rushed to the scene. The *Sheffield*'s system, designed to detect radar signals from Soviet-bloc missiles, proved ineffective against a different kind of military foe. In the South Atlantic, the Argentinean Navy used French-made Exocet missiles--with technological differences which proved fatal to the *Sheffield.*

On May 4 while the *Sheffield* was transmitting a telex to London, the ship's air-defense system failed to detect an incoming Exocet. The missile tore a huge hole in the *Sheffield* and set the vessel ablaze. The captain ordered his crew to abandon ship when it became apparent that the *Sheffield* would sink. Twenty British sailors died in the incident.

Later a spokesman for the British Ministry of Defence explained that the *Sheffield*'s computer failed to identify the incoming Exocet because the missile was transmitting radar beams on the same frequency as the doomed ship's communications system! Apparently the ship was unable to defend itself while its communication system was in use!

American naval vessels have suffered similarly deadly consequences from their reliance on computer technology. The *USS Stark* was assigned to perform routine patrol duty in the Persian Gulf in the spring of 1987. On Sunday, May 17, at 1:00 p.m. (EDT) an American Awacs (early warning airplane) reported that it had detected a single plane, assumed to be Iraqi (friendly to America at the time), flying south over the gulf. Crews on the *Stark* and the nearby *USS Coontz* began to monitor the Iraqi plane's movements. A short time later the *USS Lasalle* radioed the *Stark* to inquire whether its crew was monitoring the Iraqi Mirage.

After being placed on alert status, the *Stark*'s electronic and weapons systems reported at 2:06 p.m. that the Mirage had switched on its fire-control radar as if seeking a target. At 2:09 p.m. the *Stark* transmitted a radio warning to the Iraqi warplane. At the same time a crewman spotted a missile heading toward the *Stark.* The ship activated its own fire-control radar and locked onto what the system perceived to be an attacking plane. A few seconds past 2:10 p.m. a missile struck the *Stark*, hitting the hull on the port (left) side but failing to explode. Twenty-five seconds later a second missile hit the ship and exploded on impact, killing thirty-seven American sailors and wounding several others. This missile set several sections of the ship ablaze, inflicting heavy damage.

The *Stark*'s captain later told investigators that, several seconds before the missiles hit, he had turned on the ship's Phalanx gatling gun, seeking to protect his vessel from the Exocet missiles. He said that he had been surprised that the ship's sophisticated electronic warfare equipment had failed to detect the approaching missiles.

After the incident the Iraqi government claimed that the *Stark* was in a declared war zone when attacked. A spokesman explained that the Mirage pilot had mistaken the ship for an Iranian vessel. President Saddam Hussein sent a letter to President Reagan expressing "heartfelt condolences" for the accidental attack. He promised to compensate for injuries and loss of life, as well as for damages to the ship.

On March 27, 1989 Iraq agreed to pay the United States $27.3 million in compensation for families of the thirty-seven American crewman killed in the attack. An American government spokesman told reporters that a complicated formula, including each victim's seniority and his family's financial needs, would be used to divide the compensation among the families.

The Pentagon announced soon thereafter that the federal government had spent $82.9 million to repair the *Stark*, which had been returned to active duty.

Then, in mid-1988, the *USS Vincennes*, a guided-missile cruiser equipped with a computerized battle management system designed to coordinate the defense of navy battlegroups, was dispatched to the Persian Gulf. Consisting of radar, computers, and missiles, the much-touted, billion-dollar-per-unit Aegis system was supposed to be able to track hundreds of airborne objects, assess their threats, and simultaneously destroy up to twenty that it deemed most dangerous.

On July 3 the crew of the *Vincennes* reported that they had detected an unidentified aircraft which appeared to threaten the ship. Seven minutes later, after misidentifying a civilian Iran Air passenger plane as an F-14 warplane, the *Vincennes* fired two missiles, downing the airliner and killing all 290 people on board.

Three days later Pentagon briefers told U.S. senators that the American captain had acted properly in dealing with an unidentified aircraft that appeared to pose a threat to his ship--even though he acted on incomplete information. The senators were also told that Iranian F-14s had operated in the area for several days prior to the shoot-down. The *Vincennes* crew reported receiving identifying signals from the approaching aircraft indicating that it was an F-14. Computer tapes, believed to contain every bit of data recorded by sensors on the ship as well as every action taken by the Aegis system's operators, were rushed to Washington for analysis.

In Iran, emotional funerals for the victims turned into demonstrations against the United States. Accompanying the coffins, which were wrapped in the familiar green, white, and red Iranian flags, many participants carried banners reading "Revenge Revenge" and "Death to America." President Reagan's promise to compensate the victims' families did little to tone down the hate rhetoric.

It soon became apparent that events, as recalled by the crew, differed substantially from those the computer had recorded. A navy investigative report highlighted some examples of such differences: A crew member testified that the Iranian airliner was approaching the *Vincennes* at a speed of 445 knots, an altitude of 7,800 feet, and descending. The computer recorded that the plane was moving at 380 knots, at 12,000 feet, and ascending. Although many of the crew remembered the radio transponder registering as a Mode II, a code used by Iranian fighter planes, the computer had recorded it as Mode III, a code used to designate both civilian and military aircraft. None of the Aegis records indicated that the airplane was descending.

The official report concluded that the cruiser and its Aegis weapons system had performed as intended. The report attributed much of the confusion about the plane's classification to the fact that the ship was receiving signals from two planes, one civilian and one military, at the time of the incident. The Pentagon report also charged that officers in the *Vincennes*' control room had provided erroneous information when they reported the Iranian aircraft to be descending.

When the Iranian airplane was first detected, the *Vincennes*, because it was being fired upon by Iranian attack boats, was turning so sharply that objects were falling from shelves and desk tops. Some crew members reported later that the events caused them to remember the earlier unprovoked attack on the *USS Stark* that had killed thirty-seven American sailors. When the crew of the *Vincennes* mistakenly concluded that an F-14 was attacking, the automated system proceeded to defend the ship.

The Pentagon report also charged that Iranian officials had erred in allowing a civilian airliner to take off from a joint military/civilian facility and fly into an area where a gunfight was in progress. One of the report's recommendations was to improve the readability of the Aegis system's computer displays, making it easier for crew members to monitor range and altitude information.

In early December the International Civil Aviation Organization (ICAO) suggested that the U.S. Navy had taken inadequate precautions to keep civilian aircraft safe from combat operations in the Persian Gulf. This later report also found that the *Vincennes* and the *Sides*, another American warship in the immediate vicinity, had issued a total of eleven warnings to Iran Air Flight 655 in the five minutes prior to the firing of the missiles. However, seven of the warnings were transmitted on a military channel inaccessible to the civilian airliner's crew. Only one of the remaining four warnings was deemed sufficiently clear to constitute an understandable warning specifically directed to Flight 655--this one was transmitted only thirty-nine seconds before the *Vincennes* fired its missiles. Although the Iranian air traffic controllers should have heard all of the warnings transmitted, investigators found no evidence that they relayed even one to the doomed airliner.

The ICAO blamed the American Navy and issued a recommendation calling for military units to monitor civilian air traffic control frequencies and communicate directly with civilian controllers in future emergency situations.

Although President Reagan promised compensation, he steadfastly refused to pay reparations to the Iranian government. He insisted that payments could only go to the families of victims. Congress opposed payments and Reagan ended his presidency with the matter unresolved.

Law enforcement officials speculated that a later incident involving Sharon Rogers, wife of *Vincennes* Captain Will C. Rogers III, probably was an act of revenge for the incident. On March 10, 1989, while her vehicle was stopped at a traffic signal in San Diego, Mrs. Rogers thought she heard an explosion followed by the smell of smoke. When she opened her driver's door, she discovered the rear portion of the van engulfed in flames. FBI agents investigating the incident, fearing that the bombing of the van was the work of terrorists, moved Will and Sharon Rogers to "protective seclusion."

All of the preceding events have involved multiple deaths. Computer systems have also played significant roles in countless individual deaths. The following incidents are typical of those reported over the past twenty-five years.

In 1975, Frank Booth, director of the Brevard County Emergency office in Florida, had driven to Tallahassee to attend his father's funeral. He pulled his new Chrysler onto the shoulder of the highway, attracting the attention of a passing state trooper.

The trooper radioed dispatch requesting information regarding the car's license number. The computer reportedly responded that a car bearing the same license number appeared in its stolen vehicle file.

Press reports indicate that the trooper approached Booth's car with his weapon drawn and cocked. In the next few seconds Booth was shot and killed.

Within a few days of the tragedy, news reports revealed that the tag number had indeed been reported stolen--four years earlier. The same number had been used on license plates of different colors issued to other drivers in 1972 and 1973 before it had been issued as an orange-on-white tag in 1974 to victim Frank Booth. The four-year-old stolen vehicle report had never been deleted from the computer files.

The appallingly tragic circumstances surrounding the 1976 death of eighty-two-year-old Sophia Easer of Munhall, Pennsylvania, caused the death of an unknown woman to be reported nationally and internationally. Simply put, after a utility company's computer generated a service shutoff notice and a worker cut off the gas used to heat her home, Sophia Easer froze to death. Her body was discovered on January 19, 1976. On her dining table lay a check payable to Equitable Gas for $71.68, the total amount the company said was past due.

An inquiry reported that the service shutoff notice was routed to Equitable Gas Company's credit department to be verified and approved. The company claimed to have an unwritten policy that in cases involving elderly or disabled customers, the gas would not be cut off. The same policy also reportedly prohibited cutting off gas to any customers on days when the temperature was predicted to drop below twenty degrees.

The unwritten policy failed to protect Sophia Easer that tragic January 5, a day when the temperature ranged between nine and nineteen degrees. When a gas company employee's knock on Ms. Easer's door attracted no response, he cut off the gas supply to the residence. Friends speculated later that Ms. Easer, who was partially deaf, probably did not hear the knock.

Irate citizens demanded that someone should be punished for Ms. Easer's death. An assistant district attorney explained to reporters that he could not file criminal charges against the utility firm because a company could not commit involuntary manslaughter.

The Allegheny County coroner said that both Equitable Gas Company and the Public Utilities Commission were responsible for Easer's death, because they did not have proper guidelines covering utility shutoffs.

Ms. Easer apparently possessed sufficient funds to pay her utility bill. On December 1, 1977 *United Press International* reported that Easer had left an estate valued at $292,000. After taxes of $85,945 the estate was divided among six cousins.

In April 1976, a Yonkers, New York police communications employee reportedly entered a routine inquiry for a National Crime Information Center (NCIC) computer search for information on Steven Karagianis. The computer flashed back the code "CW" which the inexperienced communications employee mistakenly thought meant "currently wanted." When he relayed the misinformation to the policeman who had stopped Karagianis for running a red light, the officer brought Karagianis to the station.

The accused young man protested that an earlier warrant had been cleared and that he should not be jailed. The same communications employee reportedly repeated the same computer inquiry. Again he misinterpreted the "CW" response to mean currently wanted, and Karagianis was locked in a cell.

Approximately ninety minutes later, jail employees discovered that Karagianis had committed suicide.

A subsequent inquiry revealed that the "CW" code actually meant "cleared wanted." Karagianis had been picked up in November 1975 and charged with violating probation on an earlier, minor drug offense. After he appeared in court in January and the charge was dismissed, someone should have instructed the computer to cancel Karagianis's warrant for probation violation. Apparently no one did. The inquiry concluded that the warrant was finally cleared on March 9. However, the misinterpretation of the CW code caused Karagianis's incarceration, which probably led to his suicide in the Yonkers jail.

At Ford Motor Company's casting plant in Flat Rock, Michigan on January 25, 1979, a robot struck and killed Robert Williams. After the robot, which automatically stored and retrieved metal castings, malfunctioned, Williams apparently climbed into a storage rack to attempt repairs. A robotic arm struck his head, killing him instantly. Coworkers discovered his body a half-hour later.

A Wayne County Circuit Court jury, in August 1983, ordered Litton Industries, manufacturers of the automated storage and retrieval system, to pay the victim's family $10 million.

In a similar incident in Japan, a robot reportedly killed Kenji Urada, an employee at the Akashi plant of Kawasaki Heavy Industries. Factory officials reported that the robot apparently malfunctioned. They said that Urada climbed over a fence and reset the robot's controls to "manual" operations so he could repair it. A company spokesman said that he thought that Urada had accidentally touched the robot's controls, resetting a switch from "manual" to "on", causing the robot to pin Urada against a huge machine, crushing him to death.

Investigators said that opening the gate to enter the work area should automatically have shut off the robot's electrical power supply, rendering it completely harmless.

In Texas, federal and state investigators concluded that faulty software in a radiation-therapy device killed bus driver Verdon Kidd by delivering an overly-intense radiation beam. According to the *Wall Street Journal*, January 28, 1987, the regulators charged that the machine, designed to treat skin cancer, unexplainedly delivered a radiation dosage eighty times more potent than Kidd's prescribed dosage.

Faulty computer systems have even killed animals. At the University of Southern California's Andrus Gerontology Center, a computerized climate control system malfunctioned in the summer of 1980, killing more than 1,500 laboratory mice. Specifically bred for the study of the effects of aging on the body and brain, many of the mice were thirty months old, considered the equivalent to eighty years in humans.

The computer, which was supposed to maintain a temperature range of seventy-two to seventy-eight degrees Fahrenheit, allowed the temperature to rise to 106 degrees. Officials declined to speculate about the cause of the accident. They announced it would cost about $7,000 to replace the annihilated mice.

While everyone realizes that computers can save lives, few can imagine the countless ways in which inadequately controlled computers can cause the loss of life. Imaginative people, who recognize the nearly unlimited possibilities, could well make computers their murder weapon of choice!

12

HOW ADVERSELY HAVE COMPUTER PROBLEMS IMPACTED SPACE EXPLORATION?

The Soviet Union launched *Sputnik 1* into earth orbit on October 4, 1957. From that moment, outer space became an expensive playing field on which the world's superpowers would compete for more than three decades.

Then, on November 3, the Soviets launched *Sputnik 2* carrying a dog named Laika. They certainly had captured the world's attention.

America rushed to launch its first satellite, *Explorer I*, on January 31, 1958. Cape Canaveral, Florida would become a place-name as well known as Wall Street. The space race, even without defined missions for either team, had definitely begun.

Americans had become sufficiently curious about space by the 1950s for the federal government to create NASA (the National Aeronautics and Space Administration) in 1958. Scientists were desperately eager to determine whether man could survive and function in the weightlessness of space without suffering adverse effects on the human system.

From space exploration's infancy, NASA automated, to the extent possible, such critical and complex tasks as navigation, maneuvering vehicles in space, maintenance of life support systems, etc. As space exploration became more ambitious, scientists found it necessary to automate even more facets of each mission. Computer technology was advancing at a pace that seemed entwined with advances in space exploration.

President John F. Kennedy, during an address to Congress on May 25, 1961, issued a thirty-word challenge that forever changed America, the world, even the universe: "I believe that this nation should commit itself to achieving the goal, before this decade is out, of landing a man on the moon and returning him safely to earth." Kennedy's challenge, which defined and focused America's space goals, would culminate in one of the greatest historical events of all time.

Exploring the idea of a manned flight to the moon, NASA commissioned the Jet Propulsion Labs to design an unmanned spacecraft capable of journeying to the moon to take close-up photographs just prior to crashing on the lunar surface. The resulting Ranger program attempted to launch its first space vehicle in 1961.

Despite the nation's massive new commitment to its space program, for three years the Ranger program experienced failure after failure.

Ranger IV, America's tenth attempt to send a spacecraft into the vicinity of the moon, was launched on April 23, 1962. The 730-pound spacecraft carried a television camera that scientists expected to transmit pictures of its journey back to earth. It would also attempt to soft-land on the moon a battery-powered seismometer, capable of relaying to earth data of moonquakes and meteorite strikes.

Ranger IV's solar panels, designed to prevent the craft from tumbling in space as well as to provide electrical current to the onboard computer, were supposed to deploy in flight and lock onto the sun.

A few hours after the launch, engineers announced that the solar panels had failed to open. *Ranger IV*, without electricity from the solar panels, would soon drain its battery backup power supply and cease to function. The badly crippled craft, without performing any of its planned tasks, would then crash onto the moon. Seeking to salvage at least something from the failed mission, a NASA engineer reminded reporters that America had finally sent a device that at least *reached* the moon!

The next attempt, designated *Ranger V*, also ended badly when its power system failed before the craft reached the moon. Without electrical power the craft's computer could not function.

Cameras aboard *Ranger VI* failed.

Ranger VII, launched on July 28, 1964, finally performed as scientists intended--it transmitted 4,308 black-and-white photos to earth before crashing into an area of the moon known as the Sea of Clouds. The photos revealed details of the moon's surface that earth's most powerful telescopes could not. Rocks as small as ten inches wide could be clearly seen in the photos transmitted by *Ranger VII*.

The following year *Ranger VIII* photographed the Sea of Tranquility and *Ranger IX* transmitted extensive pictures of the highlands near the previously photographed Sea of Clouds. The photos conveyed the sense that the moon's surface was smooth enough to accommodate a landing craft. Ranger missions provided earth scientists with more than 17,000 photographs, revealing more detailed information in two years than had been learned in all previous history.

The early, well-publicized automation problems failed to deter those committed to meeting the Kennedy challenge, even though some critics argued that computer technology was not sufficiently advanced to be reliable for manned space exploration.

When one considers today just how heavily space exploration has depended upon computer technology, the number of automation failures statistically has been remarkably small. Even though it is probable that some computer failures were never publicly revealed, NASA's public space launches and recoveries would have made it extremely difficult to cover up significant computer problems associated with these events.

During the same period that the Ranger program sought to photograph the moon's surface, NASA began its Mercury program. Named for the Greek god whose name was probably known by more Americans than any other mythological being, Mercury would attempt to determine whether man could build and fly space vehicles capable of carrying humans into space and returning them safely to earth.

On May 5, 1961, Alan Shepard, Jr., became the first American to be launched into space when a Mercury spacecraft carried him on a fifteen-minute, 302 miles long, suborbital flight.

On February 20, 1962, John Glenn became the first American to orbit earth . When problems developed with the automatic control of his capsule's altitude, Glenn reverted to manual control and piloted his *Friendship 7* to the planned splashdown recovery area.

During Gordon Cooper's May 16, 1963 return to earth after twenty-two orbits of the earth, an electrical power failure on *Faith 7* prevented his use of automated features. Using manual reentry procedures, he piloted the capsule to a Pacific splashdown a mere four miles from the waiting recovery ship. Cooper's was the final space flight in the Mercury Project.

NASA's Gemini Project provided America's next space spectaculars. Named for the third constellation of the zodiac and its twin stars, Castor and Pollux, Gemini was designed to demonstrate, with a two-man spacecraft, that astronauts could survive in space and steer the craft through complex maneuvers similar to those required for an eventual flight to the moon. This program sought to link two vehicles in orbit, have astronauts walk in space, as well as perfect both reentry and pinpoint landing methods required by space vehicles returning to earth.

In a space spectacular apparently timed to steal headlines from the Americans, the Soviets launched *Voskhod 2* on March 18, 1965.

Almost immediately pilot Alexi Leonov donned a bulky space suit and strapped on a backpack containing an oxygen supply. He then entered an airlock, opened an outer hatch, and stepped boldly into space. By floating at the end of a five-meter (sixteen-foot) tether, Leonov entered the history books as the first human to "walk in space." Two onboard cameras recorded his twelve-minute, nine-second feat and transmitted television pictures of the event to earth.

When the *Voskhod 2* crew prepared to retrofire in order to drop their craft from orbit and return to earth the following day, its automatic orientation system, designed to use the sun as a reference point, failed. Soviet space officials instructed the crew to orbit the earth again so that Commander Pavel Belyayev would have time to manually orient the spacecraft for reentry through earth's atmosphere.

To manually adjust the craft's orientation, the two cosmonauts had to leave their seats and move around in the confined space. Their movements upset the precise balance of the vehicle during retrofire, causing it to descend in a remote, heavily forested, snowbound region, far from the landing target. Although uninjured in the rough landing, the cosmonauts were trapped in their spacecraft because they could not open the sphere to exit. Despite the bitter cold and deep snow, ground teams reached the craft and rescued the Soviet heroes the next day.

During the return to earth of *Gemini III*, after a three-orbit mission March 23, 1965, an onboard computer, reacting to readings from an inertial platform, informed Major "Gus" Grissom that his landing would fall short of its target. Major Grissom elected to rely on a series of banking maneuvers, relayed from the ground, that he thought would land the space capsule nearer the aircraft carrier deployed to recover it.

Later space officials revealed that *Gemini III*'s onboard computers had provided correct information to Grissom, but data provided him from the ground computers had been wrong. It turned out that ground computers had incorrectly interpreted the results of wind tunnel tests concerning life and gravity offset. The erroneous data caused *Gemini III* to miss its splashdown target.

Even so, *Gemini III*, the first spacecraft to change both the size and plane of its orbit, was deemed a successful mission. Perhaps it is best remembered for Walter Shirra's prank of smuggling onboard a corned beef sandwich which he presented in space to command pilot Grissom!

Two NASA announcements before the launch of *Gemini IV* prompted more than 1,000 news media representatives to request accreditation for covering the flight from Houston. For the first time, the newly-inaugurated Mission Control Center would assume responsibility for a space flight. During *Gemini IV*'s mission, America would demonstrate that she had caught up with the USSR by having astronaut Edward White take the first American space walk.

The new Mission Control Building, situated on the outskirts of Houston, had been built and equipped to handle the increasingly complex Gemini and Apollo space flights. The seven-million-dollar building was equipped with state-of-the-art electronic equipment costing more than a hundred million dollars. Engineers boasted that the Houston Center contained more than 10,000 miles of wires with more than two million cross-connections.

Launched on June 3, 1965, *Gemini IV* functioned essentially as planned for three days. Using a tether which secured him to the spacecraft and supplied him with both oxygen to breathe and coolants for his space suit, Edward White took a space walk lasting just over twenty minutes. Although he attempted no work during his time outside the space-craft, White returned physically exhausted and sweating profusely, with his helmet's faceplate fogged.

Late in the third day of the mission, *Gemini IV* "...lost its electronic brain," as the *New York Times* so succinctly described its computer failure.

A three-column headline in the *Times'* June 7 edition announced "Gemini to Return Today; Failure of Its Computer May Alter Re-entry Plan." Quoting Gemini mission director Christopher Kraft, Jr., the article indicated that the previous day's computer failure would have "...absolutely no effect on the safety of the flight." Nevertheless a vast recovery team of twenty-one ships, one hundred planes and approximately 7,000 service personnel was dispatched to the designated space capsule recovery site in the Atlantic Ocean south of Bermuda. In the event of a splashdown outside the anticipated area, the Department of Defense alerted nearly 700 merchant ships to be ready to assist in the astronauts' recovery.

As the flight neared its end, with its computer still out of service, NASA officials concluded that *Gemini IV* command pilot Major James McDivitt could not maneuver the capsule to land as planned near the aircraft carrier *Wasp*. They decided that Mission Control would "talk" the craft down, meaning that McDivitt would rely on voice rather than computer instructions.

Late Sunday when NASA publicly announced that the computer aboard *Gemini IV* had failed, an IBM executive reportedly attempted to cancel a special two-page advertisement the firm had scheduled to run in major newspapers across America the following day. Carefully planned to coincide with the conclusion of the *Gemini IV* mission, the advertisement trumpeted the capability of IBM's fifty-nine pound computer, which was smaller than a hatbox and required no more electricity than a reading lamp. The ad noted that NASA had been sufficiently impressed with the computer to install one on every Gemini spacecraft.

Many early newspapers were already being printed when IBM attempted to stop the ad. Although IBM declined to reveal how many papers had planned to run the ad, it did appear in several, including *The Wall Street Journal*, *The New York Times*, *The Los Angeles Times*, *The Herald Tribune*, and *The Chicago Tribune*.

The computer's failure probably contributed to the spacecraft's missing its targeted splashdown area by fifty-six miles on Monday, June 7 at 1:14 p.m. EDT. Within one hour a helicopter had plucked the astronauts safely from the sea and deposited them on the aircraft carrier *Wasp*.

Several weeks after *Gemini IV*'s computer failure, IBM engineers explained that the astronauts' inability to turn off the computer had caused unintended changes in its memory. Its resulting failure to perform as expected prevented the astronauts from navigating to their designated landing site, instead plunging the spacecraft into a ballistic trajectory. Although they were unable to pinpoint the cause of the earlier computer failure, the engineers expressed confidence that a second manual switch installed on the device would prevent any recurrence. The computer with two switches would be used on the next Gemini craft.

Faulty computer data caused *Gemini V* to splash down 103 miles off target, instead of near the carrier *Lake Champlain*, southwest of Bermuda. A NASA spokesman told reporters that "human error" had caused the ground computer to accumulate incorrect data during the eight-day flight. When the erroneous data was transmitted from the ground computer to the one aboard the spacecraft, that computer instructed the astronauts to guide *Gemini V* to a landing point far from the intended target.

Earlier, space engineers had feared that a power surge generated by a lightning strike prior to launch might have scrambled *Gemini V*'s computer's memory, but the near flawless mission indicated otherwise.

When an electrical plug fell from its socket 2.2 seconds before the liftoff of *Gemini VI*, the Titan launch vehicle automatically shut down, aborting the December 12, 1965 launch. The plug served to ground an electrical circuit keeping electricity from flowing into the missile's flight control programmer until liftoff, when the control programmer would begin its function as an autopilot.

When the plug disconnected, the flight control programmer began its own count, meaning it instructed the autopilot to take each action 2.2 seconds earlier than planned--and endangered the flight. An automated countdown sequencer sensed the situation and signaled the launch engines to shut down, abruptly halting the launch.

By the time the Gemini Project ended, Americans had invested $1,350,000,000 to launch ten Gemini missions in which astronauts had accumulated 969 hours and 56 minutes in space, accomplishing all of the project's primary goals.

From March 1965 until November 1966, when the United States conducted ten Gemini flights, the Soviets did not send a single cosmonaut into space. American scientists and politicians interpreted the Soviets' lack of activity as an almost certain indication that the Americans had taken the lead in the race to the moon.

Next came the Apollo Project, named for the son of Zeus, an archer able to hit targets at great distances. The twentieth century Apollo's target was the moon, some 250,000 miles from earth. The project's objective was to land a man on the moon and return him safely to earth. Simply put, the Apollo Project planned for the astronauts' spacecraft to lift-off from the rotating planet earth, then orbit the planet at 18,000 miles per hour. At the appropriate time their craft would accelerate to 25,000 miles per hour, break out of earth's orbit, then rocket a quarter-of-a-million miles to the moon. Upon reaching the moon, the spacecraft would enter orbit around it and send a smaller lunar module craft, carrying two men, to the moon's surface, while the spacecraft remained in lunar orbit. On the moon's surface astronauts would explore and photograph the surface, set up and activate scientific instruments to be left behind, collect rocks and soil samples, and fly their lunar module back to their primary spacecraft. The astronauts would then leave the moon's orbit and return to earth.

On January 27, 1967, during a practice countdown for a scheduled February 21 launch, three astronauts died in a fiery accident aboard *Apollo I* at the Kennedy Space Center. Critics complained that computers monitoring the simulation gave no early warning of the unfolding tragedy. Further, the Apollo craft lacked an automatic release button which would have permitted a hasty evacuation. To manually release the craft's cumbersome hatch required ninety seconds.

Flight Commander Virgil "Gus" Grissom, Roger Chaffee and Edward White perished in the incident, the first Americans to die while participating in space missions. A board of inquiry reported that all three had died within sixteen seconds of the fire's outbreak.

Barely three months later, the Soviet Union's *Soyuz 1*, the heaviest manned spacecraft to date, crashed, killing Cosmonaut Vladimir Komarov. The official Soviet explanation of the accident was that the parachute, meant to slow the *Soyuz* space craft as it landed on earth, had tangled, causing the craft to crash to earth at great speed. Komarov was killed on impact. However, rumor persisted that the craft's computer-controlled stabilization system had malfunctioned in orbit, making the space craft impossible to control and forcing a decision to abort the mission and return *Soyuz 1* to earth earlier than planned.

Space exploration experts reasoned that a problem as simple as a tangled parachute would not have put the *Soyuz* program on hold for a year-and-a-half, when the Russians appeared to place such a high priority on beating America in the space race. Even so, the next *Soyuz* craft was not launched until October 1968.

Back in America, *Apollo 5*, an unmanned lunar module, rocketed into orbit on January 22, 1968. Although the sixteen-ton craft carried only one computer, it achieved built-in redundancy with triplicate circuitry. In the event of a computer discrepancy, the two circuits in agreement were supposed to overrule (and ignore) the minority circuit.

Responding to commands stored in its onboard computer, shortly after liftoff the lunar module separated from the Saturn two-stage rocket. When scientists on earth noted that the lunar module's guidance system rocket had not fired for the expected thirty-eight seconds, but had stopped after only four seconds, the ground crew transmitted a new set of commands to the guidance system. They corrected the problem and caused the rocket to fire subsequently as planned.

The following day NASA reported that a programming error had caused the lunar module's guidance computer to mistakenly suspect a rocket failure, causing it prematurely to shut off the rocket's engine.

During the *Apollo 12* mission, President Kennedy's goal of landing a man on the moon came within a hair's breadth of failure on July 20, 1969, even though the *Eagle* was only eight minutes above the moon's surface. The *Eagle*'s onboard computer began to generate alarms warning that "...it was working right up to 100 percent capacity," Mission Control spokesman Christopher Kraft revealed four days later.

Everyone involved in this long-awaited moment of triumph knew that the landing attempt would have to be aborted if the computer actually overloaded. Restarting its calculations would confuse the entire man-machine interface required for the moon landing.

The computer's warnings of potential overload began when the *Eagle*'s crew began to bounce radar signals off the moon's surface to ascertain altitude and rate of descent. If these actual readings varied from those preprogrammed into the computer, the craft's flight path could be modified. At an altitude of approximately

40,000 feet above the moon's surface, the computer issued its first warning of potential overload.

A mission control officer in Houston, Stephen Bales, recommended that the astronauts stop asking their onboard computer to provide them information directly from the landing radar. Such information could be provided instead from a Houston ground-based computer. Bales reasoned that this slight change might permit *Eagle*'s onboard computer to perform its extremely critical guidance and navigational tasks without overloading.

A cockpit panel light conveyed to the *Eagle*'s crew several more warnings, the last at an altitude of 3,000 feet. In the seventh minute of the touch-and-go emergency situation, it appeared that, despite the continued warnings of potential computer overload, the Bales recommendation would avert such a catastrophe. At that point Mission Control radioed the "Go!" signal to the *Eagle*.

When the moon's surface was only 500 feet away, Armstrong saw that the auto-targeting system was going to land the craft in an area littered with rocks and boulders. Seizing the manual control, he hovered for about ninety seconds, while his eyes scanned the immediate area seeking a more suitable landing site.

At 4:17 p.m. Eastern Daylight Time, Armstrong transmitted his historic announcement "Houston, Tranquillity base here. The Eagle has landed."

At 10:56 p.m. EDT, Neil Armstrong's booted left foot stepped onto the moon's surface as he uttered words that will resound throughout history: "That's one small step for man, one giant leap for mankind."

Throughout the mission the general public remained blissfully unaware of the computer problem, which Kraft first revealed on the day the astronauts safely returned to earth. Their quarter million mile return journey landed them in the Pacific Ocean at 13 degrees 19 minutes North and 169 degrees 9 minutes West, near Johnston Island, less than two miles from the targeted splashdown.

On November 14, 1969, a momentary failure of *Apollo 12*'s electrical system and navigational computer threatened the launch of the spacecraft. Officials at the Kennedy Space Center blamed a "lightning discharge" for the temporary problem, which caused no apparent damage and failed to abort the mission.

Soon *Apollo 12* was hailed as a complete success, having accomplished all of its objectives. It proved that pinpoint landings were possible, even in rough terrain. The astronauts set up a nuclear-powered scientific observatory on the moon's surface. They even retrieved parts from a Surveyor spacecraft left on the moon in April 1967 so that scientists on earth could study how long-term exposure to the lunar environment affected the parts. The Apollo crew ventured forth on two rock-gathering expeditions, returning to earth with nearly a hundred pounds.

After a near-perfect launch, America's third moon landing mission appeared destined to succeed. Carrying astronauts James A Lovell, Jr., Fred W. Haise, Jr., and John L. Swigert, Jr., *Apollo 13* had already completed 205,000 miles of its journey when, on April 13, 1970 at 1:08 p.m. EST, the voice of Captain Lovell calmly announced "Houston, we've got a problem."

Instruments registered dangerous temperature and pressure flow changes aboard the command ship. The tank supplying oxygen to fuel cells aboard the craft had exploded, inflicting no injuries but causing extensive damage.

Three minutes of devastation had changed an ordinary moon mission into an extraordinary search for survival. The astronauts, shocked to discover that their ship's oxygen system had been destroyed, quickly learned that the situation was actually far worse than they had originally thought. Without oxygen the fuel cells could not power any of the onboard systems--all computer support, including the guidance and navigational system, life-support, etc., suddenly no longer existed.

NASA officials quickly changed the focus of *Apollo 13*'s mission from landing men on the moon, to finding how to keep the crippled spaceship functioning sufficiently to safely return the astronauts to earth. This goal could be accomplished only by continuing the journey to the moon. Then, instead of landing, the crippled vehicle had to fire its rockets so that the craft would loop around the moon and achieve a trajectory for return to earth.

Officials worried about the all-too-real possibility that the astronauts might deplete their supplies of oxygen, water or power and die in space!

Mission Control instructed the astronauts to shut down totally all systems on the command ship and retreat through a hatch to their attached lunar module. Built to accommodate two men for a brief descent to the moon's surface, the lunar craft suddenly became a "lifeboat" that NASA hoped would sustain three men for the duration of their life-threatening ordeal.

The lunar module's six storage batteries normally provided electricity the small craft required for its descent to the moon's surface and return to the orbiting command ship. Now those batteries provided the only survival hope for three cramped, cold astronauts. To conserve the batteries to the greatest extent possible, the astronauts powered down all but the most essential life-support and communications systems on the lunar module, making their temporary refuge even colder and darker.

In Houston dozens of spaceflight controllers and engineers, using numerous computers and spacecraft simulators, rushed to devise a plan they hoped would safely return the *Apollo 13* crew to earth.

Around the world, multitudes riveted attention on television screens to watch the unprecedented live drama unfold in the vastness of space. Leaders of more than a dozen nations offered to assist NASA in the recovery efforts. *Tass* reported that two Russian merchant ships had been diverted to the expected recovery area in the Pacific. Russian cosmonauts conveyed messages to the stranded Americans, wishing them a safe voyage home.

In Rome, Pope John Paul VI offered special prayers for the astronauts. In America, the Reverend Doctor Billy Graham led a national prayer vigil. Countless ordinary citizens around the world attended special services at places of worship.

NASA employees appeared to breathe a collective sigh of relief when, on April 14, at 3:43 a.m., they executed the critical firing of engines that caused the spacecraft to loop around the moon and enter a trajectory towards earth. After a fifteen-hour period that for so many seemed excruciatingly longer, the astronauts' long journey home had begun.

Television screens remained the focus of world attention for another eighty-two hours.

In preparation for an April 17 landing in the Pacific Ocean, the astronauts returned to the command ship to carry out a series of intricate maneuvers devised in Houston to aim the spacecraft for reentry into earth's atmosphere. Both the damaged service module and the lunar-module-turned-lifeboat had to be separated from the command ship prior to entering the earth's atmosphere to prevent a potential explosion that could have doomed the astronauts, now tantalizingly close to safety. Casting off first the damaged service module, in which all of the problems began, Lovell noted that the earlier explosion apparently had blown away one whole side. Then they jettisoned the lunar module, the tiny craft which undoubtedly had saved their lives.

After a near-perfect splashdown, only five miles from the recovery ship *Iwo Jima*, a helicopter quickly plucked the astronauts from the Pacific.

Four days later, Lovell told the Senate Aeronautical and Space Sciences Committee that, even though the astronauts thought that death was near, they wanted to return their crippled spacecraft as near to earth as possible before they died.

An official investigation concluded that blame for the explosion aboard *Apollo 13* should be shared by NASA, Beech Aircraft Corporation and the North American Rockwell Company. The two-month investigation involved approximately 100 tests conducted by 300 engineers, scientists and technicians. The report concluded that the accident occurred "...from an unusual combination of mistakes, coupled with a somewhat deficient design... ."

The report indicated that Beech Aircraft Corporation had installed thermostatic switches designed to carry twenty-eight volts of electricity rather than sixty-five as required by the specifications. Neither NASA nor its prime contractor for Apollo, North American Rockwell, detected the discrepancy in the switch. During the launch preparation, investigators said, the switches permanently welded shut when they were subjected to sixty-five volts of electricity; this unintended result rendered them inoperative as protective thermostats.

Tabloids, playing to superstitious readers fearing the number "13", emphasized the fact that both the mission name and the date of the explosion were 13.

Although *Apollo 13*'s mission of landing men on the moon failed, the astronauts' safe return from what many experts feared was a catastrophe certain to end in death, ranks as one of NASA's greatest triumphs.

When NASA officials used the words "very serious" to describe an electrical problem threatening *Apollo 14*'s lunar landing February 5, 1971, the public seemed surprised that astronauts again were endangered. After all, NASA had delayed the launch of this mission by a month following the harrowing flight of *Apollo 13*.

NASA reported that Houston's Mission Control engineers, monitoring the numerous systems aboard the *Apollo 14*, observed that the primary guidance computer sent a spurious signal instructing the lunar module to abort its landing descent. This command was highly irregular in that the lunar module had not yet started its descent!

Faced with the frightening possibility that a similar false signal might trigger an inadvertent abort of the actual descent, experts on earth began a frantic search for a solution they could implement before the scheduled lunar module landing, less than three hours away.

Engineers quickly determined that a switch was at fault and described the problem to mission specialists at several locations across the United States. NASA credits Donald Eyles, an engineer observing the Apollo mission from MIT's Draper Laboratory, with devising the solution that NASA chose to try. Eyles reasoned that, before *Apollo 14* began its descent to the moon's surface, program code could be entered into the craft's onboard computer instructing the electronic brain to ignore any automated abort signal. The computer would be instructed to respond only to abort commands generated by an astronaut pressing a large abort button on one of the craft's walls. If an emergency sufficiently dangerous to abort the mission should occur during the craft's descent, an astronaut would hit the red abort button and the crew would revert to an onboard backup guidance system for control of the lunar module.

After the Eyles code was tested in simulators at both Houston and Cape Kennedy, it was radioed to the *Apollo 14*, where an astronaut rapidly keyed it into the spacecraft's computer. Ground controllers also instructed Captain Alan Shepard to perform manually a throttle operation.

The lunar module proceeded to land on the moon-- flawlessly and on schedule.

However, *Apollo 14*'s troubles were not yet over. When the lunar module lifted off from the moon to return to the orbiting spacecraft, its backup guidance system abruptly failed. Because the trouble was not in the primary system, officials in Houston quickly determined that the failure probably would not prevent the astronauts' safe return.

Even Mother Nature threatened this particular mission. Some of the strongest earthquakes in recent memory rocked California, threatening the loss of electrical power to some of the computers and communications links involved in the Apollo shot. Critical computers at the Jet Propulsion Labs continued to function uninterrupted, however.

After the Apollo program ended in 1975, funding for the space efforts shriveled, threatening to cripple, or even scuttle, NASA's plans for a space shuttle program. Officials envisioned huge financial savings from fully-reusable, two-stage space vehicles. Such craft also promised to reduce the preparation time needed for each launch.

Each shuttle launch would involve three main components: an orbiter spacecraft, an external tank carrying fuel for the orbiter's engines, and solid rocket boosters to power the equipment into space. When the general requirements of the civilian sector were expanded to include the stringent requirements of the military, the anticipated cost of the shuttle program skyrocketed.

Because human pilots could never observe, evaluate and react to the tremendous flow of information from the sensors, computers maintained virtually complete control of each shuttle flight. Realizing that the equipment was not infallible, NASA officials had chosen to build redundancy into their onboard computer systems to make them more fault-tolerant. Each shuttle carried four identical computers programmed to perform exactly the same functions at precisely the same time, essentially precision marching-in-step. In situations where one computer appeared to be out-of-step with the others, it was ignored; the majority ruled. To compensate for the failure of one of the primary computers, each shuttle carried a fifth device, identical to the four, to serve as backup.

Prior to the first shuttle launch, NASA engineers and contractors developed countless computer simulations to test each craft, its computers, sensors, and crew members.

During a February 1981 test-firing preparatory to launching space shuttle *Columbia*, engineers reported discovering computer programming errors involving inaccurate timing parameters that prevented the firing of two booster rockets. *Columbia*, delayed for two months, was finally launched successfully on April 12, 1981.

On a subsequent mission, two computers aboard *Columbia* failed as the astronauts prepared to land at Edwards Air Force Base, California, on December 8, 1983. The computer failures deprived *Columbia*'s crew of guidance and navigational capabilities for slightly less than a minute; backup computers soon restored these functions. Even though astronauts restarted one of the computers, just before the flight ended, it failed again.

Mission Commander John Young said that the first computer failed when jet thrusters in the nose of the craft fired automatically. The second computer immediately took over control of the guidance and navigational systems, but when another thruster fired a few minutes later, it too failed.

A NASA spokesman hastened to explain that, despite the failure of two computers, the astronauts were never in danger. Three identical computers onboard the shuttle continued to function normally, each programmed to assume critical functions if control was passed to it. Theoretically, the astronauts could maneuver the craft to a safe landing with only one of the five computers continuing to work normally.

The faulty computers were removed from the *Columbia* and flown to an IBM facility at Owego, New York for analysis. Within two weeks the computer manufacturer announced that "tiny foreign objects" almost certainly caused the failures. Investigators reported finding in one computer a tiny sliver of solder measuring 11/1000s of an inch. In the other they reportedly discovered a piece of "extraneous matter" not otherwise identified.

Just eight minutes before launch from the Kennedy Space Center, June 25, 1984 space shuttle *Discovery*'s maiden flight was postponed. NASA reported that a backup navigational computer had failed. Engineers said that the computer made two errors approximately a half-hour before scheduled lift-off. Then, twenty minutes before launch, it would not respond to commands instructing it to change from standby to operational mode.

Although the failed computer was a backup device, intended for operational only when one of the primary computers onboard failed, NASA officials elected not to risk launching the flight without its backup computer.

Technicians reported their initial tests indicated that the balky computer had a hardware problem; they suspected the failure of an electronic component. They quickly replaced *Discovery*'s failed computer with an identical one they removed from the *Challenger*.

Discovery's problems persisted. NASA scrubbed the third attempt to launch the space shuttle on its maiden voyage, August 28, 1984, citing yet another computer problem. A spokesman explained that engineers had discovered that computer software controlling explosive devices, used to separate the shuttle orbiter from its external fuel tank and solid-fuel rocket boosters, was "incompatible" with the computer equipment aboard *Discovery*. They feared that the incompatibility might compromise the computer's ability to provide the split-second timing required to separate the devices.

Discovery finally rocketed into space for the first time on August 30.

Nearly a year later, a mere three seconds before scheduled lift-off, one of three computers controlling *Challenger*'s main engines sensed that a valve in engine number two had not closed properly, and aborted the July 11, 1985 launch.

After technicians installed a replacement valve, NASA rescheduled the lift-off for July 29. During that launch, engine number one shut down prematurely, after firing only five minutes and forty-five seconds instead of the intended nine minutes. This shortened firing placed the shuttle into an earth orbit about fifty miles lower than planned. NASA engineers blamed a computer's "inappropriate response" to the failure of two of the engine's heat sensors for the abbreviated firing and the resulting lower orbit.

A NASA spokesman explained that the computer recognized the first sensor reading and acted correctly. When the second sensor transmitted a measurement that was above the preprogrammed danger point but lower than readings the program had been instructed to consider unreasonable, the computer shut down the engine.

During the two weeks between launch attempts, another computer, meant to collect data on the scientific experiments conducted during the spaceflight, broke down. A replacement computer was substituted in time for the delayed launch.

The mission also included a computer devoted to controlling a sixty-million-dollar instrument-pointing system that would enable the astronauts to use the spacecraft as an orbiting astronomical observatory for study of the sun, stars, and distant galaxies. That computer initially refused to remain locked on target for more than a few seconds at a time. After a replacement program was loaded into the balky computer, it began to perform so well that NASA officials extended the mission by an additional day.

The space tragedy of all tragedies occurred just 73.631 seconds into what appeared to be a flawless shuttle liftoff the morning of January 28, 1986, when *Challenger* exploded, killing the seven people on board. The dead were: Francis R. Scobee; Michael J. Smith; Ronald E. McNair; Ellison S. Onizuka; Judith A Resnick; Gregory B. Jarvis; and S. Christa McAuliffe.

Millions of viewers around the globe watched the tragedy occur on live television. In the weeks following, seemingly endless rebroadcasts of the fatal liftoff permanently etched the sickening images in countless other minds.

Soon after *Challenger*'s destruction, computer experts expressed dismay that the craft's onboard computers had failed to warn of any problem prior to the deadly explosion. Spokesmen for the Johnson Space Center in Houston and IBM (the computers' manufacturer) reported that none of the numerous computers displayed any data anomaly. They said that the screens simply went blank at the moment when *Challenger* exploded. Experts wondered why the continuous stream of data relayed from the shuttle's complex system of sensors failed to report any temperature, pressure, voltage, or hydraulic changes.

Computer industry critics questioned why the five computers aboard *Challenger* were 1970's technology, operating only slightly faster than personal computers widely available at the time of the disaster. NASA countered that the computers normally operated at only seventy to eighty percent capacity, so more advanced computers were not required.

After divers recovered the computer systems from the Atlantic in mid-March, data recovery specialists said that they expected to recover from the older equipment data that would have been lost if newer devices had been in service. They explained that the 1970s computers used ferrite core memories, which stored data magnetically, and therefore retained data following power losses. By contrast, computer memory chips, used in later models to store data electronically, were extremely volatile; a power loss usually destroyed all data. A NASA spokesman claimed that this factor was one of the primary reasons that NASA decided to use the older computer technology for the shuttle program. Another was that the ferrite core memories better protected data from damage inflicted when a shuttle passed through radioactive belts just beyond the atmosphere.

After extensive study of the *Challenger* accident, safety experts concluded that, even if the shuttle system had detected the flames in the booster rocket, the tragedy could not have been averted. The astronauts simply had no way to escape quickly from the doomed shuttle. Further, the experts said that the booster rocket, once ignited, could not be shut off.

The official findings blamed a problem with O-rings used in the booster rocket for the *Challenger* disaster.

The space shuttle program was put on "hold" pending an intensive scrutiny during which agency experts sought to identify improvements to make future flights safer for space travelers. Shuttle flights resumed thirty months later with the launch of the shuttle *Discovery*, on September 19, 1988.

The crew of the shuttle *Atlantis* was scheduled to conduct scientific experiments on May 8, 1989. Instead they spent five hours replacing a failed general-purpose onboard computer with a backup device. NASA officials reported that a computer had never before been switched in an orbiting spacecraft.

The fourth attempt to launch an *Atlantis* mission, February 25, 1990, had to be postponed yet again. The launch was aborted less than a minute short of lift-off when a ground-based range-safety computer unexplainably stopped accepting input from six data sources. The Cyber computer was one of two required to monitor all phases of the launch and ascent.

If engineers had been able to correct the problem within the available six-minute window while the countdown remained on hold, *Atlantis* could have rocketed into space with its billion-dollar spy satellite. They could not. NASA later announced that technicians had identified the anomaly as a computer software problem which required several hours to fix.

Three days later *Atlantis* roared successfully into space.

NASA installed new computers on shuttle flights in 1991. With three times the memory and twice the speed of their predecessors, the new devices were half the size and weighed only half as much as the 1970s equipment they replaced. Officials said that they also expected improved reliability from the newer technology.

Following a relatively uneventful, successful launch on November 24, during their first day in orbit, the *Atlantis* crew deployed a military satellite. This was the first military shuttle mission following the Pentagon's decision to drop their traditional shroud of secrecy imposed on classified shuttle missions.

On Saturday, November 30, NASA announced that one of three navigational units onboard *Atlantis* had failed. As a safety precaution they had decided to cut short the mission and return the shuttle to earth at Edwards Air Force Base rather than to the originally planned Florida site.

A spokesman explained that the failed component contained an array of gyroscopes and other devices to provide the computer data regarding the shuttle's speed and position. Such timely and accurate information was vital to both the shuttle's safe atmosphere reentry and its landing on earth.

Even though the three-day curtailment of the mission forced the cancellation of many experiments planned for the mission, *Atlantis* landed in California without incident at 2:34 p.m., December 1.

After the debut of the space shuttle program, computers continued to create problems in other space exploration endeavors.

"Computer Failures Helped Put $100 Million Satellite Off Course," announced a January 1984, *Washington Post* headline.

A Tracking and Data Relay Satellite, launched the preceding April, veered off course and went into an orbit 10,000 miles closer to earth than planned. Officials said that a rocket misfired because instructions transmitted to the gyroscope contained errors. The guidance computer was unable to determine which craft location data was correct.

Over a three-month period NASA corrected several of the wayward satellite's problems, including the software flaw, and coaxed the satellite into its intended geo-synchronous orbit at the equator. NASA finally put into place the first of three such satellites that eventually would provide alternate communications between earth ground stations and low-orbiting satellites used for both civilian and military purposes.

On August 6, 1987, water drenched millions of dollars worth of computers and related electronic equipment in the Johnson Space Center's Mission Control Building. NASA reported that workers, installing cables in an adjacent crawlspace, accidentally ruptured a water pipe. The agency declined to estimate the cost of the damage resulting from the mishap. They did say that the deluge forced the shutdown of the computer complex for a drying-out period of several days, after which the system underwent a slow, systematic restart and test.

Although the space shuttle mission in progress on September 1, 1988 was only a simulation, the computer problem that halted it was real. During the fifty-six-hour dress rehearsal for the first shuttle mission following the *Challenger* disaster, NASA officials reported that the astronauts handled well all of the situations posed.

After the simulation's computer failure became public, NASA officials down-played the incident, stressing that the mission flight control computer had not failed.

Meanwhile, as the first in a thirty-year series of missions intended to culminate in a manned landing on Mars, the Soviets launched two probes to Phobos, one of Mars' two moons. *Phobos 1* went aloft on July 7, 1988. *Phobos 2*, reportedly containing duplicates of twenty of the twenty-two experiments aboard *Phobos 1*, was launched on July 12.

Upon completion of their six-month journey, the probes were supposed first to photograph Mars and its moon, then land two smaller explorer probes on Mars' moon's surface.

When ground controllers transmitted an erroneous signal to *Phobos 1* in September, the error shut down the attitude control system, causing the craft to lose its orientation to the sun. Without its solar-powered electrical source, the probe ceased to function and was soon lost.

Phobos 2 continued its journey and on January 29, 1989, entered an orbit 218 miles above the Martian moon. It transmitted photos of both the planet and the spaceship's namesake.

The Soviet news agency *Tass* issued a brief report on March 29 indicating that communications with *Phobos 2* had ceased mysteriously when the craft moved into position to photograph the Martian moon.

Unidentified Russian scientists, requesting anonymity, told Western reporters that *Phobos 2* had been descending to a position 164 feet above the moon's surface, a vantage point from which it was supposed to drop two small explorer craft onto Phobos. During this maneuver the craft unexplainably ceased all communications with earth.

The U.S. General Accounting Office (GAO) charged in March 1990 that poor data management practices, aggravated by inappropriate storage conditions, threaten much of the scientific data that computers have accumulated from America's space exploration. Investigators reported that hundreds of thousands of reels of computer tape were stored under "deplorable conditions," often in basements or warehouses without temperature and humidity controls. The report said that one such sub-basement storage area had flooded five years earlier. It mentioned another storage facility where auditors observed 300,000 computer tapes whose protective covers had been crushed by the steel bands used to strap them on to pallets.

GAO warned that, unless data storage improvements were implemented very soon, much of the nation's valuable and irreplaceable space exploration data might be lost forever.

Noting that the Hubble Space Telescope and the Earth Observing System were expected to generate far greater volumes of data than NASA had collected in the preceding thirty years, *Computerworld* warned in its March 19, 1990 issue that the horrendous problem could only worsen. In a subsequent story related to the government's data storage nightmare, dated February 4, 1991, the periodical observed that by the year 2001 NASA will have accumulated space data equal in volume to twenty-nine times that available in the entire collection of books at the Library of Congress!

When a computer aboard the *Mars Observer* spacecraft failed to "call home" as scheduled on August 24, 1993, chances for the success of the one-billion-dollar mission plummeted to near zero. The NASA flight director simply announced, "We've come up negative on our search for a signal." The announcement was made just minutes after the scientific community expected the spacecraft's computer to communicate with earth.

Launched from Cape Canaveral in September 1992, *Mars Observer* had traveled a virtually trouble-free 450 million miles journey to reach Mars. Then, to provide fuel required for firing the craft's propulsion rockets to place it in orbit around the planet, NASA transmitted signals instructing the craft to pump liquid helium into the propulsion system. Upon completion of this task, *Mars Observer* was supposed to switch its transmitters back on and notify NASA ground control that the task had been completed. It did not. The last contact from the space probe occurred at approximately 9:00 p.m.

Although some scientists worried publicly whether the fuel tanks had been over-pressurized and exploded, destroying the craft, NASA officials deemed this "unlikely" in view of its redundant safeguards.

NASA announced that the errant spacecraft carried backup computers for its central control, attitude control, and data processing. In addition to solar panels, *Mars Observer* carried batteries to provide electrical power.

For five days the world waited to hear from the silent spacecraft. The onboard control computer had been programmed to transmit radio communications automatically after a specified length of time during which the craft had not communicated with earth. NASA officials and scientists anxiously counted the hours and monitored the airwaves as they observed this countdown, desperately hoping that the computer would respond when the deadline came. The hoped-for call did not come.

Four years later, approximately forty seconds after lift-off from Kourou, French Guiana, faulty computer software reportedly caused a massive explosion, destroying an *Ariane V* rocket and its four Cluster spacecraft. The Cluster crafts carried scientific experiments designed to study the behavior and effects of solar winds.

Even thought these uninsured experiments reportedly were being carried without charge, the non-paying scientific customers threatened to sue the European Space Agency for the loss of their experiments.

According to the *Times of London*, July 26, 1996, "The main reason for the explosion was that software used to control *Ariane V*'s predecessor, *Ariane IV*, had been brought in for use in *Ariane V* without being tested in relevant conditions."

An inquiry board investigating the loss concluded that the guidance software and flight control systems had been tested insufficiently. The board ruled that a complete loss of guidance and altitude information had caused the explosion.

After successfully photographing Ganymede, Jupiter's frozen moon, a computer onboard spacecraft *Galileo* sensed a problem and shut itself down, August 24, 1996. Engineers at NASA's Jet Propulsion Labs in Pasadena determined that the shutdown came after a single computation was not completed as quickly as the computer required. Lab officials announced that they had corrected the problem and restarted the system in time for a second flyby, scheduled for September 6.

After a cargo vessel accidentally rammed the Russian manned space station *Mir* on June 25, 1997, scientists worried whether humans should continue to live aboard the severely damaged facility. Within four weeks the station reported four computer failures. One of the failures prevented an unmanned cargo ship carrying urgently-needed supplies from docking with *Mir* in August. Another knocked out all but essential life-support systems, making habitation even more difficult for those aboard the aging space station.

Concerned that a total computer failure might render *Mir* unable to generate electricity from its solar panels and cause it to lose its critical orientation to the sun, scientists publicly urged officials to rush a replacement computer to the crippled station.

In September NASA launched the shuttle *Atlantis*, carrying, in addition to badly needed food and water, a new central computer to replace the failing one on *Mir*.

In what must now seem an embarrassing abundance of electronic riches, Russia launched an unmanned drone cargo ship on October 5, carrying among its regular supplies another new computer! The Russians explained that this one would serve as a backup to the recently installed American computer--just in case it should fail.

13

HAVE FEDERAL GOVERNMENT COMPUTER-MODERNIZATION EFFORTS BECOME IMPOSSIBLE MISSIONS?

The federal government's willingness to pay millions of dollars for unproven technology encouraged the development of computer technology. Uncle Sam's early contracts to have computers designed and built to perform scientific calculations at Aberdeen Proving Grounds in Maryland proved successful. Soon the U.S. Census Bureau ordered a computer intended to process business data. Univac I, serial number 001, was dedicated on June 14, 1951.

These two early government successes with the new technology encouraged a wide variety of large organizations to investigate the potential uses of computers. A new industry was born. Soon the public used the words "computer" and "Univac" interchangeably.

When IBM later decided to build and sell computers, their marketing experts predicted that, over time, the firm might market as many as fifty such devices.

At that time, when computers weighed tons, filled huge rooms, consumed enormous amounts of electricity, and cost millions of dollars, it was a rare person indeed who even considered the future possibility of personal, desk-top computers costing only a few hundred dollars. Yet, by 1983, desk-top computers far more powerful than Univac I were available for less than $3,000. Today hundreds of thousands of them are in use throughout the federal government.

The following federal government computer snafus are typical of those publicized over the last twenty-five years.

The U.S. General Accounting Office (GAO), in April 1976, published a scathing indictment of the federal government computers that issued checks and made automatic decisions without human oversight or subsequent review.

GAO concluded that federal government computers annually issued unreviewed authorizations for payments or checks (excluding payroll) totaling $26 billion, unreviewed bills totaling $10 billion, and unreviewed requisitions, shipping orders, repair schedules, and disposal orders for $8 billion worth of material. Uncle Sam was spending annually at least $44 billion that no human reviewed for correctness!

The GAO report charged that an improperly programmed computer in the U.S. Navy's Aviation Supply office routinely scheduled overhauls of equipment before such work was needed. Even after auditors discovered the error, Navy personnel waited five years to correct the $3 million-a-year problem, explaining they feared Congress would notice their lower expenditures for equipment overhauls and reduce the Navy budget!

When Army computers ordered unneeded inventory items, their unreviewed actions cost taxpayers $1.3 million.

At Fort Monmouth, New Jersey, GAO said that an army computer initiated shipments of radioactive equipment without specifying that special safeguards were required.

A computer program used by the Veterans Administration reportedly overpaid veterans enrolled in on-the-job training programs. Simply stated, the computer program included an erroneous formula.

The following month, GAO issued a related, bomb-shell report titled "Managers Need to Provide Better Protection for Federal Automatic Data Processing Facilities." After investigating eighteen data processing sites in the United States and ten overseas, auditors reported that many were poorly protected against fire or flooding. They warned that prevailing security practices also made most federal government computer installations susceptible to bombings, fraud, theft, embezzlement, and human errors. Only 200 of the federal government's 9,200 computer centers were adequately protected. GAO concluded that 9,000 were inadequately safeguarded.

The Department of Health, Education and Welfare announced on July 10, 1978, that "Overpayments and payments to ineligible recipients occurred last year at a rate of 7 percent in Medicaid, 8.6 percent in AFDC and 5.2 percent in SSI." Secretary Joseph Califano told reporters that the errors totaled $1.2 billion in Medicaid, a program providing health-care funds to people near or below the poverty level. Errors costing $900 million were discovered in AFDC, a program providing Aid to Families with Dependent Children. Another $300 million in errors had occurred in SSI, the Supplemental Security Income program providing payments to blind or disabled Social Security recipients.

The disclosure, on October 16, 1978, that auditors working for the U.S. General Accounting Office had been able to insert the name "Donald Duck" on a federal government payroll computer in Washington, D.C., garnered newspaper headlines worldwide. In Paris, the story occupied the top left quarter of the Saturday-Sunday (October 28-29, 1978) edition of the *International Herald Tribune*. A prominent 3 1/2-inch square drawing of the world-famous cartoon character drew readers' attention to the story under a headline that read: "How Donald Duck Got on U.S. Payroll."

An assistant director of GAO, during testimony before a congressional committee, explained that auditors were attempting to determine whether government employees could defraud the government by introducing nonexistent employee names into computerized payroll files. The computer at the Department of Housing and Urban Development (HUD) reportedly rejected none of thirty phony names, including Mr. Duck's. Even though the maximum annual pay for U.S. civil servants at the time was $47,500, the auditors assigned Donald Duck an annual salary of $99,999.99. The computer offered no objection and computed his pay accordingly.

GAO, in 1980, charged that the Navy's centralized computer payroll system was "largely unreliable and inefficient." Auditors blamed most of the system's problems on humans rather than on equipment or software.

The Washington system, at the time, regularly paid approximately 520,000 Navy personnel. Although more than $150 million had been spent on the system's development and operation during the preceding twelve years, the audit agency concluded that most of its calculations were based on either erroneous or outdated data. According to the auditors, on each payday the faulty data caused errors in more than fifty percent of the computer-calculated payments.

The GAO report indicated that a system-wide sampling for March 1979, revealed more than $27 million in errors for that month alone.

When a benefits payment computer is not informed that a recipient has died, it will continue to issue regular payments. During the early 1980s, the Inspector General at the Department of Health and Human Services (HHS) arranged to match his agency's list of those receiving payments under the Black Lung Program with a list of people drawing Social Security benefits. The match revealed that HHS was continuing to send regular checks to 668 spouses and 240 widows to whom the Social Security computer had stopped issuing checks--because the recipients had died. The computer file match-up also identified 300 Black Lung recipients being paid too much because they were divorced. The Social Security computer knew about the divorces; the Black Lung computer did not.

The bottom line: Health & Human Services had disbursed an estimated $15,000,000 in improper payments to Black Lung Program beneficiaries whose deaths or divorces had not been entered into the payments computer.

Even after they reportedly were told that a new computer system was not yet ready for implementation, officials at the U.S. Department of Housing and Urban Development (HUD) reportedly ordered it put into service immediately. Shortly thereafter, in early 1983, instead of sending routine monthly payment notices to almost 30,000 people holding HUD loans, the computer system dispatched letters demanding immediate payment, in full, of their mortgage balances!

The U.S. Department of Commerce, as required by law, adjusted the Merit Pay of senior-grade employees at the start of each new fiscal year. In October 1982, the computer began to disburse increased amounts to those whose performance had earned them pay raises. An undetected error in the program caused widespread overpayments. By the time the auditors discovered the logic mistake nearly a year later, some employees had been overpaid $500.

U.S. Customs officials cited unspecified "computer glitches" as the cause of system outages that slowed or stopped all imports to the United States, November 20 and 21, 1989. Customs employees, accustomed to computer-calculated tariffs, had to revert to manual calculation methods. Arriving goods, subject to import quota restrictions, could not be checked against computer files, causing significant delays.

Customs officials later blamed the failure of their computer system on software problems. An electrical power failure on November 21 made matters worse, further delaying the system's restoration to service. A spokesman told reporters that the Customs Service did not have a backup system for use during emergencies.

When the U.S. Department of Justice auctioned surplus and obsolete computer equipment in September 1990, a Kentucky businessman paid $45 for a personal computer that had been used in a U.S. attorney's office. From that computer he reportedly retrieved electronic copies of sealed indictments, names of federally protected witnesses, and information about confidential informants!

Widespread press coverage of the incident triggered an investigation by GAO into computer security at the Department of Justice. In its report, GAO stated "...the unmistakable conclusion {is} that at present, one simply cannot trust that sensitive data will be safely secured at the Department of Justice."

The GAO revealed, in July 1991, that more than 100 different federal government, drug wars computer systems, scattered across almost three dozen agencies and departments, were not compatible enough to exchange information. The audit agency urged the Office of National Drug Control Policy to review all federal computerized anti-drug systems to identify modifications that would improve information exchange among organizations.

GAO also worried that most of the anti-drug systems lacked measures to ensure data accuracy. Despite the extremely sensitive nature of anti-drug data, GAO concluded that much of it was inadequately protected from outsiders.

The U.S. military spent more than a billion-and-a-half dollars on a computer system intended to streamline health care for military personnel. First used in the late 1980s, the system was tested at more than a dozen hospitals before being installed at the Walter Reed Army Medical Center in Washington, D.C. Reluctant users voiced numerous complaints about the system, as well as concerns about patient care. Many shared their views with the *Washington Post*. The public attention resulted in the introduction of substantially modified software late in 1991.

After more public complaints, the hospital commander issued guidelines permitting doctors to choose for themselves whether to continue writing prescriptions and laboratory/radiology orders as before, or to switch to the new computerized system. The *Washington Post* reported that about half of the more than 600 doctors at the hospital elected to use the computer for laboratory orders; about half stuck with traditional handwritten orders. For radiology orders approximately eighty percent elected to use the computer system. Ninety percent opted to use the computer system for pharmacy prescriptions.

The Pension Benefit Guaranty Corp (PBGC), the federal pension insurance system, at the beginning of 1993 insured pensions of more than 41 million Americans participating in 67,000 private retirement plans.

In testimony before a House of Representatives oversight panel in February 1993, a GAO spokesman reported that his agency had been unable to audit Pension Benefit's automated systems. He cited several major problems associated with the system's software, especially that used to estimate liability for future benefits and that used to account for insurance premium collections. GAO charged that PBGS's system had not performed properly since 1988, when employees attempted to modify it to process variable premiums.

Two worrisome facts emerged from the GAO testimony: The Pension Benefit system was under-funded by an estimated $50 billion. PBGC had assets of only $8.75 billion.

As federal government automated systems have grown, their computers have become inadequate for their assigned roles. Modernization efforts have created unimaginable nightmares. Although numerous other departments and agencies have had similarly frustrating experiences, Internal Revenue Service's modernization efforts have been among the most widely publicized by the news media.

Computer modernization on such a massive scale as needed at IRS is a challenge that perhaps is like attempting to replace New York City's entire subway system and, at the same time, build a twelve-lane Interstate highway section across Manhattan--without disrupting existing subway operations, street traffic, water and sewer service, utility service, communications links, or adversely affecting any residence or business!! Even the most optimistic thinker must not expect everything to turn out as planned.

"...the most publicized foul-up in computer history..." is how *Information Week*, in its issue of March 9, 1987, described the 1985 situation at Internal Revenue Service, resulting from one of the agency's computer modernization attempts.

IRS's efforts to switch from Honeywell and Control Data computers, some of which were at least twenty-years-old, to new Sperry equipment, simply did not go as envisioned. The equipment changeover required IRS's three hundred programmers to rewrite the logic for 1,500 computer programs, totaling 3.5 million lines of code, into a different programming language--in record time. Heady expectations for any team.

Sperry Corporation won a competitive government contract award of $103 million to install eleven computers at IRS computer centers across the United States. An inordinate number of computer tape-drive breakdowns prevented the timely recording of taxpayer data to computer files, and made it unavailable for either computer inquiry or timely processing.

The agency's backlog of unprocessed tax refunds focused much unfavorable media attention on IRS during the tax-filing season of 1985. The agency reported that phone personnel fielded more than four million complaints. An unknown number of additional callers simply gave up without ever reaching an IRS switchboard.

Monday morning quarterbackers said that the nationwide delays in processing tax returns in 1985 occurred, in part, because the computer system changeover actually resulted in slower processing speeds. They charged that IRS planners failed to allow sufficient time to test and implement the new system prior to the January deluge of tax returns. The situation was exacerbated when the agency had to provide space for the new equipment. To accommodate the new hardware, they had to remove the old computer equipment--shutting down the old system before the new one was running successfully. Knowledgeable systems professionals rank this move as a major "no-no."

Government auditors later reported that the catastrophic computer disaster of 1985 had cost American taxpayers $21 million in unplanned interest costs that IRS had to pay taxpayers. They estimated that the agency also lost productivity valued at an additional $39 million.

Information Week reported that because of the computer debacle IRS spent $10 billion in overtime pay--a number that seems inordinately high, even suspect.

Worth magazine later reported that during the 1985 disastrous tax return processing season, IRS employees in Philadelphia hid unprocessed tax returns in the ceiling, so supervisors would not realize that processing quotas were not being met!

IRS reprogrammed the tax processing steps for the new computers, but for document processing, the system's design was nearly identical to the original, in operation since the early 1960s.

As with any large and complex system, unexpected and embarrassing programming errors continued to pop up from time to time. The *Associated Press* reported in 1984 that an IRS public affairs spokesperson blamed a computer for assessing a $205 penalty on a couple in Mesquite, Texas, whose nearly $9,000 tax payment was one cent less than the amount the computer said they owed! That a one-cent unpaid balance could trigger such a penalty, attracted wide news media attention.

IRS also drew flack in January 1985, when officials in Philadelphia revealed that more than $300 million in withholding taxes, paid in 1984, had not been posted to their computer files. The computer, unaware that payment had been received, proceeded to generate several thousand notices to companies in the mid-Atlantic states, threatening to seize property for nonpayment of taxes. In breaking the story on January 30, the *Philadelphia Inquirer* reported more than 500 instances of local companies asking banks to provide proof that their taxes had been paid on schedule.

Computerworld, in its February 13, 1989, issue, reported that "a programming error" had caused a one-week delay in mailing 450,000 refund checks.

Later the same year, the General Accounting Office (GAO) questioned IRS's ability to continue to operate their existing system as they added newer computer operations onto such an archaic system's design. Technology from the 1960s was based on computer tape processing of batches of documents. By the 1980s, processing required online systems, providing instant responses to inquiries; such systems required massive computer disk files. GAO noted that optical scanning technology had been perfected to the point that IRS could upgrade their system and cease to keypunch data from individual and business tax returns.

A brief chronology of IRS's efforts to upgrade their computer systems should start with their first attempt, undertaken in the late 1960s. Citizens protested so vehemently over perceived privacy and security concerns that the White House eventually halted that project.

The agency initiated a second computer system modernization effort in 1982, intending to automate many clerical tasks, link related data, and make information more rapidly and universally accessible to employees. IRS's parent organization, the Treasury Department, vetoed this effort.

Perhaps believing the old saw that "the third time is a charm," IRS officials, in 1986, began yet another attempt to upgrade their grossly outmoded computer systems. By 1988 they had won grudging approval for the Tax System Modernization, estimated to cost $4.4 billion and require ten years to complete.

In 1994 IRS awarded a $1.3 billion multi-year contract to IBM for work on their Document Processing System, intended to scan and record data from incoming tax documents. This was a critical piece of their Tax System Modernization. Hounded by constant complaints from Congress, politicians, the General Accounting Office, and others, IRS canceled the Document Processing System contract in October 1996, after spending approximately $300 million.

During this time GAO continued to report IRS's computer and management problems to Congress--and the news media. GAO's audit of IRS's 1992 fiscal year financial statements reportedly found $200 billion in misstatements and errors. According to the audit report, IRS had incomplete records for approximately $800 million in taxpayer assets seized in that year alone.

Perhaps the most sobering discovery in this first-ever audit of IRS's financial statements was that the agency was unable to identify an estimated ten million businesses and individuals failing to file tax returns each year! GAO estimated that as a result, IRS failed to collect an incredible $127 billion in yearly taxes due!

Computer-generated dunning notices demanding immediate payment of $68 billion (yes, billion) from each of several stunned taxpayers were revealed in the *Wall Street Journal*, August 4, 1993. The brief article mentioned that 4,623 erroneous notices resulted from a computer program change intended to instruct the computer not to bill victims of the massive floods in the Midwest at a time when their lives were already extremely stressful.

At Internal Revenue Service, day-to-day tax processing operations must continue as usual while any systems changes are undertaken. Employees must continue daily interaction with the public, even as they process two hundred million individual and business tax returns, during which they handle annually more than two billion pieces of paper. They field more than 110,000,000 phone inquiries from taxpayers each year. They also collect $1.5 trillion in taxes. Like most organizations, IRS probably has 100% of available staff hours obligated to existing work. This means that employees who are adequately knowledgeable about computer technology, the organization, and its new system's requirements, are simply not available in sufficient number to undertake massive system changes.

Congress and the news media appear to rate many of IRS's attempts to improve computer systems as total failures, when, in fact, their efforts have accomplished a great deal. For example, following the 1985 near-collapse of their total system, IRS increased the power and capacity of their computers and installed a high-speed data transmission network linking IRS facilities across the country. After processing the huge backlog of tax returns, they modified their hastily-written programs, increasing the number of individual tax returns the system could process each week from 4.5 million to 6 million--a performance improvement of one third. The agency also moved many clerical processing steps onto the computers, eliminating 4,500 clerical positions. IRS also launched, then improved and expanded, a system to accommodate electronic filing of tax returns. They upgraded their computers' ability to screen electronically-filed returns, enabling them to detect and reject suspicious or seriously defective returns.

IRS's efforts to create an acceptable electronic tax filing capability have been belittled by politicians and journalists. Auditors reported that during the 1991 tax season, $42.9 million in phony refunds were claimed. The value of fraudulent electronically-filed claims rose to nearly $50 million in 1993. IRS had improved their ability to spot fraud and prevent payment of many false claims. During the first quarter of 1994, IRS said that citizens filed more than 12.5 million electronic returns. Nevertheless, GAO warned

Congress that IRS simply could not demonstrate that an electronic tax filing system could be adequately safeguarded from fraud. The news media widely reported Congressional criticism of the Cyberfile system as being inefficient, poorly managed, insecure, and mismanaged. IRS officials, finally caving in to the pressure, announced in September 1996, that they were scrapping the system, in which they had invested more than $17 million.

Citizens must find it impossible to differentiate between valid criticism of IRS's automation efforts and that motivated by political considerations. For example, did presidential candidate Ross Perot really believe that the United States could function without an organization such as Internal Revenue Service? Did candidate Bob Dole truly think that the IRS could do its job with one-third fewer employees? Did Congress expect improved agency performance to result from the 11% budget cut they imposed on IRS in 1996?

Is anyone today really naive enough to think that it is possible to modernize or otherwise change such complex computer systems without encountering major unexpected problems? Get real!

The Social Security Administration's computer systems also have drawn much adverse criticism for decades.

On an August day in 1975, a computer at Social Security Administration (SSA) issued checks disbursing erroneous overpayments totaling more than $10,516,000! An agency spokesman said that they resulted from a programming error, which caused the Supplemental Security Income (SSI) computer unexplainably to branch to a section of the program used to compute catch-up payments for clients who had been underpaid for the entire year. A computer giving away more than ten million dollars in a single day attracted wide news media coverage.

SSA first issued checks under the SSI program on January 1, 1974. In its first eighteen months of operation, the computer system made unwarranted payments totaling more than $400 million. More correctly stated, this is the amount discovered by auditors searching for duplicate payments, overpayments, and payments made to ineligible recipients. At a time when more than four million citizens were receiving monthly SSI checks, no one knows how many errors the auditors failed to detect.

After the SSI program had been in effect for two years, the *Washington Star* estimated that SSI's error rate over the last six months had been 24.2%. The *Star* also reported that the erroneous overpayments for the program's first two years totaled $547 million. The agency revealed, a short time after the *Star*'s report, that the officially determined error rate for the period had been 24.8%.

In a later issue, the *Star* reported, May 7, 1976, that new audits of the SSI system revealed overpayments of $622 million during its first twenty-seven months of operation--in effect, the computer system was giving away an average of more than a million dollars every business day! And, when compared to the regular Social Security system which issued nearly ten times as many checks, the SSI program was rather insignificant.

Commissioner James Cardwell spent much of this period attempting to persuade Congress to approve a $550 million overhaul of all of SSA's computer operations. The U.S. General Accounting Office (GAO) told Congress that SSA was using only 40% of the capacity of its seventeen current mainframe computers. Cardwell argued that, for the past fifteen years, congressionally-mandated programs had forced SSA to rapidly patch old systems, resulting in instances where patches of computer code had been applied over previously patched code. He warned that patches upon patches upon patches could lead to a possible breakdown of the agency's ability to issue thirty-four million monthly checks, unless Congress approved the overhaul plan.

Then, in July 1977, the audit agency of the Department of Health, Education, and Welfare (SSA's parent organization), concluded that SSA's computer systems were susceptible to fraud and abuse. At the time, the agency's computers contained sensitive personal data on twenty-seven million Americans who had applied for benefits. Applicants' financial and medical data were deemed especially sensitive, since they could be accessed by more than 2,200 computer terminals in SSA field offices across America. Many of these devices, located in open work areas, could not be secured at night. The auditors expressed concern that far too many employees, whose jobs did not require computer access, knew passwords that would grant them access on demand.

Shortly after SSA had reportedly spent a half-million dollars on a new security system to protect their headquarter's computer room, the *Baltimore Evening Sun* reported, February 7, 1978, that GAO auditors had concluded that "unauthorized personnel {still} have access to the computer room and tape vault." The audit report also specifically charged that blank Social Security and Medicare cards, as well as computer tapes and disk packs, could be removed from the data center without difficulty or challenge.

Social Security officials revealed in 1978 that "a computer glitch" had caused nearly half-a-million elderly people to be paid nearly half-a-billion dollars less than they should have received. An agency spokesman told reporters that SSA was then paying benefits to forty-three million Americans; consequently, the average underpayments of $10 per month represented less than 1% of the checks being issued. He claimed that the computer programming error primarily affected retirees who had returned to work after starting to receive SSA benefits. In some instances benefit checks had been for less than they should have been for as long as a decade. He promised that the agency would quickly recompute payments for all those affected, and pay the recipients or their survivors any money due.

Congressman Jack Brooks, upon emerging from a hearing of the House Subcommittee on Legislation and National Security on

September 23, 1981, warned that the agency was facing an imminent disaster "...when the Social Security Administration simply won't be able to get out the checks." Some of those testifying before the subcommittee said that, despite deteriorating computer support, dedicated SSA data processing employees managed to compute, print, and mail thirty-six million benefit checks each month, most of them correct. Others told the Congress that they thought that SSA's computer systems reflected extremely poor planning, coupled with monumental bureaucratic bungling and inefficiency.

Commissioner John A. Svahn testified that developing a long-term solution to the agency's computer problems was his top administrative priority.

The subcommittee also heard testimony charging that the SSA systems staff lacked the technical knowledge and skills required to modernize the agency's automated systems. Several other major problems were cited, including antiquated equipment dependent upon magnetic tape processing, programs with too many undocumented patches or changes, inadequate controls and security safeguards, lack of upper-level management support for automation efforts, low morale, and a shortage of programmers and systems analysts knowledgeable about newer computer technology.

Over the decades numerous stories have surfaced charging that SSA's computers prematurely recorded deaths of recipients. In some instances the computers, erroneously insisting that people were dead, stopped their benefits. The computers sometimes even started paying benefits to the still-living retirees' beneficiaries.

Medicare computers also frequently have prematurely recorded "deaths" of countless, still-living citizens. Accordingly, the computers then refused to pay for their medical treatment, contending that such costs were "incurred after entitlement ended"--even though the SSA computer routinely deducted Medicare premiums from the benefits it continued to pay the same people.

Commissioner Svahn said, in February 1983, that he suspected that SSA computers had paid as much as $100 million to recipients--after they died. He revealed that, in 1982, the agency had determined that more than 5,000 recipients, listed by the Medicare computer file as deceased, continued to draw Social Security benefits. Investigators discovered that numbers of those listed as dead in the Medicare computer files actually were still alive. A subsequent computer file match, involving only a small sample of the database, reportedly identified 1,411 confirmed cases in which SSA benefits had been paid to those deceased. In one confirmed case, the computer continued to issue checks, which someone cashed, for eighteen years--until the error was discovered.

Faced with the fact that SSA computers were generating (known) overpayments exceeding $1.2 billion a year by 1982, Congress agreed to support a $479 million expenditure over five years to improve the agency's computer systems.

That massive modernization effort would involve rewriting 1,376 computer programs containing more than twelve million lines of Cobol code. The agency would also have to convert magnetic tape master files containing more than 240 million records, while continuing day-to-day functions: recording wage earnings and withholdings for most American workers, processing 120 million health claims and inquiries, processing seven million new Social Security claims, and handling ten million annual Social Security Card applications. More importantly, nearly forty million Americans would expect their current monthly payments to arrive on time.

The modernization plan called for replacing twenty-six large-scale computers, many of them more than twenty years old. The agency would also construct a new, $75 million building to house their impressive new computer center.

Congress and the public, apparently assuming that the computer crisis was being adequately addressed, quickly turned their attention to debating the solvency of the Social Security fund.

GAO auditors reported to Congress in 1987 that SSA's software development efforts were two years behind schedule and $200 million over budget.

Industry critics complained that the agency was rushing to install 22,000 obsolete dumb terminals when powerful personal computers would offer greater benefits for about the same cost.

In an extremely rare unanimous vote, Congress, in August 1994, voted to separate the Social Security Administration from its parent organization, the Department of Health and Human Services, thus creating an independent agency. Politicians maintained that the new agency would be less subject to political manipulation and easier to manage. SSA, with 64,000 employees at its Baltimore headquarters and 1,300 field offices, had an annual budget of $325 billion. As an independent agency, SSA could submit its budget requests directly to Congress rather than through the White House's Office of Management and Budget.

Because of the agency's heavy dependence upon computers, Social Security Administration managers will forever have to attempt to improve their automated systems as resources permit, let their systems stagnate when resources are withheld, and constantly defend the agency against every type of criticism about their automated systems.

The chapter titled *Do Computers Compromise Air Traffic Safety?* chronicles the Federal Aviation Administration's computer modernization efforts.

For its use of computers over the past three decades, the FBI's computer systems have drawn vastly different criticism from those discussed earlier in this chapter.

The FBI established the National Crime Information Center (NCIC), in January 1967, to provide computer-based inquiry and response capabilities to local, state, and federal criminal justice agencies nationwide. Computer files provided almost instant information about wanted felons, missing persons, stolen vehicles, vehicles used in felony crimes, stolen vehicle parts or license plates, identifiable stolen property, and criminal histories. Civil libertarians vehemently objected to the very idea of such computerized data bases. Newspapers parlayed the opposition into major news stories. Court battles raged.

The NCIC computer system prevailed, gaining such wide acceptance that today almost everyone has learned, perhaps from viewing television cop shows, exactly what a check of NCIC involves. Despite continued public opposition, and frequent criticism of faulty or erroneous data, NCIC became an accepted part of law enforcement across America. By 1990, NCIC records exceeded forty million. The 60,000 authorized users were submitting an average of eleven electronic inquiries per second to the antiquated computer system, whose technology was nearly twenty-five years old.

Congress finally, reluctantly, approved a modernization plan for NCIC's computer system. Scheduled for completion in March 1995, the replacement computer system was expected to handle up to eighty-two inquiries per second. It promised to complete most searches and provide results within five seconds to users anywhere in the nation.

Six companies submitted proposals seeking the lucrative government contract. Agency officials evaluating the proposals selected Harris Corporation to create the new system, called NCIC-2000, at a cost of $47 million. Observers speculated that Harris would also sell some 11,000 computer terminals to various criminal justice agencies, generating an additional $100 million for the contractor.

The new system would permit law enforcement personnel, using a miniature scanning device carried in police cars, to transmit an electronic fingerprint image to NCIC for instant identification. A central computer, containing approximately a quarter-million fingerprints of wanted felons and missing persons, should provide a response directly to the inquiring vehicle in less than a minute.

But...all did not go as planned. NCIC-2000 was far from ready for use on its scheduled 1995 completion date.

The *Los Angeles Times* reported, December 12, 1996, that the FBI's latest cost estimates for NCIC-2000 had risen to $183.2 million. Noting that the contract had been amended eight times, the article also reported that the targeted completion date had slipped to July 1999.

News reports have sometimes confused details of FBI's different automation efforts. While the NCIC-2000 system, intended to automate only the fingerprints of wanted felons and missing persons, involves a computer database of approximately 250,000 records, the Bureau has also been engaged in a parallel effort to computerize its massive repository of some 40,000,000 sets of fingerprints. This more massive system, known as the Integrated Automated Fingerprint Identification System, promises to provide local police use of an electronic scanning device which captures images of a person's fingerprints and immediately transmits them electronically to the FBI. Within two hours, the results of each search will be transmitted back to the local law enforcement officer who submitted the query. Such fingerprint searches, which now officially take "weeks" to process, sometimes require actual waits of up to five months.

An FBI spokesman told reporters, in August 1997, that the estimated cost for this gigantic system had been revised upwards from the original figure of $520 million to a more realistic $640 million. As with any large computer system, the true cost cannot be determined until the new system is operational.

Some system upgrades attract far less news media attention. The recent situation at the Health Care Financing Administration is a prime example. Concerned with gross inadequacies in widely dispersed Medicare systems, run by seventy-two private insurance companies, the federal government contracted with GTE to consolidate and modernize the processing.

What appeared to be a reasonably straight-forward task became undoable. Simply put, the inability of federal personnel to document for the GTE staff exactly what each part of the antiquated system was supposed to do, made it impossible for GTE to create a valid replacement system.

Frustrated Medicare officials, complaining that the problem-plagued project was over budget and behind schedule, announced termination of the contract on September 15, 1997. Internal documents indicate that the agency "invested" more than $100 million in the new computer system before canceling the project.

14

HOW COMMON ARE COMPUTER FOUL-UPS?

Thousands of computer errors, snafus, goofs, glitches, etc., encompassing almost every type of endeavor, have occurred over the nearly five decades since electronic brains first appeared. Interesting stories that simply don't fit any of the preceding subject groupings are presented in this final chapter.

In the 1960s, when big insurance companies appeared to be unconcerned with smaller charges, a computer at one of the larger firms always tacked on a payment of $25, coded as "circumcision," for all newborns. Someone apparently had decided that, even though not all males are circumcised at birth, simply paying the same fee was an easy way to handle the situation. Several years into the practice an auditor noticed this procedure and concluded that the insurance company was paying an unnecessary third of a million dollars per year in circumcision fees. He reported that the computer program failed to take into account the sex of each newborn--it paid the same circumcision fee for baby girls!

Major forms of computer input in the 1960s included punched cards, and punched paper tapes. When excited sports fans need confetti, paper is paper! During the 1969 New York City ticker-tape parade for baseball's new World Champions, the Mets, enthusiastic onlookers in several skyscrapers reportedly tossed computer cards and paper tape, along with the traditional confetti, onto the team. Businesses later reported that critical computer cards and tape containing accounting, inventory, and payroll data had been thrown as confetti.

When a computer at Ford Motor Credit indicated in 1970 that a customer had not sent his car payment on time, the customer submitted proof that he had. Yet a second time the customer disproved the computer's assertion that his payment was late. When the computer made its third late payment accusation, the justifiably irate customer refused to provide further proof of his timeliness.

Ford repossessed the man's automobile. He filed suit against Ford. The judge hearing the case, ruled that a business is responsible for correctly operating its computers. He ordered Ford to pay punitive damages of $5,000 and to reimburse the customer for the fair market value of his vehicle.

The *New York Times* reported in its February 22, 1970 issue that a computer program, used by the U.S. Army to create family allotment checks for Army personnel, did not automatically cancel the payments when a member's military service ended. The loss incurred from the unintended continuing payments to dependents reportedly exceeded $100 million.

Lotteries have depended upon computer and telecommunications technology for more than three decades. Floods associated with Hurricane Agnes, in June 1972, submerged Pennsylvania's reserve supply of forty-five million lottery tickets in nine feet of water. The flooded computer facility near Harrisburg's airport also housed rented computer equipment. Lottery officials announced that, because of the flooding in the capital, the drawing for June's final jackpot would be held in Gettysburg. Following that drawing, officials announced suspension of lottery ticket sales pending receipt of new ticket supplies and replacement computer equipment. Pennsylvania resumed lottery sales on August 10 for a drawing scheduled for August 23.

State Farm Insurance, citing a computer error, attempted in a Colorado court to escape liability for a policyholder's accident. The Colorado Tenth Circuit Court of Appeals ruled in 1972 that the computer's automatic renewal of the policy, following the company's acceptance of a late payment, constituted a binding business agreement between the firm and its client. The court ruled that the insurance company must pay the policyholder's claim.

In Durham, North Carolina a computer paid a city employee $31 an hour instead of the correct rate of $3.12, according to a *Computerworld* report, April 18, 1973. The computational error remained unreported by the employee and undetected by city officials until it was discovered in a routine year-end audit.

During the late 1960s and early 1970s law enforcement computer systems proliferated dramatically. Computer file queries became routine procedure. Police asked for identification from a man hitchhiking near Las Vegas in 1974. When they submitted a query to the FBI's NCIC (National Crime Information Center) files, that computer reported that law enforcement officials in Monterey, California had issued a felony warrant for the man. The hitchhiker told the police that the warrant was no longer valid. Skeptical, the police announced that they were taking him in. While searching the man's duffle bag, police found a disassembled shotgun.

Three days later Monterey Police confirmed that the warrant was indeed out of date; they said that they had no further interest in the jailed man. Las Vegas Police then turned their prisoner over to federal authorities to be charged with possession of an unregistered firearm. A federal judge eventually ruled that the shotgun, found after a search based on erroneous computer data, could not be admitted as evidence against the man.

The New York State Lottery revealed that a programming error apparently caused a computer to print hundreds of duplicate and triplicate tickets for a special Halloween drawing in 1975.

This incident, closely following a recent rash of criticism against another of the state's games, prompted Governor Carey, on October 22, to halt all of the state's lottery games pending an inquiry.

Critics chose the occasion to remind the public that lottery advocates had pushed the state to initiate a lottery in 1967, claiming it would provide $300 million each year for education. They charged that so far it had never produced more than $54 million in a single year and that money had been deposited in the state's general fund.

Following an independent consulting company's investigation of the computer fiasco, Governor Carey announced on November 28 an extensive overhaul of the state's lottery games and dismissal of the entire 324-person Lottery Commission Staff!

When a Nevada businessman repossessed a trailer in Stockton, California in 1978, the angry purchaser filed theft charges against him, prompting police to create an NCIC computer record. Although a California court dismissed the theft charges, the local police apparently neglected to purge the computer record in Washington, D.C.

Months later, police in Tempe, Arizona stopped the businessman for a minor traffic violation. The NCIC computer, responding to the police inquiry, indicated that a warrant had been issued charging the man with grand theft. After being jailed overnight, the man was transferred to the Maricopa County Sheriff's office, which handled extraditions. When the sheriff's staff finally learned that the computer record had been wrong, they released the motorist at approximately 11:00 p.m.

Following the 1964 primary elections, the three national television networks teamed with the two major wire services in a combined, cost-shared effort to collect and provide raw returns in future elections. From a huge computer system in New York City, their News Election Service (NES) would provide such information to the networks, their affiliates, the wire services, and local newspapers. A team of researchers would collect data across the entire nation and make it available from the single electronic database.

NES appeared to serve the news industry well until intermittent system failures plagued the system on November 7, 1978. Election results that night were delivered both slower and later than expectations based on earlier years' performance.

The lateness of data from NES forced election forecasters to delay declaring contest winners, even in many local races. Although they expected to be able to announce by midnight which party had won control of the U.S. House of Representatives, the networks had to wait until after 1:30 a.m. for that announcement.

Both NBC and CBS had planned that night to test new election forecasting systems being developed for use in the 1980 presidential race. Because both their systems relied heavily on NES for raw election data, neither network achieved the test results hoped for in the 1978 election.

Even though the malfunctioning NES computer declared John Warner the winner of a close Virginia race for the U.S. Senate, that prediction was called into question when someone observed that the same computer had also listed nonexistent precincts for the state!

The Oklahoma City motor vehicle registration computer supposedly prohibited inquiries using blank spaces within the license number sequence. However, the computer did not reject inquiries containing blanks; instead, it always spewed out the record of a Guthrie, Oklahoma land appraiser in response! This unexplained computer glitch caused the same man to be accused of burning a building, stealing a car, leaving an accident scene, and failing to pay numerous traffic tickets! By June 1980 he had been the subject of almost two dozen arrest warrants! He finally persuaded officials, who had come to know him through their many encounters, to have someone fix the computer program so the system would stop "fingering" him every time someone made an erroneous inquiry.

From the time that new computer equipment was installed in the New York City Public Library in 1980, employees complained that the system experienced a higher-than-usual processing error rate. The disk drives appeared to wear out prematurely; two had to be replaced in less than a year. Their read/write heads frequently slipped out of alignment and crashed into the disk surfaces, destroying both the data and the disks. Puzzled engineers could find no cause for the disk drive problems.

The failure of two disk drives on August 24, 1982, threatened to adversely affect every one of the library's 2,500 employees; without the drives, library employees could not process the payroll.

Library officials responded to the emergency by activating an existing disaster plan which permitted library officials to acquire sufficient time at a Hoboken, New Jersey computer facility to run the payroll system and print the checks.

Consulting engineers, investigating the most recent failures, began to suspect that the library's marble floors might be causing the anomaly. To cushion the vibrations created by rapidly spinning disks, most installations used raised, more flexible floors. Rather than install raised flooring, engineers decided they could confirm their suspicion by simply installing heavy rubber casters under the disk drives. All problems and errors immediately vanished.

Over the years hundreds of organizations had discovered that static, generated when operators walked on carpeted computer-room floors, frequently caused data errors or damage. Various solutions had been found, including the use of anti-static spray on the carpet, replacement with a blend of materials less prone to static, placing special anti-static mats in front of susceptible devices, even requiring employees to wear devices designed to "ground" them, preventing the build-up and transfer of static electricity to the equipment.

In Northbrook, Illinois acid flowing through the floor of a plating company threatened to damage the A.C. Nielsen Company's computer situated on the floor below. Even though the plating company had taken the precaution of coating their facility's floor with epoxy to prevent leakage, the plating acid ate through the epoxy and started to flow into Nielsen's computer center.

Nielsen employees came up with a novel temporary solution to the unique threat of the 1980s: they installed lead tanks to protect their computer equipment until they could arrange to move it to another facility.

Police in Montebello, California wondered, in May 1980, why two men were loitering near a closed business establishment after midnight. They radioed a request to check the computer for warrants. The computer indicated that one of the loiterers was wanted for possession of PCP. After arresting and searching the man, police said they found a packet of the drug.

Even though police later discovered that the warrant had been canceled six months preceding the arrest, prosecutors proceeded to trial. The man was convicted in Los Angeles Superior Court and sentenced to serve ninety days in jail, then remain on probation for three years.

Since computers were first used in 1960 political campaigns, concerned citizens have worried whether it is unethical and deceptive for politicians to use computers to convey selected portions of their political beliefs to targeted constituents. They could easily customize their speeches and correspondence to say whatever their advisors knew that a particular group wanted to hear from a candidate. Advanced word processing capabilities made it easy to create personalized letters emphasizing points on which the voter and the candidate agreed, and neglecting to mention those issues on which they did not.

Advisors now routinely employ computers to provide safe answers to hot issue question--answers which frequently shade the answers differently for responding to questions from different groups or locations.

An article in the September 22, 1980 issue of *Computerworld* quoted Professor John Cragan of Illinois State University as saying "...you can take any idiot, parade him around the country for twelve months and get him elected."

New York State's Attorney General Robert Abrams decided that the state's proposal to use computer terminals for computerized poker and blackjack video games would violate the state's constitution and lottery laws prohibiting casino gambling. His September 1981 report said that "...each computer terminal could itself become a minicasinio."

Abrams' decision effectively ended lottery officials' plans to place 300 terminals in hotels, bars, off-track betting parlors, and transportation centers around the state.

Their proclamation, addressed to New York City Mayor Edward Koch, vowed: "We didn't pay King George, and we won't pay you." The two dozen citizens wearing militiamen costumes, carrying muskets, alternately singing Revolutionary War songs, and marching to fifes and drums, belied the fact that it actually was September 2, 1981.

The protestors had journeyed from their homes in Massachusetts to New York's City Hall to protest a "computer error" that sent them letters demanding payment of $70,000 in New York City parking tickets. One victim said he was being dunned for $26,000 covering tickets issued him from 1975 through 1978, even though several years earlier he had turned in the license plate with the offending number. He said that, prior to joining the protest group, he had not visited New York City in more than fifteen years.

Describing an election day foul-up in the nation's capital, the *Washington Post* headline of November 5, 1981 read "Computer Tape Errors Are Blamed For Balloting Problems in District." The article reported numerous problems resulting from a grossly inaccurate master list of Washington citizens registered to vote. Although it was legally required to be available for public inspection at least two weeks before the election, the *Post* said that the error-filled computer printout had been delivered to election officials only on the Friday preceding Tuesday's election. The late receipt forced clerks to work the weekend making copies needed at 137 locations.

The Board of Elections chairman told the *Post* that his office had approximately one million voter registration cards on file; he believed that approximately 273,000 were currently valid.

A computer failure in Richmond, Virginia forced the state's lawmakers to hold an extraordinary Sunday session to complete their 1983 legislative calendar. After lawmakers agreed on a new state budget, the computer refused to print the document. Because it was Saturday, state employees said they were unable to arrange immediate repairs for their equipment. Even so, they managed to make the printed budget available by Sunday morning, enabling the legislature to complete its business and adjourn for the year on February 27, 1983.

The Labor Department announced in 1983 its plans to have a robot weight dust samples collected from coal mines during safety inspections. Four employees responsible for weighing the samples would be reassigned within the Pittsburgh laboratory.

Claiming that the future employment of the reassigned employees was uncertain, the president of a union local filed an unfair labor practice charge against the use of a robot to replace the four human workers.

A *Washington Post* news aide, dutifully taking notes on a laptop computer borrowed from his employer, became the center of attention at a meeting of the Fairfax, Virginia Board of Supervisors on January 23, 1984. Suddenly his laptop's built-in speaker commenced to play loudly "Amazing Grace". After the startled, embarrassed aide figured out how to stop the unexpected hymn, the meeting resumed.

Back at work, the news aide learned that the laptop had last been used by a reporter sent to cover events in San Salvador. On the plane, she had discovered how to key in music and play it back through the computer's speakers. To amuse herself during the long flight she had keyed in several tunes, which she had simply forgotten to erase before returning the computer to her employer when the assignment ended.

Computer problems prevented New Jersey lottery winners from collecting their prizes in mid-June 1984. Lottery officials explained that, without their computers, they could not determine who should be paid and how much each person was due.

Three days later Lotto agents announced they could validate tickets and pay winnings. The lottery contractor appeared either unable to determine or unwilling to reveal what actually caused the computer disruption.

Following an August 1984 move of two Sperry mainframe computers into a new data processing center in Austin, employees of the Texas Department of Human Resources reported an unexpectedly high incidence of equipment malfunctions. Investigators concluded that the movers had not been sufficiently gentle with the thirty tape drives and one hundred and fifty disk drives. Technicians succeeded in adjusting and calibrating the shook-up equipment so that the computer system returned to its normal level of performance within three days after the move.

Liquor became a scarce commodity across the entire state of New Hampshire in the fall of 1984. State officials blamed a computer for bare shelves in the seventy state-run liquor stores. They explained that a computer system used to distribute goods to the stores was causing bottle inventory quantities to be treated as case quantities, misleading the system to think resupply was not needed. Further, the computer equipment reportedly lacked sufficient memory to work fast enough to complete all of the massive system's tasks in a timely fashion. Consequently, vital information about low inventories was not being communicated to warehouses. When warehouses failed to ship, store stocks ran out completely.

Systems specialists studying the dilemma decided they could fix the system's ills by increasing the main computer's capacity, installing additional disk drives, and adding new, faster communications links. To compensate for earlier system's lapses, humans had to work overtime catching up on store deliveries and requisitioning new warehouse stocks from alcohol manufacturers.

City officials wondered why a computer printout indicated that hundreds of telephone calls were being made from a Fayetteville, North Carolina Sanitation and Fleet Maintenance building at night, when the building was supposed to be dark and deserted. In January 1985, police, assigned to investigate the mystery, said they were relieved to discover that all of the calls were local. They were also astounded to learn that all of the calls were to the local Coca-Cola bottling company! They decided to pay that firm a visit.

At the bottling plant they learned that newly-installed drink machines contained computer equipment enabling them to automatically call the local bottler's computer to report the number of soft-drinks sold. The bottler's computer would use the sales information to schedule refills of the vending machines.

Technicians cited "a manufacturer's flaw" as the cause of the two machines' far too numerous phone calls. Replacement drink dispensers were installed.

When Boston's Museum of Fine Arts expanded its computer room in March 1987, dust created by the renovation efforts caused the computer equipment to cease functioning. After technicians had identified construction dust as the cause of the system's failure, museum officials moved operations to a temporary, leased computer facility for the duration of their remodeling project.

A mere three days after the Connecticut State Lottery switched to a new computer system, a "glitch" forced the shutdown of the state-wide system.

Two Hartford lottery ticket sellers observed that the terminals remained "live" instead of shutting down for the official 8:05 p.m. drawing on Monday, May 9, 1988. They decided to test the system by playing a number which the computer should have accepted only for the next day's drawing. The computer instead issued a ticket with Monday's date--even though the winning number had already been announced. The men then reportedly ordered their terminals to issue several tickets bearing the day's winning number. The terminals complied!

The next morning the lottery sellers took their winning tickets to a lottery office, completed the required forms, and received checks for $6,750.30 each. They requested to speak with lottery officials about irregularities in the system.   After the sellers explained what had happened, officials immediately ordered all terminals shut down pending a check of the computer system.

Declining to reveal what anomaly caused the terminals to remain functional after winning numbers were announced, lottery officials simply announced late Wednesday that the Connecticut lottery was again "up and running."

With Californians waiting in line to play for the state's largest jackpot to date, $26 million, a severed communications cable shut down more than 1,500 lottery terminals and halted ticket sales across a wide swath of California. MCI Communications reported that a highway worker grading the roadside accidentally cut the one-and-a-quarter-inch fiber-optic cable connecting northern California with a computer switch in Hayward.   Lottery officials hastened to reassure ticket purchasers that the June 1988 incident would not interfere with the lottery's operation and that no data had been lost when the cable was cut. Despite the downtime, lottery sales for the week approached $20 million.

Five months later, on Saturday, November 26, 1988, a computer crash put all 4,375 Lotto terminals out of service; some remained down for the entire critical final two hours of the week's sales.

Officials said that recently installed telecommunications software malfunctioned, preventing terminals from accepting bets. Even though the software problem reportedly was fixed and the computer appeared to be working normally within ten minutes, a computer operator reportedly loaded an incorrect backup program, again rendering the computer incapable of recognizing individual lottery terminals.

For the November snafu the California Lottery imposed a fine of $208,500 against Gtech Corporation, the contractor operating the games for the state.

A mis-keyed number in the federal budget for fiscal year 1989 deprived a federal library of one million dollars, which Congress had voted for expansion of computer-based technical information maintained by the Department of Agriculture. Meant to expand computer-accessible data that the National Agricultural Library maintained on food safety, ground water contamination, and research projects using animals, the money definitely was included in the department's appropriation. However, while the appropriations bill was being prepared for presidential signature, a typographical error reduced the amount approved for the library from $14 million to $13 million. Because the president signed into law a document containing the reduced amount, a keying error short-changed the National Agricultural Library a million dollars!

Newport, Rhode Island officials cited a computer error as the cause of 5,600 motorists with past-due parking tickets receiving notices instructing them to report to municipal court on October 19, 1989, at 9:00 a.m. Even though the notices clearly stated that the motorists had to appear in court, only 200 of the 5,600 citizens actually showed up as directed.

Shortly after a half-million gallons of heating oil spilled into waters off Staten Island, New York in January 1990, Exxon officials reported that their computer system (about which they declined to provide specifics) had failed to sound appropriate alarms designed to alert employees that a spillage had started.

Delaware lottery agents must have thought that Christmas had arrived a few days early. A jammed computer printer prevented Delaware's 265 lottery ticket terminals from shutting down as they were supposed to immediately prior to the drawing on December 21, 1990. Winning numbers appeared on television screens while the terminals remained "live." Observant clerks across the state quickly keyed in nearly 500 tickets bearing the just-drawn winning number!

Luckily, the computer time-stamped each ticket sold, enabling lottery officials to weed out and disqualify those sold after the winning number had been drawn and televised.

The *Los Angeles Times* reported in its January 10, 1991 issue that officials in Long Beach were blaming a computer programming error for their police department's poor record on solving serious crimes.

The article noted that the department frequently appeared at the bottom of the California Department of Justice's list ranking police departments according to their crime-solving rate. A police spokesman explained that the computer program used at Long Beach erroneously listed crimes as cleared only when the case was solved during the month in which the crime occurred. Cases solved in later months were not being counted among those cleared. Consequently the recently-published statistics for 1990, which indicated that Long Beach solved 14.2% of its cases against a statewide average of 22%, failed to reflect the department's actual performance.

Fire extensively damaged the American Embassy in Moscow on March 28, 1991. A State Department spokeswoman admitted that Soviet fire fighters had been permitted unescorted access to portions of the huge, highly security-sensitive building. She confirmed that employees had reported soon after the fire that computer disks were missing from several offices. She appeared to be attempting to downplay their importance.

"Computer Glitch 'Kills' Constitution", proclaimed a *Washington Post* headline on Sunday, June 30, 1991. The article, by Douglas Farah, reported that Colombia's new constitution might not be approved because "...a computer apparently ate the text."

Meeting in Bogota for several months, the constitutional assembly had approved a new charter containing more than 400 articles. After the text was keyed into a computer, the paper documents reportedly had been discarded. Before the text was printed from the computer, a technician apparently accidentally erased the entire document from the computer's memory! Without a copy of the document, delegates could not complete their debate and vote on the new constitution. To further exacerbate matters, the assembly's authority was scheduled to expire at midnight on July 4. If the new constitution had not been accepted by that deadline, their weeks of effort would be in vain. Assembly members sat idle for more than forty-eight hours, awaiting government employees' attempts to recreate an acceptable copy of the document.

Noting that several versions of the computer snafu were circulating in the capital, reporter Farah appeared to favor one claiming that the man entrusted to handle the critical computer task had taken a computer programming course only through correspondence.

Considering the foregoing circumstances reported on June 30, a subsequent Farah report in the *Post* on July 5 appeared to deem unnewsworthy the document's rescue from the computer netherworld. Under a headline reading "Colombia's New Constitution Goes Into Effect," he devoted fifteen column-inches to the changes the new document would bring to Colombia, failing even to mention the computer fiasco.

A summer 1991 thunderstorm created a scene in Prince Georges County, Maryland that has become common across America. While an estimated 200 customers shopped in a Giant Food store, lightning knocked out electrical power. Without electricity the computerized scanners used at the check-out counters were out of service. Because individual cans, boxes, and packages no longer include prices, checkout clerks could not revert to calculators during the emergency.

Uncertain how long it might be before power was restored and they could check out, frustrated customers abandoned their loaded shopping carts and left the store. This situation created still another crisis for store employees who had to rush to reshelve the many perishable items in the carts--frozen foods, meats, and dairy products.

In the Philippines a computer reportedly fouled up a May 1992 Pepsi promotional campaign. Advertisements promised that one lucky person would find a number, printed inside a Pepsi bottle cap, that could be turned in to claim a grand prize worth approximately $38,000.

When their computer selected the winning number, Pepsi officials announced it was "349." They expected one person to step forward and be declared the winner. Imagine their surprise when several thousand people appeared with Pepsi bottle caps bearing the number 349! Embarrassed officials later announced that their computer "had goofed"; it had selected a number that had been imprinted in half-a-million bottle caps!

"Outrageous" was the word U.S. Supreme Court Justice John Paul Stevens used in 1995 to describe "the offense to the dignity of the citizen who is arrested, hand-cuffed and searched on a public street simply because some bureaucrat has failed to maintain an accurate computer data base..." He was referring to the Arizona vs. Evans ruling, dated March 1.

Police in Phoenix had stopped a man driving the wrong way on a one-way street. When a computer check indicated an outstanding warrant, the man was arrested. During a search the police found marijuana. Police later discovered that the warrant listed in the computer had been squashed seventeen days before the man's arrest; his record had remained in the computer database because of a court clerk's error.

The Arizona Supreme Court ruled that the evidence must be excluded because it had been illegally seized based on an error in the computer files.

The U.S. Supreme Court ruled that evidence seized by the police, who had relied on an erroneous computer report of a valid arrest warrant, could be used in court in cases where the computer error was made by a court employee rather than a law-enforcement official.

In Queens, New York, after a computer erroneously identified the black 1989 Nissan in which he was sitting in front of his home as stolen, undercover police reportedly ordered Lebert Folkes to get out of the car. Although stories vary greatly about what happened next, Folkes somehow suffered a gunshot to his face. Doctors at Jamaica Hospital said that the bullet passed through the man's cheek and reported Folkes in stable condition.

A story in the *New York Times*, February 13, 1996, reported that the car, which belonged to Folkes's sister Iona, had been stolen on January 15 and recovered the following day. She said that she had asked the police three different times to delete the car from their computerized list of stolen vehicles. Apparently they had not.

When the South Carolina legislature enacted property tax relief resulting in tax rollbacks, no one thought to reprogram an Orangeburg County computer that distributed money to schools. In October 1996 officials discovered the error and demanded that eight schools districts each repay funds they had been overpaid, amounts ranging from $51,000 to $1,000,000.

Thousands of wedding-gift shoppers were denied access to bridal registries in 230 American cities in March, 1997, when computerized systems failed. In its April 2, 1997 issue, *Investor's Business Daily* reported that computer terminals connected to Federated Department Stores' bridal registry experienced intermittent outages over several days in March. Shoppers, expecting simply to go to their local Macy's, Lazarus, Burdines, or Goldsmith's, where they could press a button to view a list of items the bridge and groom wanted, were disappointed. The computer outage also prevented customers from seeing which of the listed gifts other shoppers had already bought for each couple.

As sales of wedding gifts plummeted, Federated reported it had more than thirty computer systems professionals working to identify, analyze, and correct the system's problems. After six days, the system was restored to service when technicians replaced recently upgraded network cards that had failed to communicate properly with the computer database.

INDEX

A. C. Nielsen Co., 8, 233
Aegis System, 169, 170, 172
Aeromexico, 104, 128
Aid for Families With Dependent Children, 208
Agnes (tropical storm), 155
AID, 26
Airbus, 131, 132, 133, 134
Air Canada, 123
Air Florida, 99
Air Force (U.S.), 35, 36, 38, 39, 47, 81, 97, 100, 102, 104, 106
Air France, 132
Air New Zealand, 107, 166, 167
Air traffic control computer failures, 97, 99, 100, 101, 102, 103, 104, 105, 106, 107, 108, 109, 110, 111, 112, 113
Alabama Power Company, 149
Alicia (hurricane), 149, 150
AMC theaters, 31
A. M. Castle & Company, 159
America On Line, 28
American Airlines, 110, 128, 129, 130
American Stock Exchange, 78, 79, 142
Amtrak, 122, 123
Andrus Gerontology Center, 176
Apollo Project, 114, 185, 186, 187, 189, 190, 192, 193, 194
Applied Data Research, 83, 228
Ariane rocket, 204
Armstrong, Neil, 188
Army (U.S.), 33, 35, 207, 229
Arthur Anderson and Company, 20
AT&T, 52, 52, 53, 54, 55, 56, 142
A-320, 131, 132, 133, 134, 135

Bales, Stephen, 188
Banamex, 64, 161
Bangalore, 133
Bank of America, 19, 65, 163
Bank of New York, 64, 65
Barclays Bank, 72, 73
Bart System, 162, 163, 164
Basis Information Technologies, 153, 154
Beech Aircraft Corporation, 192
Black Lung Program, 209
blizzard, 165
Booth, Frank, 172, 173
Bosnia, 47

Boston Museum of Fine Arts, 237
British Airline Pilots Assn., 97
British Airways, 132, 135
Brookline, Mass., 12
Brown, David, 84
Bureau of Engraving & Printing, 12
Burnett, Diane, 74

California Federal Savings & Loan, 61, 68, 164
California Police Information Network, 162
California State Government, 14, 15, 16
Campanelli, Inc., 84
Census Bureau, 92, 93, 206
Chaffee, Roger, 186
Challenger explosion, 198, 199, 201
Chemical Bank, 71, 78, 161
Chesapeake & Potomac Telephone Company, 56, 57, 88
Chicago Board of Trade, 138, 139, 143, 147, 160
Chicago Mercantile Exchange, 139, 140
China, 16
Citibank, 78, 79
CNA Corporation, 117
Coca Cola, 237
Cohen, William S., 25
Colombia's constitution, 241
Commerce Department (U.S.), 210
Commodities Exchange, 79, 161
Commonwealth Edison, 143, 160
Concorde, 100
confetti, 227
Consolidated Edison, 77, 78, 79, 80
Coontz (U.S. Navy vessel), 168
Cooper, Gordon, 180
Coopers & Lybrand, 11
Corning Glass Works, 31, 155
Customs Service (U.S.), 12, 16, 210

Daiwa Bank, 63, 88
Dallas payroll, 9
Defense Finance & Accounting Service, 35
Delta Airlines, 99, 102, 128, 129
Del Monte Corporation, 85
Department of Agriculture (U.S.), 20, 26
Department of Defense (U.S.), 33, 34

Department of Justice (U.S.), 211
Depository Trust Company, 160
Detroit Metropolitan Airport, 109
Dime Savings Bank, 151
Distant Early Warning (DEW), 43
District of Columbia Government, 17
District of Columbia National Bank, 62
Dominicks Finer Foods, 91
Donald Duck, 208
DSC Communications Corporation, 58

earthquakes, 64, 68
Easer, Sophia, 173, 174
Eastern Airlines, 102
E-Com, 13
Economic Development Administration, 7
electromagnetic pulses (EMP), 48
Electronic Data Systems, 15, 70, 116
Environmental Protection Agency, 25
Equitable Gas Company, 173, 174
Erwin Consulting Ecologists, 80
Exocet missiles, 168
Explorer I, 177
Exxon, 240
Eyles, Donald, 193

FAA, 26, 96, 107, 111, 112, 113, 114, 115, 116, 117, 118, 119, 136
Fahnestock, 160
Falcon, 103
FBI, 223, 224, 225
Federal Reserve Bank, 41, 60, 63, 64, 65, 68, 76, 77, 78, 79
Fiona, 73
First Data Resources, 72
First Federal Savings & Loan, 151, 152]
First Interstate Bank of Arizona, 62
First Interstate Bank of California, 89
First National Bank of Birmingham, 149
First National Bank of Chicago, 71
Florida Power & Light Company, 78
Florists Transworld Union, 91

Foley's Department Store, 9
Folkes, Lebert, 243
Ford Motor Company, 175, 228
Fran (hurricane), 152
Frederic (hurricane), 148, 149
Frontier Airlines, 98

Galileo, 205
Gary (U.S. Navy vessel), 40
Gemini Project, 180, 181, 182, 183, 184, 185
General Accounting Office (GAO), 12, 15, 23, 25, 33, 34, 47, 114, 202, 203, 207, 208, 209, 211, 212, 214, 215, 216, 217, 219, 220, 223
General Services Administration (GSA), 6, 81, 115
Giant Food, 242
Glenn, John, 180
Gloria (hurricane), 150, 151
Goddard Space Flight Center, 95
Goldman, Sachs and Company, 95
Goodyear Blimp, 10
Grissom, "Gus", 181, 186

Habsheim Airport, 131
Haise, Fred W., Jr., 189
Hall, Deborah, 62
Hardees, 152
Haines, Thomas, 31
Harris Corporation, 116
Hartford (Connecticut), 23
Hayes, Charles, 19
H. C. Prange Company, 94
Health & Human Services Dept. (U.S.), 209, 210, 223]
Health, Education, and Welfare Dept. (U.S.), 208, 219
Hewlett-Packard, 164
Household Financial Services, 158
Housing and Urban Development Dept. (U.S.), 208, 210

Hughes Aircraft Company, 115
Hugo (hurricane), 151, 152

Illinois Bell, 52, 91
Immigration & Naturalization Service (U.S.), 15, 26
Indian Airlines, 132, 133
Intel, 23, 26
International Civil Aviation Authority, 125, 128, 171, 172
Intuit, Inc., 24
Iowa Department of Social Services, 10
IRS, 6, 24, 26, 212, 213, 214, 215, 216, 217
Izvestia, 127, 128
Jarvis, Gregory B., 198
Jet Propulsion Labs, 178
JFK Airport, 96, 111
Johnson Space Center, 95, 182, 193, 198, 201

Karagianis, Steven, 174, 175
Kawasaki Heavy Industries, 175
Kennedy Space Center, 189, 193, 196
Kentucky State Government, 12
Kidd, Verdon, 176
Komarov, Vladimir, 186
Korean Air Lines, 36, 124, 125, 126, 127
Kraft, Christopher, Jr., 183, 187, 189
Kuwait, 21

LaGuardia Airport, 96, 111
Lauda Air, 135
LAX, 109, 129
Leesburg Air Traffic Control Center, 97, 99, 108, 109
Lehigh County (Pennsylvania), 37
Leonov, Alexi, 181
Lewis, Peter, 32
Lincoln (U.S. Navy vessel), 48
Litton Industries, 175

London Stock Exchange, 143, 144, 145
Loral Corporation, 117, 118
Lotteries, 229, 230, 234, 236, 238, 239, 240
Lotus Development Corporation, 14
Loveless, Kilena, 121, 122
Lovell, James A., 189, 191, 192
Lutheran Brotherhood Building, 10

Manufacturers Hanover, 79
Mars Observer, 203
Maryland's Energy Assistance Program, 10
Mazda Motors, 156
McAuliffe, S. Christa, 198
McDivitt, James, 183
MCI, 58, 116
McKesson Corporation, 157
McNair, Ronald E., 198
Medicaid, 208
Medicare, 221, 226
Merchant Bank, 148
Mercury Program, 180
Merrill Lynch, 139
Metro System (Washington, D.C.), 121, 122
Mexico City earthquake, 161
MGM Grant Hotel, 84
Microsoft Network, 29
Mir, 205
Mitsubishi Bank, 63, 88
Montana State Auditor, 13
Monterey (U.S. Navy vessel), 47
Morgan Guaranty & Trust Co., 78
Mulhouse, France, 131

Nasdaq, 146
National Agricultural Library, 239
National Bank of Washington, 60
National Institutes of Heatlh, 22, 26, 77
National Semiconductor Corporation, 41
National Spinning Company, 153

National Weather Service, 154, 155
National Westminster Bank, 72, 160
NASA, 177, 178, 179, 180, 190, 191, 192, 193, 194, 195, 196, 197, 198, 199, 200, 201, 203, 204, 205
NATO, 47
Navy (U.S.), 41, 49, 171, 207, 209
NCIC, 224, 225, 229, 230
New Hampshire Welfare System, 9
New Jersey Bell, 51
New Orleans Police Department, 158
Newark Airport, 80, 98, 111
Newbridge Communications, 145, 146
News Election Service, 231
NOAA, 92
Norad, 43, 44, 45, 46, 47
Normandy (U.S. Navy vessel), 47
North American Rockwell, 192
Northwest Airlines, 104, 109, 137
Norwest National Bank, 85
New Jersey Department of Motor Vehicles, 13
New York City Public Library, 232
New York State Income Tax, 11
NTSB, 104, 106, 109, 123, 136
NYSE, 76, 78, 138, 140, 141, 142

Oakland Airport, 105, 112
O'Hare International Airport, 89, 97, 98, 101, 105, 129
Olympic Games, 27
Onizuka, Ellison S., 198
Ontarios Department of Education, 8
Ontrack Data International, 21
Oxford House Hotel, 6

Pacific Bell Telephone, 57, 88
Pacific Telesis Group, 29
Pan American World Airways, 107
Patriot missile, 42
PCBs, 86, 142
Pennsylvania Emergency Management Agency, 37
Pension Benefit Guarantee Corporation, 212
Pentagon fire, 81
Pepsi, 242
Persian Gulf War, 21, 42
Phobos, 202
Pikeville National Bank, 156
Piper Archer, 103, 104, 128
Pogo, 3
Postal Service (U.S.), 13, 87, 155
Premier Systems, 66

Quotron, 141

Ranger missions, 178, 179
Raytheon Company, 119
Reagan, President, 106, 169, 170, 172
Resnick, Judith A., 198
Riverside Hospital, 93
robot, 175, 176, 235
Rockport, Illinois, 154
Rogers, Will C. (Captain), 172
Royal Bank of Scotland, 73

Saber System, 128, 130
Saddam Hussein, 169
Santa Monica Freeway, 121
Scobee, Francis R., 198
Scud missile, 42
Securities & Exchange Commission, 141
Securities Industry Automation Corporation, 142
Security Pacific Bank, 63, 69
seven nines, 118
Shalikashvili, John, General, 34
Sheffield (HMS), 36, 167, 168
Shepard, Alan, Jr., 180, 194
Shirra, Walter, 182
Sides (U.S. Navy vessel), 171
SkyWest, 109
Smith, Michael J., 198

Social Security Administration, 26, 209, 218, 219, 220, 221, 222
South Central Bell, 157, 158
South Dakota State Government, 12
Southwestern Bell, 107
Soyuz flights, 186, 187
Space Shuttle program, 194, 195, 196, 197, 198, 199, 200
Sprint, 51
Sputnik, 177
SSI Program, 218, 219
Stapleton Airport, 98, 123
Stark (U.S. Navy vessel), 168, 169
State Department (U.S.), 240
State Farm Insurance, 229
Steinberg, Inc., 94
Stockholm Stock Market, 139
Strasbourg, 134
Strategic Air Command, 41
Sun Microsystems, 18
Swigert, John L., Jr., 189

Tandem Computer, 22
Taurus System, 143, 144, 145
Telecomp, 150
Texas Instrument, 39
Todd Shipyards, 40
Tomahawk missiles, 47, 48
Toronto Stock Exchange, 147
Tracking & Data Relay Satellite, 201
Treasury Department (U.S.), 12, 63
TRW, 21, 116
TSB, 74

United Airlines, 123, 136
Univac I, 93, 206
Urada, Kenji, 175
U. S. Administrators, 88
USAir, 109
U. S. Electrical Motors, 151
U. S. Home Corporation, 150

U. S. Military Personnel Records Center, 83
U. S. News, 28
United Technology, 152
United Telecommunications, 51

Veterans Administration, 31, 207
Vicennes (U.S. Navy vessel), 42, 169, 170, 171
Vinick, James, 51
Virgin Islands, 17
Volkswagen, 83
Voskhod, 181

Walker, David, 108
Walter Reed Army Hospital, 211
Washington State Government, 29, 30, 86
wedding gifts, 243, 244
Wells Fargo Bank, 69, 163
White, Edward, 182, 186
Williams, Robert, 175

Year 2000 problem, 30
Yeltsin, Boris, 127, 128
Young, John, 195

Zimmerman, Donald, 102

DO YOU KNOW OF OTHER MAJOR COMPUTER SNAFUS?

Readers are invited to submit information about other major computer blunders, errors, failures, glitches, goofs, malfunctions, snafus, etc., for possible inclusion in a follow-up book the author is planning. Please submit as much information as possible, including the name and location of the victim company or organization, names of individuals involved, date (or year) when incident occurred or became known, plus a brief explanation of what happened. Copies of articles or news-clippings about such incidents are also welcome (please indicate publication name and issue date for each item sent). All submissions should include sender's name, address, and e-mail address (if any). Those comfortable with doing so are encouraged to include their telephone number so a researcher or the author can call to discuss an incident, should they desire.

Author especially wants to learn about incidents which have not previously been widely publicized--those swept under the rug in government agencies and major corporations. Individuals desiring to relate first-hand knowledge of (or participation in) such incidents are encouraged to write detailed letters to the author, addressed in care of the publisher. Please indicate how researchers can corroborate the stories. Your e-mail address and telephone number will be appreciated, but are not required.

The *first contributor* of each recommendation the author uses in his new book will receive one free copy of the work, inscribed by the author, if desired. Those hoping to receive a free copy obviously must include their name and mailing address with their submission. Further, the author will list names of *first contributors* in the new book's acknowledgements (unless contributor specifically asks not to be listed).

E-mail submissions to: ChicoraPub@aol.com *or mail to:* H. McDaniel, % Chicora Publishing, Inc., *350 Wesley Street, Suite 702, Myrtle Beach, SC 29579.*